I ha
D

westland

From the author of the bestsellers
Stay Hungry Stay Foolish and *Connect the Dots*

I have a
Dream

RASHMI BANSAL

The inspiring stories of
20 social entrepreneurs who found new ways
to solve old problems.

westland

westland ltd

Venkat Towers, 165, P.H. Road, Maduravoyal, Chennai 600 095

No. 38/10 (New No. 5), Raghava Nagar, New Timber Yard Layout, Bangalore 560 026

Survey No. A-9, II Floor, Moula Ali Industrial Area, Moula Ali, Hyderabad 500 040

23/181, Anand Nagar, Nehru Road, Santacruz East, Mumbai 400 055

4322/3, Ansari Road, Daryaganj, New Delhi 110 002

First published by westland ltd 2011

10 9 8 7 6 5 4 3 2

ISBN: 978-93-80658-38-4

CONTENT, PAGE DESIGN AND TYPESETTING BY

JAM Venture Publishing Pvt Ltd,

Email: mail@rashmibansal.in

COVER DESIGN

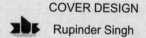 Rupinder Singh

Inside book formatting and typesetting by Ram Das Lal

Printed at HT Media Limited, Noida

Disclaimer

DEDICATED TO

My daughter Nivedita.
With all my love.

ACKNOWLEDGEMENTS

My deepest gratitude to Sunil Handa – teacher, friend, philosopher and guide. And also, the best publisher any author could have.

To Deepak Gandhi, for believing in me, working with me, making this happen.

My friend Piyul Mukerjee, for being my best critic, and best friend.

The students of LEM at IIM Ahmedabad, as well as Surya Ragunaathan, Swastik Nigam, Nupur Maskara and Saurabh Datar, for the painstaking work of proofreading.

Madan Mohan, for laying out endless 'versions' of pages. And never once saying 'bas ho gaya'.

To Vipul Patel and Rajiv Mehta at Eklavya Foundation, for solid support and attention to every detail. Aapka bahut bahut shukriya.

To my transcription team – Nikhil Sahasrabudhe, Surya Ragunaathan, Mihir Jha, Sanjeev Priyam Chandran, Mansee Tewari and Avinash Agarwal. Thank you for all the love and perfection you put into the work!

Rupinder Singh, for an outstanding cover design.

To Apoorva Dixit, for being such a wonderful virtual assistant. And to Pranav Shah, Paras Shah and Sania Aggarwal – you guys help me rock online!

My daughter Nivedita, for making me wise and keeping me innocent. And grounded, at all times.

To Yatin, for teaching me important life lessons. And putting me on a more spiritual path in life.

My mother for her unconditional love, and practical day-to-day support. Without which I could never have had a career.

Not to forget my domestic help – past and present – who make my life manageable and more comfortable.

Last but not the least, a big thank you to my new publishers – Westland. In particular, Gautam Padmanabhan and Paul Vinay Kumar. For their patience and sweetness, at all times.

And but of course, all the wonderful men and women in this book. For sharing their amazing, inspirational journeys.

I hope you look up from this book. And take one small step, in the same direction.

For yourself, your fellow man, for all of mankind.

ACKNOWLEDGEMENTS

" I have a dream... That one day all of God's children will be able to join hands and sing... Free at last! Free at last! Thank God Almighty, we are free at last! "

– Martin Luther King Jr, speaking on 28th August, 1963, at the Lincoln Memorial, Washington D.C.

AUTHOR'S NOTE

There are two kinds of people in the world. Those who think, and those who feel.

The 'thinkers' see a child begging on the street and say to themselves, "That's not my problem."

Those who feel, however, will give that child something. If not a coin, at least a moment of compassion.

Thinkers believe the world is a neat place, with boundaries.

"My house"

"My family"

"My community"

"My welfare"

That's where the boundary ends.

But, those who feel see the entire world as One.

Beggar and bourgeoise, sinner and saint. We are all inter-connected, in ways we cannot understand.

And hence, in serving another, we are only serving ourselves.

For too long now we – the 'middle class' of India – have chosen to be thinkers.

We have deadened our hearts and our minds to the poor, the hungry, the homeless and the hopeless.

Because that problem is really not 'ours'.

And the small minority who feels, it's doing the best it can. But it is never enough!

Magar hawa ka rukh badal raha hai.

I see now, a new breed of people. Thinking-feeling individuals who look a problem in the eye and declare war.

These people think like entrepreneurs but feel and work for the cause of society.

And hence, they are 'social entrepreneurs'.

These are people like you and me, not Mother Teresa. They are using the principles of business, to create a better world.

A world where profit does not equal greed. Where people come together for a greater common cause. A world where 'I' does not mean crushing 'them'.

Because the bank balance you have here on earth will remain, when you depart.

Your *karma*, you carry forward.

So no matter what your problem in life is, spare a moment for someone else.

Spread love, laughter and goodwill.

The more you give, the more you will get back.

January 2011

Mumbai

Rashmi Bansal

AUTHOR'S NOTE

CONTENTS

– RAINMAKERS

– CHANGEMAKERS

– THE SPIRITUAL CAPITALIST

RAINMAKERS

Social enterprises which generate revenues but where profit is not the primary motive. This is a new breed of entrepreneurs, a new model of 'doing good' and not mere charity.

CASTE AWAY

p02

Bindeshwar Pathak – born 1943

Sulabh International

When Bindeshwar was a young boy, his grandmother once made him eat cowdung to 'purify' himself, after contact with an untouchable. The same Brahmin boy grew up to lead a movement we know as 'Sulabh'. A revolution in toilets and a rightful place in society, for those who once cleaned them.

RAGS TO RICHES

p32

Anita Ahuja – born 1960

Conserve India

Like many well-to-do women in Delhi, Anita Ahuja took up social work. But, deeply moved by the plight of ragpickers, she decided to do something to improve their lives. Today. Anita and her husband Shalabh run a unique income-generation program – recycling plastic waste to create beautiful export-quality handbags.

BEYOND PROFIT

p46

Vineet Rai – born 1971

Aavishkaar Social Venture Fund

Quite by accident, 25 year old Vineet Rai became CEO of GIAN – a network to support grassroots innovation. From there came the idea of setting up a micro-venture fund for rural entrepreneurs. Today, Aavishkar supports 23 companies which generate profits – and returns to investors - but also address important social issues.

WEAVE THE PEOPLE

p64

Sumita Ghose – born 1960

Rangsutra

Sumita married an idealistic young IRMA graduate - Sanjoy Ghose – and made a career in the NGO sector. In 1998, Sanjoy was murdered by ULFA; Sumita had to pull herself together and chart a new course. Today, she runs Rangsutra, a for-profit venture which sources craft and textiles from villages and retails through Fabindia.

CONTENTS

RAINMAKERS

Social enterprises which generate revenues but where profit is not the primary motive. This is a new breed of entrepreneurs, a new model of 'doing good' and not mere charity.

p78 ## COUNTRY ROADS

Saloni Malhotra – born 1981

DesiCrew

As a 23 year old engineering graduate Saloni decided to do something different with her life. Three dots in her head – 'rural', 'technology' and 'business' – connected to form DesiCrew, India's first rural BPO. The project has also became a feather in the cap of IIT Madras, which incubated the idea.

p92 ## MOVING MOUNTAINS

Ishita Khanna – born 1977

Spiti Ecosphere

Ishita is young, idealistic and passionate about conservation. But, she believes it must go hand in hand with development. Through Ecosphere, Ishita promotes eco-tourism and berry processing – economic incentives to mountain folk to preserve their majestic heritage.

p102 ## PRODIGAL SUN

Harish Hande – born 1967

SELCO

Harish Hande is a 'mad' scientist. As a PhD student, he spent two years living in rural Sri Lanka and India, before starting Selco, a company which makes solar lighting suitable – and affordable – for villagers. Selco has installed 120,000 systems in Karnataka, and plans to take the mission national, in the near future.

p118 ## TREE OF LIFE

Santosh Parulekar – born 1969

Pipal Tree

Santosh was a well-settled IT professional until one fine day the job demanded he go out and learn all there was to know – about microfinance. Today, he runs a unique social enterprise which transforms poorly educated rural youth into highly skilled construction workers.

CONTENTS

RAINMAKERS

Social enterprises which generate revenues but where profit is not the primary motive. This is a new breed of entrepreneurs, a new model of 'doing good' and not mere charity.

p134   **TEACH A MAN TO FISH**

Dinabandhu Sahoo – born 1961

Project Chilika

Dinabandhu Sahoo is a marine biologist who's stepped out of his laboratory, into the real world. Through Project Chilika Sahoo has trained villagers in Orissa to 'farm the ocean'. Sowing the seeds of a 'Blue Revolution', a new hope for millions across the world.

p144   **THE HUNGRY TIDE**

Anand Kumar – born 1973

Super 30

Anand Kumar is a mathematics teacher who ran his own coaching classes. But in 2002, his classroom turned into a unique social experiment, tutoring poor but meritorious students for IIT JEE. In 2008, all the students of 'Super 30' cracked the exam, igniting hope in the heart of darkness. A hunger to succeed, in gaons and gullies across India.

p158   **THE SOUND OF SILENCE**

Dhruv Lakra – born 1980

Mirakle Couriers

Dhruv Lakra could have become an investment banker. Instead, he invested in a very offbeat idea – a courier service employing the deaf. In a short span of two years, Mirakle Couriers is a robust business, competing with the best. And Dhruv dreams of making it as big as FedEx, but keeping that social edge.

CONTENTS

CHANGEMAKERS

A single person is all it takes to start a movement. While the world laments 'what is', the changemaker takes a small step towards making it as it should be.

p174   **THE SCIENTIFIC SOCIALIST**

Madhav Chavan – born 1954

Pratham

Born into a political family, Madhav Chavan almost became a Communist leader. But a PhD in the US made him question Marxist ideals. Madhav returned to India and made 'education' his life's mission. Today, Pratham is the largest NGO in this sector, working with the govenment to impact millions of children across India.

p202   **THE NAKED TRUTH**

Anshu Gupta – born 1970

Goonj

Trained as a mass communication professional, Anshu Gupta decided to communicate an entirely unusual message to the masses. Through systematic collection, sorting and delivery Goonj reaches every scrap of waste clothing from urban India to someone   out there. To use with dignity, wear with pride.

p216   **THE ART OF WAR**

Trilochan Sastry – born 1960

Association for Democratic Reforms (ADR)

An IIT-IIM graduate, Trilochan Sastry could have been one of the many armchair critics who despair about the state of the nation. But his simple, courageous act of filing a PIL raised the standards of Public Life. And is slowly but surely changing the way we elect our leaders.

p238   **THE GIRL IN THE MIRROR**

Shaheen Mistri – born 1971

Akanksha

As a student, Shaheen Mistri got her friends to volunteer their time teaching kids from the slums. That small initiative with 15 children in a single borrowed classroom now covers 3500 children in 58 centres and 6 schools. And continues to inspire the youth to do their bit, for a better India.

CONTENTS

CHANGEMAKERS

A single person is all it takes to start a movement. While the world laments 'what is', the changemaker takes a small step towards making it as it should be.

p262   **INTO THAT HEAVEN OF FREEDOM**

Arvind Kejriwal – born 1968

Parivartan

As an IRS officer, Arvind Kejriwal waged a secret war against his own department. This campaign – under the banner 'Parivartan' – later pioneered the use of RTI (Right to Information Act) to empower citizens. Arvind's dream is to see 'true democracy', where ordinary people regain the right to govern themselves.

p282   **INNER ENGINEERING**

Bhushan Punani – born 1954

Blind Person's Association (BPA)

As a young MBA, Bhushan made the unconventional choice of joining Blind Person's Association. To see if management principles could be applied to the social sector. 31 years later, the scale at which BPA operates makes the answer to that question a resounding 'yes'.

CONTENTS

THE SPIRITUAL CAPITALIST

The ideal of service may be old-fashioned. But there are individuals who still choose to live by it. Because they believe purity of purpose and selflessness of spirit can transcend every limitation.

p302

SOUL FOOD

Madhu Pandit Dasa – born 1956

Akshaya Patra

As a student at IIT, Madhu Pandit once came close to committing suicide. Then, he discovered Krishna and embraced the spiritual path. As head of ISKCON Bangalore, Madhu is now leading Akshaya Patra. A movement which combines missionary zeal and modern management, to feed 1 million hungry children everyday.

p320

ALL IN THE FAMILY

Vinayak Lohani – born 1978

Parivaar Ashram

An IIM Calcutta graduate, Vinayak turned his back on corporate India to do something of service to humanity. That something is Parivaar Ashram, a residential facility for orphans, tribals and daughters of prostitutes. Today, Vinayak leads a 'household' of over 500 children.

p338

LEAD, KINDLY LIGHT

Shreesh Jadhav – born 1968

Belur Math

Shreesh Jadhav graduated from IIT, knowing he did not want a conventional career. He toyed with social work   but ultimately found his calling - as a monk. Through the path of renunciation, Shreesh holds up a candle. A light of hope in the darkness of a selfish, me-first world.

CONTENTS

RAINMAKERS

Social enterprises which generate revenues but where profit is not the primary motive. This is a new breed of entrepreneurs, a new model of 'doing good' and not mere charity.

CASTE
AWAY

Bindeshwar Pathak,
Sulabh International

When Bindeshwar was a young boy, his grandmother once made him eat cowdung to 'purify' himself, after contact with an untouchable. The same Brahmin boy grew up to lead a movement we know as 'Sulabh'. A revolution in toilets and a rightful place in society, for those who once cleaned them.

I have many beautiful memories of summers spent in my 'native place'.

But the one thing I'd rather forget is the toilet.

The toilet from hell.

It was a raised platform with a hole. No flush, no sanitation, no escape from that god-awful stench.

My aunt would say, "Put Vicks, you won't smell anything".

Fat chance of that!

For days, I would simply not *use* the toilet. But how long could one hold back?

Thoughts like these cross my mind on a beautiful February morning under a gorgeous blue sky. I am at the Sulabh complex near Palam in New Delhi, home to the world's only museum dedicated to toilets.

And to the one man who's made it his mission to bring sanity to this country's archaic systems - both social and sanitary.

Bindeshwar Pathak is a sprightly sixty-something. Dressed in khadi *kurta* and white churidar pyjama, he looks like a village headmaster. And each morning, he plays that part, as he leads the 'morning assembly' at the Sulabh campus.

"*Aao sab mil jul ke banayein sulabh sukhad sansaaar*...!" sings the Sulabh family.

Over hot tea and *pakoras*.

In his expansive air conditioned office.

With a lilting Bihari accent.

Bindeshwar Pathak shares his story.

And it is simply amazing, it is breath taking, it is so honest, almost too-good-to-be-true.

As Bindeshwar himself would say, "*Hai ki nai?*"

Jee, hai to sahi. Aur agar hai to hamare desh mein aage ki peedhi ke liye hope hai.

A single person can move mountains, perform miracles. And that person could be you...

CASTE AWAY

Bindeshwar Pathak,
Sulabh International

Bindeshwar Pathak was born in Rampur Baghel village in Vaishali district of Bihar.

"*Brahman parivar se hum aate hain..* by birth. Of course I don't believe in all this caste system thing." But that, was to come later.

Bindeshwar's grandfather was a famous astrologer, his father an ayurvedic doctor. Prosperous, respected family.

Bindeshwar was the proverbial child with the silver spoon. He grew up in a sprawling house with a large compound. There were nine rooms including a *pooja ghar*, a room where only *atta* was ground and a well to draw water.

But, no toilet.

Every morning at 4 am, there was chaos in the house. All the women in the house had to complete their ablutions before sunrise.

"As a child, even though asleep I was aware of all the activity. Someone picking up a bucket, someone filling water..."

In case a woman in the house fell sick she would have to relieve herself in a straw basket or *mitti ka bartan* lined with ash.

Young Bindeshwar noticed all this, and felt something was not 'quite right'.

"Many ladies had headaches because during the day, they had to control the call of nature." Besides, they were never 'safe' – there were snakes in the grass (both literally and figuratively!).

Bindeshwar studied in four different schools – none of which had a toilet. Or female students.

His first memory of a '*pakka* toilet' is a *pakhana* used by the village zamindar, some distance from his house.

"It smelt so bad we would all hold our breath as we passed by it."

It was cleaned by a scavenger lady, who lived outside the village. An 'untouchable'. In the same village there was a 'Dome'* family. Young Bindeshwar happened to touch a member of this family and all hell broke loose at home.

"*Dadi* made me swallow cowdung, cow urine, *gangajal*, sand… She called some boys to hold me down and stuff it all down my throat. My mother pleaded in vain to let me go, she thought I might die."

Dadi had a simple response: "*Ghar mein rahega kaise*?"

It was a long time ago and yet, this is *not* ancient history. In some parts of India, I'm sure, this might even be living history. The same India where *balika vadhu* is not a character on TV but the girl next door…

The sum total of the story so far is this: *Yeh sab us zamaane mein common tha.*

Lack of toilets.

Rampant disease.

Chhooaa-chhooth.

"Of course I never imagined that a time would come when I would be working to solve all these problems."

Millions of people experienced these very same things, yet, there is only one Bindeshwar Pathak. Was he different, even as a child? Where did he get the idea that change was even possible?

Well, the reality is actually rather mundane. Young Bindeshwar had no idea what he wanted to do in life. In fact, like many many young people even today, his ambitions were guided by circumstances.

---

* *Domes were considered lower caste and known for making straw baskets.*

"People want the caste system to end,
which is not possible. What will happen
is, the importance and the rigidity of the
caste system will reduce. It has already
happened in West Bengal."

The family faced a reversal of fortune; property had to be sold.

"My heart said, let me do something which would allow us to hold our heads high once again! And bring financial stability."

Education was the escape route. Bindeshwar stood first in B N College, Patna and decided that his future lay in becoming a lecturer. A career with respectability and stability. The doctor-engineer equivalent of today.

After a degree in B A Sociology (Honours), Bindeshwar wanted to specialise – of all things – in Criminology. Why? Because it was a new subject and people said it would help him become IPS or CID.

"I really wanted to be a lecturer. At that age you know how it is, no? You go whichever way the wind blows."

Besides, there were no lecturers in the field of Criminology yet. So it seemed like a 'sure shot' way to get his dream job.

Bindeshwar was at the top of the class upto the terminal exam. But in the finals, somehow, he scored very low marks in three papers and stood fourth. In fact, he could not even get a first class overall.

Bindeshwar was shattered. This, he says, was the 'turning point' of his life.

"Yeh mahatvapoorna hai ki jeevan mein mod aane lagte hain. Pehle ek, phir doosra, phir teesra...ab kis mod pe atkenge aap, ye kehena mushkil hai."

And that is why you try a little bit, of everything.

Bindeshwar first became a schoolteacher, then worked at various odd jobs and eventually joined the family business – selling ayurvedic medicines.

"This is my personal observation, but at that time I felt that in India, in our culture, businessmen were not held in high esteem."

You might have lots of money, a hundred cars, even ships to your name. But you did not command *respect*.

Bindeshwar recalls an incident where an acquaintance of his would ask him to alight from the rickshaw a hundred metres away from his office.

When he would reach the same office a few minutes later the man would ask, "*Kab aaye aap?*"

This bemused young Bindeshwar – *ho kya raha hai?*

The man explained: "You are a supplier of medicines, I can't be seen entering my office with you."

His words affected Bindeshwar deeply.

"I felt, this means the work I am doing is not respectable. *Jab kisike saath hum chal nahi sakte… to yeh kaam karne layak nahi hai.*"

It was December 1967. Bindeshwar decided to once again pursue his dream. He applied to study his favourite subject – *apraadh vigyaan* or Criminology – at Sagar University in Madhya Pradesh. And got selected.

In June 1968, Bindeshwar set off for Sagar. The train stopped at Hajipur junction, and he got off the train to have a cup of tea. Bindeshwar's cousin brother was at the station and asked where he was going.

Oddly enough, Bindeshwar had actually bought a ticket to Lucknow – in the opposite direction. He'd never traveled long distance and simply had no clue. In the age of Google Maps it sounds rather… laughable. But the point about being lost is that you are waiting to be found. And it is far more common than knowing exactly where you want to go…

As Bindeshwar puts it, "Some people are absolutely certain – they think straight. "*Mujhe toh yehi karna hai aur waise hi kiya usne*". But most people, if you see, they set out to do something and ended up doing something quite different!"

And that is exactly what happened in his case.

Bindeshwar told the cousin – and his lawyer friend – that he was on his way to Sagar to do an MSc and hopefully become a lecturer. In those days a lecturer earned a princely sum of ₹ 450 – per month.

Vakeelsaab said he had a better idea. He knew of an organization called the 'Bihar Gandhi Janma Shatabdi Samiti', which was planning how to celebrate Bapu's centenary the following year – 1969. Would Bindeshwar like a 'permanent job' there, for 600 rupees a month?

"*Hum tumhe dilwa denge kaam*," was the promise.

Ignoring Bindeshwar's protests, the two pulled out his luggage and bedroll from the train.

"Now you won't believe it, but I was pulling my luggage one way, and they were pulling it the other way. And in those days I was quite the weakling, just 48 kgs in weight. So you can guess who prevailed!"

And that is how Bindeshwar Pathak came to be in Patna. Years later, he was invited to Sagar University, to deliver the annual Dr Harisingh Gaur memorial lecture.

"The title of my lecture was: *Adhtees baras mein Sagar ki yatra*. Or how I reached Sagar after 38 years! I said that in the normal course, a man would reach Sagar from Bihar in 1-2 days. So why it took me 38 years – all the things that happened in between – let me share that with you!"

And what a fascinating journey it has been.

Patna, 1968. Young Bindeshwar meets Saryu Prasad, general secretary of the Gandhi Shatabdi Samiti. Prasad had been MLA of Hajipur from 1952-57; at the time *vakeelsaab* worked as his election agent. Confidently, he went up to Prasad and put forth his *sifarish*.

All very well but the General Secretary declared there was no job available. *Lekin vakeelsaab kahaan haar maanne waale thhe.* Every morning he would take Bindeshwar to Prasad's house. There would be *chai-nashta, idhar udhar ki baatein* and then, the very same *sifarish* would be repeated.

Meanwhile Bindeshwar also explored the option of going to Sagar – as originally planned.

"I called the registrar, and said I had been delayed. He said, 'No need to come now – we have allotted your seat to someone else'."

> **"In Oriental philosophy wealth is not revered, knowledge is. I mean not just in India but China, Japan, Bangladesh, Burma, Laos, Cambodia, African countries. In Western philosophy, it is exactly the opposite."**

Stuck between a rock and a hard place. Bindeshwar could only wait. And hope. Ultimately Prasadji relented and gave the young man a job. Translator from English to Hindi, Hindi to English.

"*Kitni meri tankha rahi hogi, isko aaj tak koi aadmi guess nahi kar paaya hai,*" he chuckles.

"*Kaaran yeh… ki maine kaam kiya bina tankha ke.*"

Ah, a job with no pay at all. But still, a job. Bindeshwar spent four months living off the money he had planned to use for his studies – at Sagar University. Eventually, Prasadji recognised the young man's talent and sincerity, and started paying ₹ 200 per month.

Bindeshwar now worked with the sub-committee known as 'Gandhi Sandesh Prachar'. A book titled '*Gandhiji ko Saadar Pranaam*' was released. Bindeshwar did not see much merit in the book but the secretary had already placed an order. Some internal politics ensued and Bindeshwar was transferred. To the scavenging cell.

A punishment posting.

And the starting point of Bindeshwar's real journey.

His life's work.

"I was told, '*Gandhiji ka ek sapna tha, tum usko pura karo*'."

Bindeshwar recalled the childhood incident when dadi made him eat *gobar* and *gaumutra* (cow urine) to 'purify' him after he'd come in contact with an 'untouchable'. "*To inke saath hum kaam kaise karenge*", was the question on Bindeshwar's mind.

Then came the fact that he was not an engineer. So how would he solve this problem?

The system of scavengers cleaning 'bucket toilets' could not be wished away. You had to provide an alternative.

The Brahmin community used to make fun of me, "*Haan bhai, bhangiji aa jaaiye, aa jaaiye*. We've heard that these days you are doing the work of a *bhangi*."

As he was mulling over this *ghor samasya*, his background in sociology came in handy.

"The people you want to work with, you have to build a rapport with that community. Only then, will they open up and share their problems with you. *Nahin toh aap nahin jaan sakte*."

It was not enough to do a one-off interview. You need to *immerse* yourself in that world.

And that is how a Brahmin came to live in a colony of untouchables in Bettiah. As he went in search of a room on rent, Bindeshwar met Bhola Raut – a member of Parliament from that area.

"As soon as I entered the room, he stood up. He said, 'You can't be serious! You will stay in our home? *Yeh kaise ho sakta hai*'?"

Bindeshwar stayed true to his word. But his unorthodox actions had caused major upheaval at home.

"*Pitaji bahut dukhi thhe*. Father-in-law *toh bahut hi dukhi thhe*. I can't tell you the kind of things they used to say. I faced all kinds of taunts and insults, but bore it all quietly."

Bindeshwar stayed on – for three whole months – and two incidents he observed during that period left an indelible impression on his mind.

The first involved a *nayi naveli dulhan*. The very first day she reached her marital home, her *saas, sasur*, and husband were all forcing her to go and clean the latrine (*pakhana*).

"She was crying and crying… I don't have words to describe the depths of her sorrow. *Humaare aankh se bhi aansu aa gaye tab. Lekin woh log maane hi nahin*."

The young bride had no choice.

The second incident took place ten days later. A bull charged towards a young boy in the marketplace. At first, several people rushed forward, to rescue him.

Then someone shouted, "This boy is from the scavenger colony!"

And suddenly the crowd dispersed. Bindeshwar and his friend happened to be passing by and tried to intervene. They found some bricks lying on the roadside and managed to scare off the animal. But the boy was grievously wounded. He died on the way to the hospital.

These two incidents shook Bindeshwar to the core. It was a deep and fundamental shift – he no longer cared what *anyone* thought.

"That was when I decided, I had to do it. I would dedicate my life to fulfilling the dream of Mahatma Gandhi."

Remained the problem with father-in-law.

Sasurji said, "I am not worried about you, but I am worried for my daughter – what will happen to her? This is not what we expected from a son-in-law who is a graduate from Patna University!"

Bindeshwar replied that he was determined to rewrite history. And nothing would stop him from completing that mission. His solution was practical.

"*Jab tak hum safal nahin hote hain, tab tak apni ladki ki chinta aap kariye. Aur jab hum safal ho jaayenge, toh swabhavik hai ki hum chinta unki karenge.*"

A mission is a madness. A mountain that must be conquered alone. But help and 'equipment' comes in many, unexpected forms, along the way.

When leaving Patna for Bettiah – to live in the scavenger's colony – Saryu Prasad had given Bindeshwar a valuable book. It was a volume published by the World Health Organisation (WHO) titled 'Excreta Disposal in Rural Areas and Small Communities'.

He added, "I see a spark in you. Take up this work. I don't know where or how, but you will find a way!"

Nor did Bindeshwar himself know. He had but a hazy idea – and kept searching.

Around this time Rajendra Lal Das presented Bindeshwar with a book he had authored. Das was part of the Sarvodaya Movement and his book outlined what a better toilet system should be like.

The books, the immersion experience, the questions running around in Bindeshwar's mind – all of it came together, Like *amrit* produced out of *sagar manthan*; the constant churning of thoughts and ideas brought forth an answer.

The WHO handbook had a sentence which struck Bindeshwar, in particular. It noted that 'out of the heterogeneous mass of latrine designs produced over the world pit privy* is the most practical and universally applicable type'. The word 'universal' being most important.

But, universal did not mean 'ready for use'. Much invention, innovation and development followed.

"Kuch toh humne WHO ki book se liya aur kuch usme joda, toh innovation ho gaya. Aur bahut si baatein usmein nahi thi jisko humne create kiya toh invention ho gaya. Phir develop karke diya logon ko, government ko – isliye development bhi ho gaya."

You take a seed planted by someone else and water it. The fruits of the labour are just as sweet!

"I realised that the most important thing in life is application of mind. *Hai nahi*? Knowledge can be borrowed but where and how to apply it, you have to figure out."

Application of mind is the basis of all the technology created at Sulabh. Their model is simple: low cost, needs little water, turns waste into a resource. Can be built quickly, locally and needs no scavengers to maintain.

Simply put, Sulabh is a twin-pit, pour-flush compost toilet.

A deeply sloping toilet pan was developed to enable effective 'flushing' with just a mug of water. The pan is connected to two pits by a Y shaped channel. As soon as one pit is filled up – it may take months, or years, depending on usage – the excreta is sent to the second pit.

No sewer lines, no septic tank required. What's more, the waste in the first pit turns into valuable fertiliser during the 'rest period'. No odour, no pathogens, no manual cleaning required.

And it did not take a crack team to 'R & D' this. Bindeshwar pretty much did the job himself.

---

* *Pit privy is what we know as 'Indian style toilet'.*

> "In my experience, five things are most important in life: Vision, mission, commitment, capabilities and efficiency. You need all five to come together to make a big success of any idea."

"I have made pans with my own hands and polished them", he recalls. The initial work happened over a few months; perfecting the design took 2-3 years. Over the decades it got a little better, more variations, different building material. But the essential idea – even today – is the same.

The simplicity of Sulabh was both its greatest strength. And its greatest weakness.

When Bindeshwar approached the government with his initial prototype, the first reaction was, "This won't work! *Phaltu hai*, humbug *hai*!"

By now of course you know, Bindeshwar was not one to give up so easily.

He met the local administration in Patna. There were two IAS officers in charge. One was Ramesh Chandra Arora – an engineer. He rejected the Sulabh design outright.

"He said, "I have studied engineering and never come across anything like this. It cannot work."

Then he asked Bindeshwar, "Are *you* an engineer?"

Bindeshwar replied, "No I am not. But why don't you test our design, see if it works?"

Arora retorted, "As long as I am in charge of Patna city I won't allow money to be wasted on such a toilet."

But the second gentleman – one Mr P S Kohli who was not an engineer – came to the rescue.

He said, "If Pathakji is saying he has a new idea, let us give him a chance. Let us make 200 Sulabh Shauchalays in Patna. If it works, it will create history. If it doesn't, we shut it down."

"Lekin naya idea aaye hi nahi, iss se hum sahmat nahi hain".

Kohli being senior to Arora, the file was passed.

And thus it was that in 1970 the government of Bihar agreed – in principle – to build Sulabh toilets. A circular was sent out.

By this time Bindeshwar had formed his own *sanstha* – under the name of Sulabh.

"NGOs *dekhiye*, generally they have a love-hate relationship with the government. But with Sulabh, it's different. From the very beginning, we worked hand in hand with them."

In fact, contrary to what you might think the government was hugely supportive of organisations like Sulabh. Politicians like Shatrughan Sharan Singh and Daroga Prasad Rai – the then CM of Bihar believed the government alone could not bring about social change.

Their thinking was simple: Only if the government and NGOs worked together would there be a real impact of change or reform.

So that was a wonderful attitude – at the very top.

The second and most crucial direction came in 1971, when Bindeshwar applied for a grant of ₹ 70,000. An amount of ₹ 50,000 was sanctioned. But then, the government fell. The matter went into a loop and Bindeshwar was asked to meet Rameshwar Nath – an IAS officer.

"What you see of Sulabh today, the model we work on, is only because of that gentleman. *Nahi toh aaj Sulabh ka growth hi nahi ho sakta tha.*"

When Bindeshwar met the officer, he laughed and said, "Who are you?"

"We were not contractors, our work was much more that that. We designed the system as well as built it. Motivation, education, communication, training, follow up – Sulabh was responsible for everything."

"Sir, I am the secretary of *Sulabh Shauchalay Sanstha*. You called me to meet you."

The officer said, "I expected a seventy year old with a walking stick. A freedom fighter."

He said: "The work you are doing will create a dramatic impact in this country. But I see one danger..."

"Who was the President of the Shatabdi Samiti?" he asked.

"Governor ex-offico," replied Bindeshwar.

"And Chairman?"

"CM ex-offico."

"How much money did you request as grant?"

"Five lakhs."

"And how much was sanctioned?"

"Two and a half lakhs."

"When did you apply?"

"In April."

"When was the money disbursed?"

"In February next year."

Rameshwar Nath gave the young man a life lesson. He said, "Look. An NGO headed by the Governor and CM got half the amount it asked for. Almost one year after applying for it."

Tumhara kya hoga?

"You will take fifty thousand grant and then the finance department will raise objections. You will run around in circles, giving clarifications. After a year or two, again you will go around begging for a grant."

It won't work out.

Rameshwar advised: "Don't ask for grants. Charge money for doing your work."

And that is the model Sulabh adopted ever since. Payment on per project basis for installation of toilets. Pay per use from beneficiaries for maintaining them. No grants, subsidies, loans or donations. Sulabh is a self-sustaining organisation.

The IAS officer added a caveat: "As long as you do not misuse the funds, your organisation will flourish."

Bindeshwar assured him, "I will not misuse the funds."

The officer said, "Right now what does it matter – you will say anything! You have no money at all. A man is tempted when there is temptation."

Rameshwar Nath asked the young man for a 'guarantee'.

Not a bank guarantee, but a personal one.

"If ever you feel like being dishonest, remember me. Remember my words."

Bindeshwar Pathak considers Rameshwar Nath to be a 'messenger from God'.

There are many messages and many messengers all around us, but are we listening?

Usually not.

Of course, despite this lucky break Bindeshwar's struggles continued. Rameshwar gave the green signal but then got transferred. The next officer was violently opposed to the idea. Two years passed. The file was returned twice.

The third time the officer received the Sulabh file he wrote a note on it: "If this file is sent to me again, I will suspend the person who brings it to me."

Finally, Bindeshwar knew a Congress MLA. Through him, he sent a letter to Indira Gandhi, the Prime Minister. The letter brought to her notice a new idea which could eliminate scavenging, which was not being taken up by the state government. Those days the slogan was 'garibi hatao'.

"When the state is not releasing funds, how will poverty be eliminated?" the letter asked.

Within ten days a missive came from Indiraji, to the Bihar Chief Minister Kedar Pandey.

This created quite a stir and ultimately the CM agreed to start a pilot project in Saran district.

"Show us that it works!" was the challenge.

In 1973, ₹ 25,000 was sanctioned for the project. But just as the work was about to begin, the officer-in-charge was transferred.

> "Because I do not do *gadbad*, by and large the people in the organisation are also honest. And anyone who attempts any *gadbad* is dealt with severely; everyone knows, it's not a good idea to mess around here. You will lose your job."

The new secretary once again halted the work.

He admits, "This was the most difficult period of my life."

Not that he was a stranger to hardship. From extreme wealth to near poverty, Bindeshwar had experienced it all as he grew up.

After passing matric, he took tuitions to fund further studies. His first job – at the *Gandhi Samiti* – paid a measly two hundred rupees a month. But when the centenary celebrations were completed and the organisation wound up, Bindeshwar was back to no income at all. Plus, he now had his own *sanstha* to run – Sulabh.

So how *did* he manage?

Two things. First, he sold the little property he still owned in the village. Second, he sold his wife's jewellery. Not that there was much to begin with.

"I remember how girls whose parents could not afford a good enough dowry cried in their *sasural*. People would taunt them that their father has sent them without a fridge or a car – your family has no status. When I got married, I could not afford to buy my wife the kind of jewellery which is generally given to the bride."

It was humiliating. "*Us samay mujhe utna hi rona aaya tha.*"

Among Maithil Brahmins in those days, the wedding party was hosted in the *sasural* for upto a month.

In those days the neighbours and relatives would say, "Oh, this girl is married but does not *look* married. Look how little jewellery she is wearing."

Even those few ornaments had to be pawned, when Sulabh was in its struggle phase.

"I recalled the tears in my mother's eyes when my father had similarly pawned her jewellery. He did not have a choice then, and neither did I."

And on top of all that, Bindeshwar also borrowed ₹ 50,000. A large sum in those days.

"A hundred from here, two hundred from there, .. and I was unable to return. *Kyunki kaam toh chal hi raha tha.* There were times when I thought of commiting suicide."

And then he recalls the days when he was selling medicines which were – in some ways – worse.

Sales means travel. But there was no money to spend on hotels. So the modus operandi was simple: "I would lay my dhoti on the platform. Take off my *kurta*, fold it into a pillow and go to sleep. I used to be so tired, that I slept like a log!"

So comfort and discomfort is always, relative.

"In 1973, I was on the brink of collapse, at breaking point. That was when unexpected support arrived. A saviour, so to speak."

Bindeshwar went back to the family business of selling medicines. Because after all, one has to earn a living! One fine day he visited Arrah, a small town in Bihar, to procure an order. There, he noticed a signboard bearing the name of Ramakant Mishra – a special officer with the municipalty.

Bindeshwar knew the man slightly, and stopped by to meet him.

Mishraji asked, "What happened to your Sulabh Shauchalays? How are they doing?"

Pathak confessed he had nothing to show as the government was just not giving sanction.

"Apart from my wife, every single person opposed my choice of work. Later, of course, when I became 'successful'. they all flocked back. *Samay ke hisaab se duniya ka nazariya bhi badal jaata hai.*"

Mishraji said, "I have a lakh of rupees in my budget. We are an autonomous body, we don't need government permission. I will give you funds to start two *shauchalayas*."

And he wrote out a cheque for five hundred rupees.

He called the head clerk – Mr Keshav Upadhyaya – and asked, "*Agar yeh paisa kha gaye to*?"

The clerk replied that he did not think this young man was 'that kind'. But just in case he was wrong, they could cut the amount from his salary.

When you are a nobody, and somebody believes in you, you know. There is good in this world.

That is how the very first Sulabh Shauchalaya came into existence in August 1973. But selling the 'two pit' concept remained difficult. Bindeshwar would go door to door explaining the benefits but most people would say, "We want a septic tank."

A ward councillor called Suresh Prasad Singh came to the rescue. He asked for two of his toilets to be converted to *sulabh shauchalayas*. Word spread in the *mohalla*, then in the neighbouring town of Buxar.

And in all this – like a true entrepreneur – Bindeshwar literally got his hands dirty. Right from carrying buckets of water to pushing a *haathgaadi*, nothing was too 'menial' a job.

"Humne life mein kisi bhi kaam ko chhota nahi samjha".

Bade kaam karne waalon ka vaise yehi usool hota hai!

Meanwhile the success of Sulabh in Arrah and Buxar had its effect in Patna. The file moved forward and on 30th April, 1974, a circular went out acknowledging Sulabh as a 'catalytic agency'* between the government, local bodies and beneficiaries.

One morning Bindeshwar was sitting with the Administrator of the Patna Municipal Corporation. He was instructing the Chief Engineer to be present at 3 pm to construct a public toilet near the Reserve Bank.

"Why don't you come along?" he said to Bindeshwar.

In the afternoon the Administrator declared that the toilet block should be ready by tomorrow noon.

---

* *Government provided 50% loan and 50% grant for conversion of existing toilets; 10% of that money went to the NGO to run its operations.*

The Chief Engineer panicked. How was that possible? The man was due to retire soon, this would be a black spot on his otherwise illustrious career. In desperation, he turned towards Bindeshwar and asked, "Can you do something?"

Bindeshwar was taken off-guard but, in a fraction of a second he made a bold decision.

So far Sulabh had focused on converting bucket toilets in homes into pit privies. Here was a chance to venture into the public domain.

He smiled and said, "This? No problem at all... We'll do it by tomorrow!"

The Administrator took out his red ink pen and wrote the work order – on the Chief Engineer's left hand!

He said, "Take this to the office, get it typed and come back with ₹ 20,000."

The money was sanctioned and the Administrator said he would be back the next morning – at 7 am – to inspect the completed toilet.

Ab karein kya? Aur kaise?

The spot where the toilet block was to be built was in fact an open air toilet already. Some two to three thousand men and women used the place to relieve themselves each morning. The entire area – and miles around it – stank of human waste.

Bindeshwar had a brainwave. He sent his workers to Koliwar, a place where *lal baalu* (red sand) was available and had them bring in twenty truckloads.

By this time, it was late evening.

Next, he sent workers to all the *maalis* (gardeners) in town. They

"Children play games, eat sweets, watch cricket, go for movies, stroll in malls. But we still have children in this country who clean toilets. *Aaj bhi aise bachpan guzar rahe hain, aaj bhi kaam baaki hai.*"

were told to bring as many potted plants, bushes and trees as possible. Whatever the price.

The sand was laid out in the maidan.

The plants were placed, pots hidden, in that layer of sand.

And one pit was dug, and filled up with sweet smelling sandalwood.

The entire area looked good, and smelt good.

By now it was 4 am.

Keeping in mind the calculation of 2 cubic feet per person per year for the standard 2 pit toilet, Bindeshwar estimated the space required for 500 people. And multiplied that by 8 cubic feet.

Workers began digging and by 7 am – when the Administrator arrived, there were no toilets. But the *maidan* no longer had the spectacle of men and women displaying their bums and *lotas*. In its place was a fragrant garden and some work in progress on the toilet block.

"He became so happy, he said, 'This is looking beautiful'. And he forgot all about the actual toilets, which had not even been built!"

In reality the Administrator had instructions from the Chief Secretary to 'do something' about that ugly open air toilet in front of the Reserve Bank within two days. So toilet or no toilet, the goal had been achieved.

More important than letter, is *spirit*.

Meanwhile in ten days time, the actual toilet block was also up and ready (except for the roof – that came later). It was a pay-for-use toilet – 10 paise per visit.

"The government agreed to provide the land free of cost, and pay for the construction. The maintenance was to be covered by charging users."

The question was, would the man on the street pay? Skeptics said that in Bihar most people traveled ticketless in buses and trains – would they shell out money to use a toilet??

Bindeshwar said, "We will keep it spotlessly clean. They *will* pay."

And he was right. On the very first day 500 people lined up to use the facility! There was such a buzz about the Sulabh Shauchalay that it quickly set up pay and use toilet blocks across Patna city and then across the state.

> **"Our movement is to restore the human rights and dignity of untouchables. And to bring them into the mainstream, of society. The toilets, biogas plants, all these are means to achieve that dream."**

In 1977 a WHO official called Mr A K Roy – a sanitary engineer – came to visit. He was astounded by what Sulabh had achieved. 40,000 two-pit latrines had been installed in individual homes. And pay per use Sulabh Shauchalays had sprung all over the state.

He commented: "I joined the engineering department in 1940 and we could not achieve this. How have you done it?"

An engineer named Alberto Besa was sent across Bihar for verification. The first sentence of his report read as follows: "This is unbelievable but true…"

WHO, UNICEF and the Government of India then conducted a seminar in 1978 for chief engineers and bureaucrats across the country. The recommendation was: "The Sulabh toilet which has been successfully implemented in Bihar, must be adopted across India."

For once, Bihar was actually *leading* the way.

From 1978 onwards Sulabh spread to Bengal, Orissa, UP and then all of India. Today Sulabh has a presence even in Afghanistan and has trained professionals from 14 African countries to replicate the model.

Today, there are 7500 Sulabh Shauchalayas (public toilet complexes) and two pit latrines in 12 lakh homes across India. The model was uniform. A public-private partnership where the 'private' was Sulabh. Building the actual toilets and managing – as well as multiplying – the movement.

So, land came from the government (for public toilets).

As did funds for building them.

Users paid a small sum, so that they could be maintained.

A self-sustained model which was a win-win for all concerned.

In individual homes, the *sarkaari* support came in the form of part grant and part loan. But the evangelisation was done by Sulabh.

"Our job was to go door-to-door, explain the benefits. Motivate people to adopt the new system which did not require a scavenger."

Further, Sulabh would collect the signatures of interested parties, get their papers processed, expedite release of funds and finally, build the toilet.

To process was important. Because how else can you ensure 'customer satisfaction' across states, across geographies?

"We had to build trust, and confidence. Our workers would give a list of items required for construction which the house-owner could cross check."

Later, a Sulabh worker would follow up; find out whether the customer was fully satisfied.

Finally, a prize was also awarded to the house-owner. This not only instilled a sense of pride in the user but made the Sulabh workers accountable. Each installation was incomplete without the house-owner's stamp of approval.

Sulabh also provided a guarantee card for a five year period. If anything went wrong in that period, repair and replacement would be done free of cost.

The Sulabh organisation also grew rapidly, to make this scale up possible. As Bindeshwar puts it: *"Dheere dheere log aate chale gaye".*

Ordinary people – what are known in the social space as *karyakartas*. Because the technology was so simple, you did not need engineers or other highly educated professionals.

The seed of any organisation is sown by an individual, and then it flowers and grows into a mighty tree. In nature, the tree is grounded and every fruit and every leaf has the same odour, same flavour. But how do you grow roots and instil the fragrance of common, shared values?

Bindeshwar's answer is simple: The founder must lead by example. And create the culture, or *sanskaar* of the organisation.

"Whether it is a head of state, a school headmaster, a college principal, a librarian, *usi ke character par sanstha chalegi."*

In short, if I am a dubious type of person, I cannot expect my people to be sincere.

"The first person in any organisation – if he is honest – then the people who work for him will largely be honest. Of course there may be a few rotten apples. But they will be weeded out and punished."

But how does one monitor if workers are handing over all the cash being collected at 7500 Sulabh Shauchalays around the country? Surely there is no SAP system here to do that!

Bindeshwar pauses, then says, "*Kaha jaata hai* – 'By little mind, you cannot rule over a great empire'."

Translated into ordinary English – you cannot grow big if you believe in micro-management.

In case of Sulabh, there's a principle called 'three-monthly checks". Instead of monitoring what every *Sulabh Shauchalaya* collects every day, the money collected on any one day in a 3 month period is inspected. And taken as a benchmark.

Now the person managing that location must ensure he submits that much money, until the next three-monthly inspection occurs.

"I can't guarantee that each and every rupee is submitted. But the amount established through the random checking - that we get for sure."

Is this condoning a 'liitle' cheating. Or does one see the small amounts that slip through into workers' hands as an incentive or bonus?

Pathakji smiles.

"There is one important principle of administration… there are some things which you wilfully ignore."

You pick and choose your battles. *Ghar ki shaanti ke liye.*

And many HR heads may say 'we are family'. But *kehne ki baat hai,* how many places can you feel it. At Sulabh, you do.

There is love, compassion, nurturing, a sense of pride. And generosity of spirit as well as actual resources.

"If one of our workers – or their family members – falls sick, whether it is a heart problem or liver problem, we never turn anyone away. We don't ask, what is your income, your eligibility for funds. Whether it costs two lakhs, or four lakhs – we don't keep count."

> "The government is providing more and more reservation. But where are the jobs? I believe that if we educate these children, make them capable, they will find jobs on their own."

You cannot put a price tag – on a life.

But you can pay the price for a life because, you have resources.

Sulabh, as a self-sustaining, entrepreneurial, social organisation has annual 'revenues' of $20 million. That's right, ₹ 100-125 crores.

Bindeshwar clarifies that this is really a 'budget'. On the one hand Sulabh earns an income from building toilets in homes and in public places. On the other hand it is paid, to maintain them.

This income goes out into different directions. Firstly, money is used towards physical infrastructure – to build and maintain facilities. Secondly, on salaries – or 'honorarium'. Sulabh has 25,000 people 'associate members' on a full time basis and 10,000 on a project basis (few companies in India would match those numbers, I think!)

And thirdly, there are welfare activities. Sulabh runs its own school (Sulabh Public School*), vocational classes for young men and women and other such activities – mainly for the benefit of scavengers and their families.

"We fund the education of hundreds of children... *Bahut ladkiyon ki shaadi karwayi yahanse humne*. Even people who are not associated with Sulabh in any way come seeking help."

And rarely is anyone turned away.

The big difference between a corporate earning ₹ 100 crores in revenues and Sulabh having ₹ 100 crores as budget is that there are no 'profits' which are distributed to stakeholders. In fact, there is really no concept of profit, let alone *maximisation* of profit.

Despite 'professional management'.

---

* *Sulabh International Public School comprises 60% children of scavengers and 40% children from other classes of society.*

Take the example of the Sulabh public toilets itself. Out of 7500 such toilets, around 4000 generate little or no income. 1000 *shauchalayas* run on break even. And the remaining 2500 actually make 'a lot of money'.

It's the simple principle of 'cross subsidy'. A principle that makes no sense in the corporate sector, but serves the social sector rather well.

So what does Bindeshwar see as his lasting contribution. Is it the public toilet complexes in cities all over India, or the lakhs of two-pit toilets in homes all over the country?

Neither, he says.

These are just outward manifestations, what we *see*.

"This is a revolution – a sanitation revolution. And my mission is to fulfil the dream of Mahatma Gandhi. To make India scavenger-free. It is my mission to educate these scavengers, get them into new occupations, make them part of the mainstream."

And that dream *has* been realised. Because the same people who were once considered untouchable, dirty, unfit to be a part of society; these scavengers are now human beings.

A part of the mainstream.

Bindeshwar gives an example. Women who once had only scavenging as their source of livelihood; these women are now running small businesses.

"Who buys the goods they've made? The same people whose homes they used to enter to clean the toilets. *Memsaab* would not give them water in a glass. *Theek hai?*"

"Today, in those very same houses, they go, sit on a sofa and share a cup of tea with the lady of the house. They enter temples, where they were never allowed..."

Much progress has been made, but much is yet to be done. Sulabh estimates there are 3-4 lakh people in India who still earn their livelihood by cleaning toilets. The government says that number is 127,000.

The point, says Bindeshwar, is that they exist.

Sulabh is currently running a rehabilitation centre in Tonk (Rajasthan) in collaboration with the Ministry of Social Welfare. This is a pilot program for one year, covering 61 girls.

"Your heart will break to hear this," he says. "These girls, when they were two years old, three years, five, six or seven – they used to go with their mothers to see how toilets were cleaned. And from the age of seven, they started cleaning toilets themselves.!"

So how does one 'rehabilitate' those who were made to believe – from birth – that they had no rights. Let alone the right to dream.

Bindeshwar believes it's not just about sending an 'untouchable' to school. *Wo to zaroori hai* but more important is raising that individual's self esteem.

"Dr Ambedkar has written about the time when an inspector came to his school and asked: "Tell me the one thing which you can see, but not touch. *Aisi kaun si cheez hai jo tum dekh sakte ho, magar chhoo nahin sakte*'."

Children gave different answers.

'Sun'. 'Moon'. 'Stars'. 'Wind'.

Ambedkar said '*Paani ka ghada*' and pointed to the earthen pot with water in a corner of the classroom.

He said, "Until people of all castes do not eat together, go to the temple together, do *pooja* together, bathe in the pond together, fill water from the same well – until then I will not consider untouchability as 'abolished'."

Thus, non-traditional or '*gair paramparik*' methods are the cornerstone of Sulabh's rehabilitation program.

For example, Bindeshwar will take the women to a 5 star hotel for dinner. Why? To make them realise ki "*hum bhi yahaan aa sakte hain*".

The first time he took such a group to Delhi's Maurya hotel, the GM came rushing out and asked, "Pathakji, what is this you are doing? What will people say!"

After the meal, the same GM came and apologised; there was no cause for complaint.

"You tell me… who in this country would have the heart to take scavengers to a 5 star hotel for a meal? At a cost of ₹ 3 lakhs!"

Again, you cannot put a price tag on something intangible like a 'feeling'.

A feeling that I too am somebody in this world.

"*Samman badhane ka symbolic tareeka*", as Bindeshwar puts it. A symbolic means of improving their self esteem.

And it does not stop there. Gandhiji dreamt of a day when a scavenger – a mahila – would become President of this country.

Bindeshwar says, "President *to hum bana nahi sakte, humko adhikaar nahi hai. To hum kar kya sakte hain? Hamne aisi hi ek mahila ko Sulabh ka President bana diya ha.*"

As President of Sulabh International, Usha Chaumar is now meeting dignitaries, accepting awards, travelling the world!

Last year Usha gave a speech in the UN Trusteeship Council – in English. She walked the ramp with some of India's top models. Represented Sulabh at the World Toilet Summit 2007 held at Vigyan Bhawan in New Delhi.

"*Kal jab yahan se jaa rahi thi* she said, 'Sir – thank you. Bye bye! Good night'!" She has so much confidence, so much energy to take our movement forward."

And all because someone believed in her. Gave her that chance.

His methods are unorthodox, even eccentric. But what strikes me is that he can do exactly what he wants. The way he wants. Because Sulabh is not a typical 'NGO'.

Bindeshwar agrees wholeheartedly.

"On record I am telling you that we have a ₹ 10 crore overdraft with State Bank of India, Patna. Why? To organize the World Toilet Summit 2007 and also for the trip our women made to US. Who would take a loan from the bank to further a social cause?"

"*Rupya hoga, to dil nahin hoga,*" he adds.

Like when it comes to booking a hotel for the New York visit, Bindeshwar insists they stay right opposite the UN building. Not in a cheap place costing $30 a night, *jahan se aane jaane mein do ghanta lagega.*

It's a different way of thinking, that's for sure.

"In the corporate world, people think about how to earn more, and save more to line the pockets of shareholders. We have a different philosophy. *Hum bataa rahein hain ki, apni roti kama kar kaise logon ke beech mein baata jaaye. Kaise uska sukh bhoga jaaye*".

"We feel that the benefits of globalisation should go to the poor. *Yeh kaam mind se nahin ho sakta hai, sirf heart se ho sakta hai.*"

Aur yeh dil dhadakta hai from the Sulabh International complex on Palam Dabri Road. Very close to Delhi airport. I don't know where Bindeshwar got the inspiration from, but it's really – in a manner of speaking – the Disneyland of toilets.

As a visitor, you will be taken on a whirlwind tour – through the Sulabh Public School to the vocational training classes for scavengers; you will see actual two pit toilets, a bio-gas plant in action and – most intriguingly – the world's only 'museum' dedicated to toilets. 2.2 million people have visited this complex and gone potty over it – since 1992.

So where does all this fit in, in the larger scheme of things? Well, social reform is the main agenda of Sulabh; but so is sanitation.

Says Bindeshwar, "America, Europe and Australia *ne toh samasya ka hal nikaal diya. Lekin* Asia, Africa, Latin America, *yeh nahin nikaal paaye.*"

Samasya hai toilet ki. 2.5 billion people still do not have proper lavatories in their homes. And they cannot hope to, in the near future, because both septic tanks and sewerage do not come cheap.

Sulabh has an alternative to the sewerage system – a decentralised water treatment plant. This plant recycles water, produces biogas and produces bio-fertiliser. It can be put to use in any large complex – a housing colony, school, college or hospital.

And where did the idea come from? The home of an *adivasi*.

In 1977, Bindeshwar was at the Diplomat Hotel in New Delhi when he heard two men discussing how a tribal had connected his toilet to a biogas plant – and ran his *chulha* on this gas.

He went up to that table and asked for the tribal's address. They said the *adivasi* was 'somewhere in MP', near Indore. Through a distant connection, Bindeshwar managed to track down his location.

"I went there, saw it with my own eyes. Realised that methane was being produced and that we could try something similar with our toilets."

It's another long story. But if one had to sum it up: Application of mind is more important than knowledge.

And application of heart, is the most important... of all.

———————————

ADVICE TO YOUNG ENTREPRENEURS

Gandhi once said that he would be happy if we got freedom later, but that we need cleanliness first. The new generation should join in bringing about this revolution.

Lack of toilets is one problem, but even in a fancy restaurant you will find the food is good, restaurant is clean, but toilet is filthy. Cleanliness is a culture, which we must adopt, and propagate. As a national mission.

Secondly, we should definitely maintain our cultural heritage, the good traditions (minus the superstition and harmful practices). Also assimilate knowledge from other cultures. But we should not allow our uniqueness, our Indianness to disintegrate.

And in the end I would say, lead a life of contentment. *Santosh ka jeevan.*

These days I find more and more people are dejected, depressed. See, in this recession, even billionaires are sitting with their head in hand. *Bhai kyun?* What does it really matter?

When our family fell on hard times, one of the workers in our fields said, "*Babuwa*, I have seen you reduced to a molehill from a mountain." Later, when I started this work and made it big she said, "This is astonishing. *Phir rai se parbat bhi bante bhi dekha humne*".

I have seen you become a mountain once again.

So fortune comes and goes. One should not live for it or be attached to it.

Lastly, create your own identity, leave your own stamp in whatever you choose to take up. I told my son, to take up some work other than Sulabh. *Koi aisa kaam karo jisse tumhari pehchaan bane. Kyunki jo vyakti apne naam se jaana jata hai na, woh No. 1 vyakti hota hai.*

And to be No.1 in a field of one is a great feeling.

RAGS
TO RICHES

Anita Ahuja,
Conserve India

Like many well-to-do women in Delhi, Anita Ahuja took up social work. But, deeply moved by the plight of ragpickers, she decided to do something to improve their lives. Today. Anita and her husband Shalabh run a unique income-generation program – recycling plastic waste to create beautiful export-quality handbags.

One look at Anita Ahuja and you know she is 'South Delhi'. Casual, yet chic. Punjabi, but not *behenji*.

Well to do, cultured.

I can almost see her – mornings in the garden; afternoon kitty party; evenings at the India International Centre. NGO work a few hours a week.

Bhai bacche bade ho gaye hain, one must have something to do, no?

Anita Ahuja defies this stereotype with every gentle bone in her body. She is the dreamer who started Conserve, a social enterprise which makes world-class handbags from plastic waste – or *kachra* – collected by ragpickers.

Anita Ahuja did not plan to get into business. Neither did she plan to get into social work. In fact she started working with ragpickers only to 'reinvent herself'. To learn something, and possibly turn it into a book.

But working with the 'poorest of the poor' moved her deeply.

"These are human beings, with a right to dignity and a minimum wage", she thought. And that's what triggered the idea of creating wealth from waste.

How would she do it? No idea. Who would buy it? No idea. Has it ever been done? Who cares! *Karna hai – bas*.

Armed with the ignorance of an amateur and inspiration of an artist, Anita created something the world had never seen before. Today Conserve India's handbags are sold on high streets across the globe. What's more, the enterprise employs 300 erstwhile ragpickers.

At the Patparganj office of Conserve India, I am as mesmerised by the handbags created from Amul milk pouches, as by this story of entrepreneurship. Anita and her husband Shalabh – the technical brain of the project – have a great thing going. But it's more than a business.

It's the expression of that inner eye.

The vision of a better, more beautiful world.

RAGS
TO RICHES

Anita Ahuja,
Conserve India

Anita was born in Bhopal – daughter of a freedom fighter – at a time when life was relatively uncomplicated.

"Bhopal was a very small town and just opposite our house was the big Tajul Masjid – I could hear the *imam* in the morning. My father's name is Ram and his brother's name is Lakshman. So, we named our house, *Ram-Lakshman Nivaas*."

A Ram-Lakshman *nivaas* right opposite Tajul Masjid was not considered odd at all.

Anita grew up with, what she calls a 'very secular kind of system in place'. When she was ten years old, the family shifted to Delhi.

"Bhopal was very conservative in some ways... Delhi of course was a big city. I joined a co-education school, Modern School. I was pretty young so in a way, I grew in Delhi and... it was a very nice growing up period."

Community service was not drilled into their heads but the school did create that kind of a feeling where you were at least sensitised to various issues.

Like most women of her generation, Anita was not very ambitious.

"I joined Delhi University; did my BA and my Masters in Literature and Political Science. I was artistic but like any traditional Indian family, my parents thought it better that I go for academics rather than for art and... marriage was kind of quite uppermost in their minds."

In 1984, straight after MA, Anita got married. She was 24.

"Shalabh is an engineer from BITS, Pilani. We were dating so, you know, my parents were in a hurry (laughs)..."

"From day one, Shalabh wanted to do a business... we both believed that business creates jobs. He started a business making televisions. We were a young couple in love; I had two children very quickly after marriage..." Anita trails off.

"I don't think my mind was really shaped. That shaping up started happening gradually."

Anita's father is a lawyer but also a freedom fighter.

"He has contributed a lot to my thinking. As a lawyer, my father handled some wonderful cases like coal nationalisation, Baroda dynamite case and so on. I was exposed to politics right from childhood."

However she never had any inclination to join politics. Instead, when her kids grew older, she took up writing.

"I started writing short stories and 'middles'. My mother used to tell me that I should write more seriously; perhaps write a book. But I felt I did not have the discipline or the commitment to do it."

A thought that almost every author has before taking the plunge. But books are funny things, when they need to, they just *happen*.

"My mother passed away and something got triggered." The year was 1994. India had been through a great deal of turmoil – *rath yatra*, Babri masjid, Mandal Commission.

"For the first time the *imam* at the Tajul Masjid opposite my childhood home had closed the gates and locked it. The call for *jihad* had come, *Maha Aarti* had taken place. I saw all this and wondered, as a small town person how would I be feeling? As a Hindu; as a Muslim."

"I felt there were not enough women writers, writing on such issues... and I feel if you have a viewpoint, if you have something to say, you must express it. Whether, people agree, disagree, like it or don't like it is a different thing."

"We were already making compost – using wet waste to create a saleable product. Why not find a use for plastic waste? So I started experimenting."

And that's exactly what Anita did. It took her two years; one year to write the book and one year to get it published.

"*Flames of Fervour* was very well received, it got a lot of coverage from the media, a film got made and I was invited to numerous seminars."

But there were other issues. The book had political overtones and some people did not take kindly to it. Were the threats serious? For a young middle class couple, serious enough.

"Men are also scared but as a woman with children..."

She trails off.

"We live in a democracy. We have an independent judiciary. All those things are there, but..."

It's foolhardy to antagonise the state machinery.

As a young businessman, Shalabh had cause to worry. Did he have enough security or finances to deal with the situation?

"We didn't have that clout. I mean, we are middle class."

So, what now? Anita knew one thing for sure. She had to be *honest* in whatever she did. You can't write freely if you're constantly worrying how someone might react to it. Maybe it was the stress, or just writer's block. Anita wondered, "Do I even have anything more to say?"

"As a writer, whatever you have, whatever you know; you give it to the book. I had given everything I had at that point of time. To write another book I felt I needed to reinvent myself, learn something."

Which is how Anita got into social work. A grassroots project, she thought, would give her a window into another world. A better understanding of the human condition.

Along with some like-minded people – family and friends – Anita decided to take up a few small projects in her own locality.

"We started an NGO," and she laughs. "In Delhi 'NGO' is a very commonly used word because every family, I think, has an NGO or a foundation!"

Conserve India was registered in 1998 and the project it took up was waste collection in the surrounding locality. The idea was to separate kitchen waste and make compost in the local park. The first thing Anita realised was that nothing could be achieved alone.

"You have to be involved with your Residents' Welfare Association (RWA). Then you need to have links with the Deputy Commissioner; with the municipality, and then it grows."

Around the same time, the Chief Minister of Delhi Sheila Dikshit was launching a programme known as 'bhagidari'.

She said, "Since you're doing such a good job in these two-three localities on your own, why don't you be more active with other RWAs."

We thought, "Why not?"

Conserve started reaching out, partnering with more colonies. From Madhuban and Preet Vihar, they went as far as Safdarjang Enclave. Was it easy convincing people outside her own neighbourhood?

"There were problems. We had to meet the RWAs and convince them but since our efforts were sincere, intentions were good, it was generally quite smooth. People knew I was a writer. I had no axe to grind and I wasn't looking for a political ticket or seat."

Besides, it was clearly not about 'making money' – no one at Conserve even drew a salary. The NGO worked within the system, with the ragpickers who were already collecting waste. But, the job was now done more systematically.

"We got better carts, gave the ragpickers uniforms and identity cards. We trained the ragpickers on how to handle and segregate the waste. How to go door-to-door for collections, speak politely. Everybody liked it very much."

When people like something – they embrace it. They don't just buy your idea they buy into it.

Which is how Conserve was successful in training not just ragpickers but the ladies in the locality – and servants – on segregation.

Over time Conserve started interacting with 3000 Residents' Welfare Associations. These RWAs were across social strata and income groups and Conserve found itself working not just on waste management but everything from RTI to security and roads.

By 2002, Conserve had become a full time commitment, an *organisation* in its own right.

"We started getting grants from the Delhi Government, from the Ministry of Environment, from USAID, from World Bank."

The grants were small – ₹ 2 lakhs, ₹ 5 lakhs, the maximum ever received was ₹10 lakhs. But over a period of time Anita realised that funding usually came with strings attached. You have to make proposals on issues which the funding agency wishes to support. And these may not be the issues you want to work with.

"We realised we needed our own funding – to stand on our own feet."

The NGO needed to earn an income – but how could it be generated? And ultimately who or what was Conserve really working for? Questions which needed answers...

By this time Anita had spent over four years working with the ragpickers. And she realised that they were the poorest of the poor.

"Ragpickers live on the edge of the society. I visited their homes – cardboard shelters built on land-fill sites. They have no education, no training."

And they have language issues.

"It's not that English is a problem. They don't even speak Hindi because they have come from different parts of India and also from outside India – Bangladesh, Afghanistan. So they are treated as an 'illegal community'."

Any 'thinking' middle class person would say "none of my business". But Anita was different. She felt their pain.

"The point is, wherever they are from, they are now living here. And here to stay. They are living a sub-human existence."

It felt entirely unfair.

"When corporates do CSR, it is their
last priority. But when fair trade companies
or NGOs take up marketing programs,
then fairness is the top-most priority.
That is the difference."

"Today you need minimum ₹ 4000 per month to survive in Delhi. The ragpickers earn about ₹ 1500-2000 and are completely at the mercy of contractors."

Often, the contractor would give the ragpickers only some dry *rotis* to eat. The large majority were women, with several children. Health was a major issue; hygiene non-existent.

There are many problems in society. But every NGO has to focus on one issue; and one community which is its core constituency.

"I decided Conserve would work to improve the life of ragpickers."

But how?

While grant supported programs continued, side by side, Anita started 'playing around' with plastic waste. The typical blue-pink-yellow variety of *thailis* you see everywhere.

"We were already making compost – using wet waste to create a saleable product. Why not find a use for plastic waste collected by the ragpickers? So, I started experimenting."

Anita reseached the recycling technologies available on the internet and tried dozens of different things.

"First, I tried weaving and making carpets. But the products that came out looked home made and were very labour intensive."

Not financially viable and hard to sell. But despite getting nowhere, Anita kept going. Ultimately she developed a texture of layering the plastic bags together and it came out very nicely.

"I found I could create beautiful patterns and no one could tell this was made from plastic waste at all!"

At first Anita thought she could just make artworks and installations, have an exhibition and try and raise money. But Shalabh – being more practical of the two – realised it would not work.

"If the objective is to generate income, we have to look at starting a factory."

The first step in that direction came when Shalabh fabricated a machine which could mass-produce the plastic sheets. Artist creates, engineer automates – a fine example of left brain-right brain collaboration!

"It took us about six months; the whole process of learning how to combine the right colours and make the sheets look pretty. Because if you just put *anything* then it's just a sheet; then it doesn't sell. It looks dirty, like dirty plastic."

By trial and error Anita produced a portfolio of 200 unique designs. She calls them her 200 'paintings'.

Initially, Anita made a few simple things like wine bags and carry bags, files and, folders. To do this, she hired a few roadside tailors. The merchandise was sold at embassies which had trade fairs around Diwali season.

"Since we had already worked with the funding agencies, I knew them. So I went and put up a stall at these fairs, " recalls Anita. The ragpickers were trained to man these stalls and do the selling.

But Anita quickly realised that a wine bag or a file/folder would fetch maximum ₹ 60-100. The profit margin was slim so there wasn't much left – to share with the ragpickers.

But, the sale was not in vain. As they say, customer is queen and when she makes an outlandish demand you stop and ask yourself, "Why didn't I think of that!"

One woman said, "I really like the colours and texture. Can you make a better bag – a proper handbag – with the same fabric? I'll pay you a lot more."

And that's how Conserve started making well designed, high quality handbags. The practical, viable, 'hot selling' product she had been searching for all along.

At this time, Shalabh decided to join her full time. But what about his own business?

"He sold it. Because the handbag idea really seemed promising. We realised that with this material you can make anything – wallpaper, tiles, file-folders, footwear..."

Bahut kuch ho sakta hai. Par karne wala bhi to chahiye!

With Shalabh throwing his enthusiasm and expertise behind the venture, Conserve was poised to grow much faster. As with any idea, it all boils down to implementation. And that means getting into the basics – the *chhota chhota* details.

Conserve recruited *masterjis* who knew how to make good quality, leather handbags. They bought catalogues. And then, they got 'lucky'.

The idea of a green product with a social angle to it attracted *firang* designers. Volunteers, who offered to work for the sheer challenge of it. Purely through word of mouth.

"I was at the embassy fairs; so somebody's sister would say I want to come for a month and help out. Many of these volunteers even stayed with us!" she recalls.

Apart from designing, volunteers helped in setting up systems.

"I remember we had one volunteer who came from the UK – Andrew. He set up processes – right from how to collect the plastic to inventory and labelling."

Passion and purpose magically attract resources. A virtuous cycle from which, there is no looking back.

In 2003, Conserve participated in a trade show at Pragati Maidan. The Ministry of Textiles had given NGOs small booths and Conserve was able to book orders worth close to ₹ 30 lakhs ("which was a big amount for us!").

There were two USPs – the product was recycled but it was also very well designed. It had, after all been 'test marketed' at embassy fairs. That meant it had the quality and finish so crucial for the export market.

At the expo, Conserve learnt another important lesson. Buyers liked the product but were not too keen to place orders with an 'NGO'. Would a non-profit be able to deliver the goods? Would they be dealing with a specific person? Would it be as *accountable* as a for-profit which strives to please its clients?

"Some buyers had a series of bad experiences with NGOs. For example, the samples they received were different from the actual production."

So, they preferred to deal with private entities.

"Also NGOs have boards and funding – what happens if the funding gets over? They don't like such problems."

Anita and Shalabh decided that it made sense to form a propietorship company. What one must hold on to is 'spirit' – not form!

The first large order took Conserve 4-5 months to execute. Processes and systems were not in place. For example, to make one hundred pieces of the same style you need to mass produce sheets which looked nearly identical.

"Theoretically speaking I had understood it, but I had to start collecting 'that blue', 'that green', 'that pink' and learn to combine them in a certain way."

Logistically, it was a huge challenge.

"For example, I always did a lot of stripes and squares because if you change one stripe it doesn't make that much difference in the overall scheme of things. With plains, if there are two shades, the handbags will look different".

The technical nuances are lost on me but Anita gets so animated talking about it – I can feel the energy she's poured into the project. No mountain too high, no valley too low – when it comes to recycling plastic*! To seek more, go deeper, to explore – *that's* the hallmark of the entrepreneur.

However there's a practical side to being successful in business. You can do a zillion experiments but once you know what sells, you go after it with all you've got. Although Anita has developed 200 designs, at a typical trade show she showcases only 12, in keeping with the season and colour forecast.

It's been five years since Conserve was registered as a company and there is growth, diversification. Bigger buyers. New product lines such as footwear. And more kinds of waste being recycled such as tyres and textiles.

As requirements grew Conserve has had to look beyond ragpickers to source waste material. While it still conducts some door-to-door collection that does not yield the volumes and specific colours of plastic needed for production. So Conserve has tied up with *kabaadiwallas* and also sources directly from the industry.

But where do the ragpickers fit into all this? Well, they supply Conserve with waste but close to 300 of them are also part of the production team. The new footwear unit, for example, is

*Conserve received a 20 year patent on 'handmade recycled plastic' in Sep '10

completely staffed by ragpickers – they are being trained into 'footwear craftpersons'.

It's a process of evolution. "When they don't know anything, they do ragpicking. Then they show some skill, some interest in being part of a factory setup. We put them in training, as an assistant in some machine."

Over time, ragpickers move up to 'group leader'. While the stitching is still done by tailors, almost all other aspects are handled by former ragpickers.

"The sheets are made by the ragpickers. They are very fragile and need to be pasted with something. That's done by the ragpickers. Then there's folding, die cutting, quality checking, finishing, packing – so many operations!"

Has their life changed for the better? Certainly!

"They are very happy because they have become factory workers. You know, a person can be doing one thing only, such as putting the label. But he takes pride, feels like an important part of the process."

What's more, every worker at Conserve gets a salary of ₹ 4000*. Plus there is overtime, ESI, PF – all strange and new benefits for a community which has always lived on the edge...

Conserve India revenues are expected to touch ₹ 5 crores by 2011. With production demand increasing, the company has just moved into a new factory in Bahadurgarh.

"We are growing but a lot more has to be done. Also, because it's a fair trade company we have to balance a lot of things."

Things can move faster if you take a lot of trained people. But the emphasis here is on training the ragpickers.

And slowly Conserve is moving from being a supplier to becoming a brand. Initially, buyers would simply stick their own label onto anything sourced from Conserve. But now most of them are co-branding the bags because telling the story – its recycled heritage and social purpose – helps sell more.

I can see Anita and Shalabh are working hard. And having fun. And doing more than their bit for society. But is there any discomfort with being an NGO and 'making money'? Can you have your cake and polish off the crumbs??

* the minimum wage in Delhi is ₹ 3700 p.m.

"Yes, definitely. Conserve has a strong commercial focus because otherwise, we will not be able to sustain it socially. Today, there are more than 300 families dependent on this project. And if I am not sincere in my efforts, then… how will I support all of them?"

Few have the courage to ask – and fewer seek to answer – such questions.

ADVICE TO YOUNG ENTREPRENEURS

Your field of interest may be specialised, like mine is designing, but you must learn about accounting, marketing, legal issues, HR, Quality control etc. And not just terms from books, but in real terms.

You have to develop mental muscle, emotional muscle and physical muscle to chase all three bottom lines aggressively.

If you are chasing only money, then your family and friends end up spending it, which makes one feel "used". If you are focussed on social then the problems of poverty are so overwhelming, you burn out very fast. If it is only environmental issues then nobody is going to listen to you, you are not financially sustainable.

The secret is to find a balance.

BEYOND
PROFIT

Vineet Rai,
Aavishkaar Social Venture Fund

Quite by accident, 25-year-old Vineet Rai became CEO of GIAN – a network to support grassroots innovation. From there came the idea of setting up a micro-venture fund for rural entrepreneurs. Today, Aavishkaar supports 23 companies which generate profits – and returns to investors – but also address important social issues.

Vineet Rai's office looks more corporate than 'social'. Neat cubicles, interior-decorator colours on the walls.

Like most people I too am confused – what is this guy really all about?

Vineet Rai runs a 'social venture fund'. This fund invests in companies which have social objectives but also aim to make profits, and give investors a reasonable return. A philosophy far removed from the greed that drives a traditional VC firm!

Of course, people told Vineet,"It can't be done!"

7 years and 23 companies later, he's proved them wrong.

Aavishkaar also proves that you cannot and should not draw a line between 'social' and 'commercial'. Commerce can drive and deliver socially relevant goods and services.

And whether you start your career in the jungle or in a swanky office suite, you can become a leader of men.

Inspirer of hearts.

Creator of wealth.

In the material world and in the kingdom of Conscience.

If you bring out the best, in who you are.

BEYOND
PROFIT

Vineet Rai,
Aavishkaar Social Venture Fund

Vineet Rai was born in Jodhpur.

"My father was in the state government services. I was neither a great student nor an outstanding athelete, but aspired to be a 'stud' of some sort."

Living in Jodhpur, a place close to the border, Vineet saw convoys moving up and down, day in and day out.

"I thought that the easiest way to become a hero was to join the Army. So that was my story – just one goal, one dream. The only thing I did besides trying for the Army was to play a lot of cricket and football!"

Unfortunately the Army for some reason didn't like Vineet. He would clear the written exam with ease but get rejected in the SSB interview.

"They look for officer-like qualities and possibly they found none in me (laughs). Maybe I was too cocky, gung-ho, whatever."

It is said that if you get rejected once by the SSB, you will probably get through the second time. But Vineet had a pretty big ego.

"I wanted to get selected in the first instance. When I was rejected for NDA I said, 'Ok, I'll give the CDS and get through in the first chance'. And when I got rejected in CDS I applied for Air Force – there too I was rejected."

It was heartbreaking for somebody who had dreamt of *nothing* but a life in the army.

Vineet found himself at a career crossroad. What *else* could he do with his life? A friend suggested the obvious: an MBA.

That's when Vineet first heard of the Indian Institute of Forest Management. In fact the friend joked,"*Agar fauj main nahi liya to kam se kam jungle main hi chala jaa...* You'll still enjoy it."

"And I liked the idea. So this friend of mine – a gentleman called Jayesh Bhatia – bought my IIFM form, filled it up and paid the fees. He told me that I just had to read GMAT books and appear for the exam."

During that period Vineet also worked as a Sales Representative with a company called *'Current Tax Reporter'*, which published books on taxation. 2000 rupees a month was a pretty 'lucrative' sum for a 20-year-old back in 1991. Vineet spent the next 3 months travelling across Goa and Karnataka meeting Chartered Accountants.

"I realised that selling is not my calling and maybe I can do better things in life. But I need to find a way to move forward."

So Vineet hit the books with a vengeance, got through the exam as well as the interview (for once!). In June 1991, he arrived at the Indian Institute of Forest Management in Bhopal.

"I did not know whether Indian Institute of Forest Management teaches you forestry or management or a combination of both. After going there I realised that the institute itself did not know whether it was teaching forestry or management or a combination but ... at least the building was impressive!"

For the first three months Vineet had the burning ambition to be a gold medallist. And he was doing quite well, academically. Then he decided that too much hard work was no fun and the next 18 months were 'chill out'.

"I met Swati, who is my wife now. Thanks to her, I discovered many things about myself. Like I can do a lot of things very well, the trouble was my ability to stay fixed or attracted to something was very limited!"

But that was to change. To the surprise of many, Vineet was amongst the first in his batch to land a job. He joined Ballarpur

> **"Today I can say I had this brilliant vision but when I started Aavishkaar there was nothing. Just the belief that people in rural India need small amounts of money and can give the investor a reasonable return if they succeed."**

industries in June 1994 – with absolutely no clue what he would actually be doing on the job.

Vineet was posted at Chaudwaar, near Cuttack. A part of the world he had never seen before. Doing a job that had not been done before..

"We had taken over another company, so things were in shambles. I did not even have a place to sit – no table, no chair!"

Ballarpur is in the business of paper. The forest department outsources the management of its land to private industry, who then cut bamboo and wood and take it to their factories.

"I was technically trained but actually saw a bamboo forest for the first time in my life. It finally boils down to man management and nothing else. Plus, there was the excitement of being chased by elephants!"

Vineet spent a year in Chaudwaar. Then, he managed to get himself posted to an even more remote area.

"I made some statements which no sensible person would make in a production company. Actually, I started laughing in one of the meetings and obviously that annoyed the bosses. They sent me off to a village called Boinda, 150 kms further away."

There was a British style thatched roof building and a 7 acre farm around it. No electricity, no running water, one well to draw water from. An exciting 'Tarzan' kind of life.

"I was given two forest divisions to manage which meant I had to wake up at 4 in the morning, visit the jungle, get chased by wildlife... Put out a forest fire or two, and make sure the trucks kept moving towards the factory."

The salary was ₹6000 per month but Vineet was pleased enough to graduate from motorcycle to jeep. Besides, he had close to 2000 labourers working under his supervision as well as a couple of officers. For a 24-year-old, that was a big high.

"The problem was all those people consider you their 'father' and that can get to your head. When I woke up there would be 200 people sitting outside waiting for me..."

Vineet spent close to 20 months as lord-of-the-jungle. But in the middle of the second year, he began feeling restless. It was the same cycle of seasons, of work, of one day the same as the next.

Besides, he was now married and his wife had been patient but could not help wondering,"Is this guy out of his mind?"

So, one fine day Vineet put in his resignation and went to Delhi, in search of a job.

"I spent three months looking for a job and realised that nobody wanted a person who has been living inside a forest for the last 3 years. I didn't know what is 'internet', I could not use MS Word..."

There was also the culture shock of seeing friends working out of swanky offices.

"I needed personal rewiring!"

It was at this time that Vineet got an offer to work with Prof Anil Gupta of IIM Ahmedabad.

"Prof Gupta was looking for a research associate with a corporate and forestry background. He offered me a salary of ₹ 3000 p.m. I said for that kind of money one can survive in the forest – not in a city like Ahmedabad!"

Prof Gupta agreed to pay the princely sum of ₹ 5900 p.m. Eight months of slogging with him taught Vineet that he was not cut out for research. He was a *doer*, not just a thinker!

Luckily, for Vineet, there was a project right up his street.

At the time the government of Gujarat and Prof Gupta were setting up an institute called GIAN (Grassroots Innovations Augmentation Network).

"Why don't you apply," suggested Prof Gupta.

Vineet looked at the proposed structure and applied for the position of 'manager'. To his shock, he was hired for the post of CEO.

"That was simply because nobody else applied for the post of CEO as far as I know. I loved the idea of being a CEO, even though there was no organisation *(laughs)*".

Vineet set one condition: he would not operate from IIM Ahmedabad. His argument was that GIAN should have its own identity, stand on its own two feet.

Prof Gupta said,"Do what you feel is right."

The next four years were a huge roller coaster. GIAN set up Gujarat's first Intellectual Property Rights cell and a Grassroots Innovation design studio (a collaboration with the National Institute of Design). GIAN filed patents for 8-9 companies which were part of the Honeybee* network.

"Having done all this, around 1999-2000, I stumbled upon a very simple and very well known fact: it is very difficult to raise money in India. The smaller the amount of money, the more difficult it gets!"

To Vineet's mind this was counter-intuitive, and it started bugging him. At this time he also discovered that GIAN had originally been conceived as a venture fund. However at the time there were some issues about setting it up as a 'for-profit' venture.

To get around the problem, GIAN became an incubator.

Phir bhi, Vineet decided to explore the how, what and why of starting a 'micro-venture fund'. One which could lend between one and twenty lakh rupees to rural innovators.

"I made a presentation to both SIDBI and NABARD. They said,"It's very exciting but won't work!"

Meanwhile Prof Anil Gupta had discussed the idea with two of his ex-students. In early 2001 Vineet got a call from one of them – Ananth Nageswaran. He then flew down to Singapore to discuss the plan.

Ananth said,"There are 40 odd NRIs who want to contribute to the country. Let us set up a for-profit fund that will be accountable to investors. Here is the first $5000 – show us that it works!"

The whole thing was based on faith.

---

* Honeybee network is a loose network of organisations, individuals and NGOs which documents innovation at the grassroots level (www.honeybee.org)

"They literally gave me cash – no papers, no account, no agreement, nothing. To them everything about Aavishkaar – which is what we called it – sounded like a fantasy."

Show us proof of concept.

Is it really possible that some guy in a village has produced a brilliant machine? And can we treat him like an entrepreneur and help him scale up?

GIAN invested the $5000 with two such rural innovators, Mansukhbhai Patel – who had devised a cotton stripper – and Kailash Gajjar, with an oil machine. That two lakh rupees yielded an annualised return of around 26% in six months.

"The investors were pleasantly surprised – they were expecting to see their money go down the drain!" grins Vineet.

This small success should have been a big victory; but at this point of time strong differences arose between Vineet and Prof Anil Gupta.

"Prof Gupta felt that implementing the venture fund as a for-profit was against the basic ethics of how to deal with grass root level people. Whereas I believed that the model was delivering the goods – helping rural innovators to create a business, create an impact. And being accountable to investors."

Matters came to a head; one fine day Vineet simply quit. He had no job in hand, no idea what he would do..

"The next 4-5 months I was doing nothing – literally. Then, a gentleman called Arun Diaz whom I had met in Singapore got in touch".

He said,"Vineet I know you have quit, but can you set up Aavishkaar again?"

"Venture capitalists are driven by greed. In fact, the entire US capitalism is in shambles primarily because their system is driven by the motive of maximisation."

> **"We basically act just like investors except we put money into companies that will generate returns and address social issues at the same time."**

Vineet said,"Yes but earlier I was backed by the Government of Gujarat, IIM Ahmedabad... Now it's just me, an inexperienced 28 year old."

Arun said,"Why not?"

He went back, and promised to speak to Ananth and Arvind Singh (the two gentlemen who had contributed the original $5000).

Meanwhile Vineet signed a contract with T & M VCL – 'Tungari Manohar Venture Capital Fund'. This fund was set up by Ravi Reddy and Sandeep Tungari (co-founders of Think System Pvt Ltd) with the objective of making 'social investments'.

"Similar to what I wanted to do in Aavishkaar, but they believed that investing ₹ 20,000-30,000 doesn't work. It has to be $ 200-250,000 put into each enterprise, as a one-time grant."

Vineet moved to Mumbai to work with T & M; at the same time he registered Aavishkaar as a trust in 2001. The Singapore based investors had raised ₹ 50 lakhs – but it was not enough. As per SEBI guidelines a VC fund must have a minimum corpus of $1 million.

"I went and pleaded to SEBI... Finally they gave us a registration but only after I gave a personal affidavit stating that Aavishkaar would not make any investments until the corpus reached $1 million."

The future of the project looked bleak. Meanwhile, in 2002, T&M VCL also wound up operations, leaving Vineet without a steady income once again.

"We were completely stuck actually on all fronts. For the next 5 months we struggled. With a great effort by Ananth, some effort by Arvind – we managed to increase the corpus from ₹ 50 lakhs to a crore."

After that Vineet would go to the SEBI office everyday, asking them for permission to invest.

"Unless we invested, we knew nobody was going to give us more money. We had to show some action, some results!"

Finally, in September 2002, SEBI sent Aavishkaar the go-ahead.

"I think they basically got completely tired of seeing me everyday." (laughs)

Now came the equally difficult task of identifying socially driven enterprises – to invest in. Paul Basil, CEO of the Rural Innovations Network (RIN) suggested a company called Servals.

Servals was run by Mukundan, a 60 year old gentleman, based in Chennai. The company manufactured stove burners for low income groups – its USP was the fact that it was 30% more efficient than any other burner in the world.

On the one hand, this meant savings on kerosene (and small amounts saved made a big difference to poor people). On the other, it reduced emission of greenhouse gases and this helped protect the environment.

Vineet was sold on the project and wrote up a proposal for Aavishkaar's investment committee. All the members approved it except for one: Vijay Mahajan.

"I don't think it will work," he said flatly."But that's just my opinion!"

Vineet would not go ahead, unless there was a consensus. Ultimately he persuaded Vijay to come down to Chennai and meet Mukundan.

"Mr Mahajan changed his mind; we went ahead and made our first investment in December 2002."

Aavishkaar paid ₹ 8 lakhs for a 49% stake in Servals. And the 'drama' started. There was no company, no 'business' as such.

"Just the burner and two gentlemen – one sixty years old and the other sixty five years old. We also had a lovely presentation in which we estimated we will capture 10% of the 2 crore burners sold annually – in the next 5 years".

The actual number of burners sold in the first year was 4200.

"Our next year target was 2 lakh burners and we sold 22,000 burners. So basically the company had gone bust in the first two years!"

The investors were coming up with brilliant ideas."*Uske sath katori do, uske saath glass do!"*

Another wellwisher advised,"Get a smart IIM guy and he will run it."

One of the first professionals who joined Aavishkaar was P Pradeep, an MBA from TAPMI who came with 5 years experience in the corporate finance team of Rajshree Sugars.

He said,"Vineet, all these things won't work. The problem is we are dealing with the unorganized industry".

Both Pradeep and Vineet started selling burners themselves to figure out what was going wrong. What quickly became evident was that rural India is not really about the best product in the market. They want the best product at the cheapest price.

And unfortunately Servals was *not* the cheapest. What's more, in order to be competitively priced, the company was squeezing the dealers and distributors.

One dealer bluntly said,"Most burners are made out of scrap; they go bad in 2 months, 3 months – to the max. Yours is made of copper and lasts for 9 months! On top of that you give me less margin... why should I sell it?"

Funnily enough, all the points Vineet had listed in his investment memo as 'strengths', were actually *weaknesses* in the marketplace.

"Which meant effectively that we had to go back to the drawing board. We had to compete with that burner which dies in 2 months and yet continue to maintain quality!"

A year went by, without much to show for it. The tsunami of Dec 2004 improved Servals order book. In 2005 the company sold approximately 50,000 burners. But clearly, it was not sustainable.

Mr Mukundan remained unfazed.

"Don't worry Vineet, it will all work out", he said.

But investors were breathing down Vineet's neck – to write off the company.

"It's just ₹ 15 lakhs – cut your losses and move on."

Sensible advice, but Vineet could not abandon Servals. Along with Pradeep, he plodded on. In late 2005, there was a breakthrough. Servals discovered a new alloy which brought

"We have differences in our investment committee. Some people believe that if a company becomes profitable it is no longer 'social'."

down costs dramatically, without compromising the product in any way.

It was Mr Mukundan who made this discovery. *He* had never ever given up...

Soon enough, sales of Servals burners jumped from 10,000 a year to 10,000 a month!

The question now – how to raise capacity.

Once again, Mr Mukundan came forward with a radical idea,"Vineet, I don't believe in mass production, I believe in production by masses. Let us make the village into our production centers."

"I said brilliant vision, but we'll probably have to close down!"

But what Mukundan proposed actually made great business sense. He knew of a man called Rangaswamy Elango, the force behind the 'model village' of Kuthambakam*. Elango is an IIT Madras graduate who returned to his roots, and was elected sarpanch in 1996.

At the time Kuthumbakkam was plagued by all kinds of problems – alcoholism, caste violence and lack of basic infrastructure like drinking water and roads. The biggest issue of all was unemployment.

"Elango tackled all these issues, by making a five year development plan. He involved people in the working of the panchayat at all levels. If you go there today you will not believe what you see – it is truly a model village!"

Creation of jobs was high on Elango's priority list. He had already established a small production centre with the help of local Self Help Groups (SHGs).

* *Kuthambakkam is 45-50 km from Chennai. See www.modelvillageindia.org.in*

"We converted the centre into our main point. Kuthumbakkam now manufactures 30,000 burners a month for Servals!"

Villagers get jobs; Servals enjoys low cost, efficient production. The struggle period is over, now it's all about scaling up.

"Today Servals sells 70,000 burners a month. The company's annual turnover is ₹ 2 crores – expected to touch ₹ 3.5 crores soon. We have just raised ₹ 60 lakhs for further expansion."

Perseverance has paid off. Vineet's original investment of ₹ 8 lakhs is now worth over ₹ 1.5 crores.

Servals is just one of the 23 companies funded by Aavishkaar, a social venture fund which 'harnesses the entrepreneurial spirit at the bottom of the pyramid'. These companies range from Naveen Gram (a venture focussed on sustainable technologies related to livestock and agriculture) to Vortex Engineering, which manufactures low cost ATMs for remote regions of India.

"There is no 'normal' investment. Every person behind these companies is a story..."

A story of struggle, of determination and will power.

"I wanted to prove that you can do 'social good' with commercial thinking. Obviously we have to sweat harder; really slog and slug it out."

And that is true of not just the companies Aavishkaar invested in, but the fund itself. In 2005, Aavishkaar had a corpus of $ 1 million (Rs 4 crores). The fee to manage this fund is generally fixed at 1.5 % which would be ₹ 6 lakhs a year.

"Our annual budget was ₹ 8 lakhs, including travel, salary – everything. I worked from my home in Mumbai; Pradeep worked out of his home in Chennai and we used to meet only when somebody would invite me and pay for my air travel (*laughs*)"

"People want to test you out before they trust you. I remember how many people were convinced that 6 months *baad ye bhaag jayega*. I proved them wrong!"

> "Getting romantic about development and doing development are two different things. It needs a lot of staying power and staying power mostly comes at a cost."

While Pradeep drew ₹ 35,000 p.m. as salary, Vineet took ₹ 25,000 p.m.

"By this time my son was old enough to go to a school and I suddenly realised I would have to pay ₹ 20,000 as 'capitation fees' and ₹ 10,000 as 'deposit'... and we didn't have the money!"

It was at this time that Vijay Mahajan suggested Vineet start some income generating consulting work, on the side.

"Back in 2002, when I was at a loose end, I had registered a company by the name of 'Intellectual capital' or Intellecap."

Intellecap was actually a crazy idea which Vineet's one time flatmate Pawan Mehra had come up with. A company that would trade in 'intellectual capital'.

"Vijay's suggestion made sense. Two days later I got an email from a gentleman called Mr Gautam Ivatury, former CFO of SKS Microfinance".

He said,"The World Bank wants to outsource the management of its microfinance gateway. Would you be interested in taking up the project?"

Vineet jumped at the offer.

"I roped in Pawan – who was now in the US. We made a brilliant proposal, sent it and got selected. I'm sure nobody else was so desperate to get a $1000 per month contract!"

On 1st March, 2004, Intellecap hired its first employee – Aparajita Agarwal.

"We had a table in my home. Aparajita used to sit on one side, and I sat on the other. That's how IntelleCap and Aavishkaar functioned for close to a year!"

Intellecap slowly grew – from two people to four, six, eight... The company took whatever projects came its way to pay the salary bills that Aavishkaar could ill afford.

In 2005, Vineet realised that he *had* to raise more money for Aaviskaar – make it a sustainable entity on its own.

"I decided to burn some money of Intellecap and go on a world tour to spread some awareness about our work. And raise funds."

Vineet went to the US and Europe and returned with commitments from investors for $ 6 million. With some additional effort, this sum swelled to $11 million in June 2008, and over $15 million in January 2009.

So far Aavishkaar has disbursed $16 million to 23 investee companies.

"We grew slowly. In 2002, Aavishkaar invested in two companies, another two in 2003 and 2004. And we were involved hands on in each of them."

As Aavishkaar grew, so did IntelleCap. The company focuses on social investment advisory and social knowledge management.

"Our clients are microfinance institutions, social institutions, financial institutions, healthcare, education – all kinds of people who are in the social space".

Because of the kind of work profile it offers, Intellecap attracts graduates from India's top schools (IITs, IIMs, IRMA and IIFM) at 30%-70% of their market value.

"I told them, 'You have to run this company.' And they did a fine job of it! The top management team in IntelleCap has remained the same since we founded it."

Meanwhile the social venture story itself has exploded with two new funds being added on to the Aavishkaar family.*

While visiting Oxford's SAID School of Business in 2005, Vineet met Wim van der Beek, who was trying to set up a microfinance fund. Thus was born Aavishkaar Goodwell.

Then, in partnership with Venture East, Vineet set up the BYST Growth Fund to provide equity-like financing for businesses run by young entrepreneurs from socially disadvantaged

* Aavishkaar is now a consortium of VC funds; for the full list of companies it has invested in visit www.aavishkaar.in.

backgrounds. BYST will invest from ₹ 4 lakhs to ₹ 1 crore in each enterprise.

"We are happy with a 25-30% return. Actually, we are happy even with 12% return. So in that sense we are different from a traditional VC company".

To put it in a nutshell, Aavishkaar is *not* driven by profit maximization.

"We are looking at rational profits, profits should be enough for us to create value. We will not squeeze out people, trying to take away each and every pound of flesh."

Out of the 14 companies which Aavishkaar invested in upto 2008, seven are profitable. And Vineet has no doubt the rest will turn a corner in the next couple of years.

What about the social impact these companies have created?

"To be frank I don't believe in this idea of *measuring* social impact. How can you quantify a smile on a woman's face whose monthly income has gone up by ₹ 300?"

And that applies to the entrepreneurs as well.

"The motivation that Mr Mukundan has cannot be quantified. A 65-year-old-man with diabetes, running a company 12 hours a day, how do you quantify that?"

Is it a commercial fund with a social objective; or a social fund with a commercial angle – the debate continues at Aavishkaar. At the end of the day Vineet says he is trying to create a 'multitude of Amuls'. Coming from a private herd.

"It's not just about giving money to somebody. We want to inspire promoters to scale up but we also want them to *retain* their souls.. The spirit with which they started out to do something, to make a difference."

The spirit with which Vineet started Aavishkaar, and rewrote the definition of 'venture capital'.

"Not many understood what I was trying to do... my parents were certainly baffled! But finally I think they are happy and think that I am doing something worthwhile. My father has even gone and met Mr Mukundan and seen what we do!"

Vineet's sister thinks he is 'brilliant' whereas his wife Swati, although confused, has always been a pillar of support.

"The most wonderful thing about my wife was that she never objected, even when I did something crazy like quitting my job. She had blind and complete faith in me!"

Just like Vineet had in his idea.

Like Mukundan had in *his* idea.

Like you will need to have, in yours.

———————————

ADVICE TO YOUNG ENTREPRENEURS

Entrepreneurship is about enjoying the journey. If you do that, the result will take care of itself.

Taking risk is far more important than worrying about managing the risk as you cannot create value and wealth without risking something .

Patience is a virtue in the current world of impatient exuberance – anyone could be *rich* but to create value you need to be dedicated and spend time and effort. Wealth creation and value creation are not always synonymous – I hope young entrepreneurs learn to understand the difference.

Capitalism and Wall Street has worked hard to give a very respectable positioning to the word"Greed". However an entrepreneur must understand that greed needs to be managed and harnessed properly for it to create wealth.

Unfettered greed has terrible consequences – the economic crisis of 2008 is a great reminder of that!

WEAVE
THE PEOPLE

**Sumita Ghose,
Rangsutra**

Sumita married an idealistic young IRMA graduate –
Sanjoy Ghose – and made a career in the NGO sector.
In 1998, Sanjoy was murdered by ULFA; Sumita had to
pull herself together and chart a new course. Today, she
runs Rangsutra, a for-profit venture which sources craft
and textiles from villages and retails through Fabindia.

On the map, Lado Sarai is a part of Delhi.

On the ground, it could be anywhere in India.

Narrow, dusty lanes; tiny shops, rickshaws and cycles everywhere. Here, on the third floor of a building with no name is the office of Rangsutra. A company which connects the India of 'Balika Vadhu' with the India of *The Economic Times*.

Rangsutra is a collective which sources craft and textile products from the villages and supplies them to Urban Retail. But there are many efforts of this kind – including Khadi Gram Udyog – what's so special about this one?

Well, Rangsutra has chosen to function as a 'private company', not a co-operative. In doing so, it has broken the NGO mould, become more market-oriented, achieved a galloping growth rate and touched the lives of more people.

Rangsutra does not depend on grants or subsidies – it talks profits and dividends. A new language for the social sector in India. A language that could change the way NGOs see themselves.

On a sunny winter afternoon, in a bare room brightened up by eye-catching samples, Sumita tells me her story.

It is a story of courage, of perseverance, of never losing faith. Of the beauty of the rainbow smiling in the sky, after the darkest storm.

WEAVE

THE PEOPLE

Sumita Ghose,
Rangsutra

Sumita Ghose was born in Calcutta but grew up in Mumbai. Or Bombay, as it was called then.

"I imbibed the best of India growing up there, in the sense that both school and college gave me the feeling that it's possible to do anything."

After graduating from Elphinstone College, Sumita went on to do a master's in Economics from Mumbai University. At this time, she considered joining advertising.

"I had a bent towards writing so I thought of going and working as a copywriter. But somehow the people I met from the ad world made it seem like very creative and fun, but a little superficial."

Soon after, Sumita got married to her college sweetheart – Sanjoy Ghose – and life took a very different turn.

"Sanjoy had just graduated from IRMA and he was very charged with this idea of working in rural areas, so that's what we did. First – very briefly – we were in Anand. And then in Rajasthan."

Friends asked, "How will you adjust to life in a village?"

Being young and in love, Sumita did not 'think' too much. *Bas kar liya.*

Of course, there were adjustments. And initially, a massive 'culture shock'.

"I had grown up in Bombay, which was like this melting pot. Suddenly, you go to a rural area and realise how strongly they believe in things like 'caste'."

And there was also the 'small stuff' – like packing away the jeans, putting on a sari.

Sanjoy and Sumita were very inspired by the Amul story. After a year in Oxford, the young couple returned to India and joined the 'Urmul' dairy – a co-operative similar to Amul – in Rajasthan. The year was 1985.

"Urmul dairy was very profitable in those days and they wanted to invest some of their profits in providing health services for their members. At the time there were health services for the cows, but nothing for the villagers. No government hospital for miles!"

And so, Urmul had registered a trust and invited professionals to take up this task. It was this challenge that brought Sanjoy and Sumita to Loonkaransar, 60 km from Bikaner.

"We came up with an innovative way to fund these services – from contributions made by members of the milk co-operative. The idea was that for every litre of milk that you give, which costs ₹ 3 per litre, put aside 3 paisa for health services."

However the richer farmers who controlled the dairy opposed the scheme. Services like ante and post-natal care and TB drugs were needed by the poor – who had no cattle – and hence would not be 'paying'.

"That model did not work, so we had to charge money. Later, we started getting government and international funds to do the work."

Right away, it was clear that finding a doctor to work full-time would be difficult. So what was the way out?

"Initially we were targetting mainly pregnant women and young mothers so we decided to work with the village midwives. We also created a team of paramedics by training locals in areas such as immunisation."

And it worked beautifully.

The scheme kicked off in 1986. But then in 1987 there was a bad drought – the worst seen this century – and the 'cattle economy' was literally wiped out. There was no point in talking about health when people did not have food to eat!

> ## "The country is so different and diverse and both – in terms of its richness as well as its problems – which is why we went to work in the villages in the first place."

"That's when we entered into this whole area of hand-craft. People needed *some* kind of work, and we found the women had *charkhas*. So we got wool, and got them to start spinning."

But what was to be done with this cloth? It was coarse and had no buyers!

"We found some weavers who made the famous 'pattoos' and got them to come and train the weavers in our area. And we linked up with NID (National Institute of Design) to learn how to make a finer quality product, better designs."

Then, Sumita discovered that some of the villagers were very skilled in hand embroidery. Mainly, women who had come over to the Indian side after the 1971 war, as refugees.

"The Urmul Trust organised this entire effort. We sourced the raw material and we sold as a collective – so that we could get a better rate for the products. In NGO terminology, we became an 'income generation' program."

Of course, initially they made losses. But the project was supported by the government of Rajasthan and funding agencies like Oxfam, so *kaam chalta raha.*

"Over time, some of these activities did become revenue generating, and we stopped taking grants. By this time – 1993 – I had stopped working with Urmul and moved on to other things."

After eight years in Rajasthan, Sumita wanted to get back to city life, for some time. The couple had two children – age 5 and 6 – who had never been to school. There *was* no good school in Loonkaransar..

So Sanjoy continued with Urmul, while the family shifted to Delhi. Sumita spent the next two years with the United Nations, organising the international Women's Conference in Beijing, in 1995.

"30,000 women from all over the world attended this conference. We took 200 women from the villages, gave them a voice." By this time, Sanjoy had also quit the Urmul Trust and was wondering what to do next. Living and working in Delhi was not very appealing. Neither was starting a city-based NGO, or working for a funding agency.

"We decided to go back and work in another state at the grassroot level. This time, we chose Assam. Partly because I felt a connection, having spent the first five years of my life in Guwahati." Sanjoy and Sumita zeroed in on an area known as Majuli in Jorhat district. Sumita had a fellowship from the MacArthur foundation, while Sanjoy was the general secretary of AVARD (Association of Voluntary Agencies in Rural Development) – a network of NGOs.

"We shifted to Assam in 1996, and though we'd worked in Rajasthan, in the villages, everything here was different."

And circumstances were different, as well. There was the luxury of a six-member team, and six months to 'study' and understand the place.

"I was very keen to make every woman a weaver because my fellowship was related to women's livelihood and health. But that same year there was a major flood. Since we had a doctor on our team, we decided to focus on immediate concerns like diarrhoea."

At the same time, Sanjoy and Sumita decided not to follow the Urmul model of 'service delivery'. Because, that made the villagers dependent on outsiders.

Their focus shifted to advocacy; creating awareness about existing government programs, and reaching them to the people.

One of the major problems in Assam is land erosion. To tackle this, Sanjoy and Sumita worked with scientists from the University in Dibrugarh to find new, better ways to build embankments. But it wasn't just a question of Man vs Nature...

"It was a big racket. Every year, you build the embankments; the rains come and wash it all away. Certain contractors made a lot of money doing this!"

Not only did Sanjoy and Sumita take on this mafia with their work on the ground, they wrote about it in the newspapers. And that's when they started getting threats from ULFA (United Liberation Front of Assam).

'We realised that although they are supposedly anti-state they were hand in glove at all levels. But, we never took the threat seriously."

It was a very costly mistake.

On the 4th of July, 1997, Sanjoy Ghose was abducted by ULFA militants. He was never seen again.

But why did these young activists become *such* a big threat? Because in just one year and three months, Sanjoy and Sumita had managed to mobilise 30,000 locals to participate in a movement to build their own embankments.

"All said and done, the ULFA played on peoples' sympathy. That government does not do anything for you, so 'support us, join the revolution'. If villagers start taking constructive action, it is detrimental to their cause..."

Sanjoy's untimely and tragic death resulted in the project folding up. The team disbanded, Sumita relocated to Gurgaon with her kids. Difficult as it was, life had to go on...

"I still had the MacArthur fellowship, but I changed the topic to 'conflict resolution'. I did a comparative study of different movements – those which had used violence and those which had not."

Sumita reached an important conclusion: non-violent movements empower women. Whereas violent struggles – like in Kashmir – have the opposite effect.

"I researched this area for two to three years and then got involved with the 'Hunger Project', an organisation based in the US."

The Hunger Project aims to reduce hunger but they try to do it through various means. Such as working with women, at the micro level. And through them, influence the agendas of local self-governments.

"I worked with women panchayat leaders, developing and building their leadership capacities. That was really good work, interesting work."

In 2001, Sumita got a Fulbright fellowship and spent a year at the

"Men wear the same clothes whether in villages or cities, but as a woman you have to adjust and balance."

Eastern Mennonite University in the US. An institution which does not preach any religion, but is based on faith.

"This is where I first got the idea of Rangsutra. I was writing papers, pondering on conflict resolution, and I realised that every conflict is an opportunity for change."

You can either choose to be put down by it or to accept it and improve the situation. By tuning out the noise and understanding, what is *really* going on.

And at this time of retreat and reflection, Sumita was also struck by the increasing gap between 'India Shining' and the India where electricity was yet to reach. The heart of India, still beating in its thousands of villages.

"I was writing a paper on organisations as part of my course. That's when I thought of this whole idea of doing something to make a difference in the textile and craft industry."

In the traditional model, artisan creates – gets a pittance. Fancy shop sells – makes a killing. Could that model be tweaked, to make it more 'fair' and yet commercially viable?

Now although Sumita had left Rajasthan in 1993, she had remained in touch with the weavers.

"I used to organise exhibitions for them in Delhi every year and I was also in touch with weavers from Assam, West Bengal and Uttarakhand. I felt that we should all get together and retail through a small shop."

By selling through exhibitions and supplying small quantities to retail outlets – including Fabindia – the Urmul Trust was making revenues of ₹ 1 crore a year. And it had taken ten years to get there.

"The weavers were happy – they were getting orders, selling their stuff and even getting a bonus. But there was no 'business plan', no targets."

"Anyone with a little bit of intelligence and feeling of humanity will know that one is dependent on the other. The retailer cannot exist without the artisan and vice versa."

Actually, Urmul Trust was doing many different things – health, education, environment, drinking water. So the hand-craft effort was not being given enough attention. So much *more* could be done with it...

When Sumita returned to India in December 2002, it was once again time for the annual Urmul exhibition. This time she decided to do something more 'concrete'.

"Initially I thought of a co-operative because that is the traditional way of thinking. Then, I met with Amrita Patel, who now heads Amul."

Amrita said, "In Rajasthan, co-operatives are mired in red tape. Why don't you think of becoming a 'producer company' instead?"

Taking her advice, Sumita registered Rangsutra as a producer company in December 2004.

What is a 'producer company'? Simply a company where producers are shareholders. It functions like a company in all ways, except that it does not exist *for* giving dividend.

"Well, you do give back some of the dividends to your shareholders – who are the artisans and producers. But part of the profits are also re-invested, to build capacities of others."

So the producer company has a social objective, in addition to business goals.

Which is great, but the limitation with a producer company is that it does not allow financial investors. If you are not a producer, you cannot be a shareholder. The structure indicates an inherent distrust of the 'capitalist'.

"Woh to sirf paisa kamaana chahta hai, usey hamare kaam aur hamare social objective se koi matlab nahin."

Which means you need your own capital to start. But neither Sumita nor the artisans had the funds.

"Ten of us put in ten thousand rupees each and that's all the capital we had to start with. Rupees one lakh."

Sumita tried to access funds from banks, but they had little or no idea what a producer company was! Banks would not open an account. And getting a loan was impossible, because there was no balance sheet to show.

At the same time, Rangsutra was no longer eligible for grants. After all it was not an NGO now, but a profit-making organisation!

"The year 2005 we worked as a producer company, doing most of the same things we did as an NGO. We couldn't really take it much further."

That's when Sumita met Vineet Rai, from Aavishkaar Social Venture Fund.

"Both Vineet and I are Ashoka* fellows – that was the connection. Vineet managed to convince me that it really does not matter whether you are a 'producer company' or a private company, as long as you have the same interests at heart." The point is, you have more flexibility – to operate, to raise funds. And thus in 2006, Rangsutra was registered as a private company. And at this point, Fabindia also entered the picture.

"We had been supplying to Fabindia in small bits and pieces over the years and I had been in contact with William Bissell. In fact, he had been supportive of the producer company as well."

Rangsutra now created a completely new structure, with four-way shareholding.

Sumita has a 20% stake, Fabindia** has 30% and Aavishkar 23%. The balance shareholding is with artisans.

"It was a big task getting the artisans to agree but when Fabindia and Aavishkaar came in – and I myself borrowed quite a large sum and invested in the company – they realised we were serious."

1060 artisans are now 'owners' of Rangsutra – they were offered shares at a price of ₹ 100. Whereas Aavishkaar and Fabindia bought their stakes at a premium. Sounds like an ideal set up but of course, there are issues.

Ashoka is a global organisation which awards fellowships to leading social entrepreneurs. See www.ashoka.org
** Fabindia's holding is via subsidiary AMFPL, Artisans Microfinance Pvt Ltd.*

"It's been a real challenge getting people who are traditionally seen as 'labour' to feel and behave like equals. Like 'management'. It is a bit of walking the tight rope!"

Lekin dheere dheere, ho raha hai.

"We just had a board meeting about two weeks ago and it's a fact that Fabindia has a stronger voice there, they come with more power. But at the end of the day even the artisans can say, 'This price does not work for us, we are not doing social work' and they also understand that."

Then there is the issue of mindset. Making people shift from an 'NGO' style of working to a business style, aimed at making profits.

"At the end of the exhibitions Urmul used to be left with a lot of unsolds. As an NGO you can bear the loss because you are subsidised by grants. But now I have to think a hundred times and make sure we produce only what sells!"

Rangsutra focuses on its USPs – hand embroidery, extra weft weaving and now a unique form of tie and dye. With the help of designers (one full timer, based in Bikaner and others who freelance), the company creates a range of products. These are then shown to the 'selection committee' at Fab India – currently Rangsutra's biggest client.

The bigger concern is delivering on time, and ensuring quality.

"Just yesterday I was having this heated argument with a weaver I've known for 20 years", laughs Sumita.

She said, "When you took the order, you said three months were more than enough. In fact you asked for two months and I gave you one month extra! *Par kaam abhi tak khatam nahin hua*?" The weaver replied, "There was a death in the village – no one worked 20 days."

And this is not a one-off incident. So how does Sumita tackle it? "I am at it – all the time!" she sighs. "Actually, I am finding the women much more forward and progressive in their thinking. They want to earn more, do more."

How much they earn, of course, depends on how much they work. On average, a woman would put in 4 to 5 hours a day and earn ₹ 3000-4000 in a month.

"There is enough work for her to go upto 8 hours a day but it would be bad for the eyes, and of course she has other responsibilities. Looking after the children, the cattle, the cooking and even drawing water."

The 'working woman' balancing act – no matter where she may be!

Interestingly, most of the shareholders of Rangsutra are women, and first-time 'investors'.

"They did not have much money, so they would buy five shares for ₹ 500 but, they were very enthusiastic about owning shares!"

It is this energy and zeal which has propelled Rangsutra's remarkable growth. Sales have grown from ₹ 26 lakhs in 2007 to ₹ 1.5 crores in 2008, and crossed ₹ 4 crores in 2009. The company is hoping to cross ₹ 8 crores by March 2011.

Last year Rangsutra even declared a dividend of 10%. And there are social returns, as well.

"We have been able to provide continuous work to all our artisan shareholders – as much as they wanted – which is a great thing. In a year of drought our people don't have to join NREGA. They are earning enough sitting at home."

Apart from thousand odd shareholders, Rangsutra also employs 1000 other artisans. And as the company continues to grow, that number will only go up.

Already, Rangsutra is working with artisans in Jaisalmer and Barmer district. NGOs and Self Helf Groups (SHGs) from other parts of India are also keen to become part of Rangsutra and access a bigger market.

"I know we have to scale up, but don't want to become a 'sourcing agency' *ki yahan se, wahan se, kahin se bhi maal le liya*. We need to develop leaders in the villages, at the organisation level to function as a collective."

To co-ordinate the various groups working for it, Rangsutra now has 21 employees and an office in Bikaner. The Delhi office is a 'sampling unit' with a *masterji* at work, which Sumita visits a couple of times in a week.

"People were not willing to give Rangsutra money but willing to loan *me* money. So I borrowed, and invested in the company."

"Like all my artisans, I am home-based," she smiles. "Less carbon footprint!"

Eco-friendly efforts like using natural dyes make Rangsutra products more 'ethical'. And could help the company expand overseas.

"The next step is building a Rangsutra 'brand' but we don't plan to set up a retail chain. We are exploring other alternatives like 'shop in shop' and selling through the internet."

And the future could lie not just in textiles and craft, but drawing on other aspects of rural life. Farm products is one possibility, especially organic foods.

"The other area we are keen to venture into is rural tourism, which we have started in a small way in Bikaner. We are targetting people who want to know more about the people and the place, beyond the palaces and forts."

And going beyond, working as a 'change agent', there are many possibilities. D.Light Design*, a company in the business of affordable lighting solutions, is keen to link up with Rangsutra. D.Light needs a channel to distribute its products, such as 'Kiran' which is the world's cheapest solar lantern.

"It would really be a wonderful thing for the villagers – women will be able to get two hours extra work done, children can study better. We are exploring how to take this forward."

Let there be light.

The light of hope, of change and transformation. In holding this lantern, Sumita too has found herself changed.

"People thought I was a complete idiot to leave a good job in an international NGO, take a loan and start Rangsutra. After all I had two children to raise and I had never managed a business..."

But she's done it; proved them wrong.

"You know I also faced criticism at NGO forums, for going outside the co-operative mould. But this model works – I am glad I took the risk!"

A journey which began in Rajasthan 25 years ago, has come full circle.

The man who took the risk, who started this grand adventure, is no longer with us. Wherever he is, he would be proud.

---

* *D.Light Design is a venture started in 2006 by Sam Goldman and Ned Tozun, both MBAs in Social Entrepeneurship from Stanford University.*

ADVICE TO YOUNG ENTREPRENEURS

There are so many opportunities and so many things that can be done!

We started off with the spinning and weaving, now we're thinking of rural tourism and organic food. The sky is the limit! Demand for ethnic, natural and hand-crafted products sourced from villages is only growing.

All you need is little bit of creativity and it helps to have a team. Maybe get a couple of years experience.

And also you should spend some time in the villages, in the 'real' India. Learn about the richness of the place, appreciate all that can be learned from there.

We worked in Bikaner, for a very low salary. But what we got from the people there was priceless. The connections made cannot be measured in terms of money...

I know it was the social capital I built from years spent in Rajasthan that is responsible for Rangsutra's success today.

Then of course a social business – like any other – must find a market for its products. And focus on quality and delivery to its customers. No one is going to buy from you just because your fabric is woven by a rural artisan.

You need a spirit of adventure, risk taking and drive. It is never too early to start. And never too late either. I began very late!

COUNTRY
ROADS

Saloni Malhotra,
DesiCrew

As a 23-year-old engineering graduate Saloni decided to do something different with her life. Three dots in her head – 'rural', 'technology' and 'business' – connected to form DesiCrew, India's first rural BPO. The project has also became a feather in the cap of IIT Madras, which incubated the idea.

Saloni Malhotra is polite, petite and soft-spoken. In fact, she looks like she might still be in college.

"It is a problem sometimes," she admits. "People in this industry are expected to have some white hair – it gives the client confidence!"

But Prof Ashok Jhunjhunwala of IIT Madras needed no such 'proof'. He met a young woman of 23 with a crazy dream and decided she was up to the challenge.

The challenge of setting up a business, with a social objective.

She failed the first time.

And the second time.

But in its third avatar, DesiCrew got it right.

Today, the company is a sustainable, profitable 'rural BPO'. In the process, it has brought income, empowerment and exposure to young people in mofussil towns and villages. Giving them a reason to stay rooted, and yet stay relevant.

And it all began in the head of a young woman who had never visited a village.

A dream took Saloni from Delhi to the dusty roads of Tamil Nadu.

A dream can take you *anywhere*.

COUNTRY ROADS

Saloni Malhotra,
DesiCrew

Saloni Malhotra grew up in Delhi.

"I attended a small convent school in Delhi called Carmel Convent. Both my parents are doctors – my father is a professor with AIIMS while my mother has a private practice."

However Saloni chose to take up engineering. Like many students from Delhi, she came to Bharti Vidyapeeth in Pune to study.

"I was very keen on extra curricular activities in college. I got involved with a group called Leo club (a junior wing of the 'Lions Club'). We took up a lot of development activities and became one of the 'star' performing clubs in Pune."

Saloni joined the Leo Club as a team member and exited as President of the club.

"We grew the club from seven to sixty people and that's where I realised I enjoy doing something which is in the development space but at the same time involves ideating, fundraising and running like a business."

Saloni realised, *this* is the thing that I want to do for the rest of my life. But what could she do as a fresh young BTech? "I thought it was very unfair to go and talk to parents and say, 'I want to start an NGO'. So I decided to get some experience in a small start-up."

The start-up was Webchutney – an interactive agency. It didn't really matter *what* she was doing because the idea was to learn *ki apna business chalana kya hota hai.*

"I joined in the business development profile and worked there for a brief period. When I left I had some sort of idea as to what I wanted to start but still wasn't very sure..."

At this point Saloni's parents said, "If you want to do something, do it now or go for your MBA."

Saloni was very clear she did *not* want to do an MBA. So, that was one 'option' out of the way.

"I sat at home for 6 months trying to figure out what I wanted to start. Then, I heard Professor Ashok Jhunjunwala speak at a conference. I found him fascinating and sent across a résumé introducing myself."

The year was 2003, Saloni was all of 23 years old.

"I had done some research and found out that he was one of the key persons promoting the concept of a 'social business'. So I was really kicked when he actually took the trouble to reply back!"

Saloni went down to IIT Madras, to meet him.

"I had an idea, but I wasn't sure if it was feasible. When we met, I shared the idea with him and he asked me a thousand different questions. That conversation was a turning point for me."

Saloni had three 'dots' in her head – 'rural', 'business' and 'technology'. But she didn't know what was the best way to *join* them.

Prof Jhunjhunwala said, "Instead of thinking of selling things to people in the village, we should look for ways to *infuse* money into rural areas."

That was a pretty radical idea. But what non-farm goods can one buy from villages?

"We had likes of the Khadi Village Industries, Fab India and Lijjat papad. All of them support rural artisans, women working from home."

But the other model creating waves in urban India at the time was outsourcing.

"We were seeing educated people migrating from small towns to large cities in search of jobs. This was putting a lot of pressure on the city, and on the migrants themselves."

"Lots of people speak English in Tamil Nadu, even in the villages. That is one of the reasons that I chose Tamil Nadu – it is easier to sell in the BPO business."

Was it possible to turn that model on its head? Combine rural manpower with communication technology to start 'outsourcing' work to the villages? And if so, what kind of services could be provided?

This idea excited Saloni, and Prof Jhunjhunwala lent physical and mentoring support.

He said, "I will give you space to work, and to network. We are already doing development work in villages, we can give you access to those places."

There was just one caveat.

"I will give you two years to do the groundwork. But you can't come back with a paper saying 'this cannot be done'. I want a live company."

When opportunity knocks, you can't just stare at it through the peephole. You must open the door and welcome it in your life. Which is what Saloni did.

Pro Jhunjhunwala asked one last question, "Would you like to work from Delhi or Chennai?"

Trick question, but Saloni was clear.

"In my mind I knew it had to be Chennai. So I said, 'I have come with my bag and I am staying here'."

He said, "OK then, start from tomorrow!"

And that's what happened.

"I didn't go back to Delhi. At that time I was travelling, trying to find what I wanted to do. I had fixed appointments with various people, to visit them and understand different rural models."

Even as she was completing these explorations, the tsunami struck Tamil Nadu. Saloni joined in the relief operations. Finally, in January 2004, she began 'work'.

Rather, she began working on ways to turn a dream, into reality.

"I remembered my first day in the engineering college hostel when I met a girl from Sangli for whom Computer Engineering was her passport to a better life. It made me realise that the computer is more than an electronic device."

And entrepreneurship is more than having a great idea. Ideas are like seeds which need plenty of water and sunshine – to grow. And IIT provided just that.

Moreover, the tag came with a stipend and 'parent value'.

"I could say to my folks, 'See, I am doing something at IIT'!" grins Saloni.

It's a different thing that this 'something' was very loosely defined.

"IIT Madras did not have a formal incubator at that time*, so they used to hire people as Research Associates. If the idea took off, then they would spin it into a company."

In fact, Saloni's Rural ITeS project was the first 'incubatee' and like all experiments, this one had its share of trial and error. Lots of errors!

"The first model we tried flopped at the end of year one," she shrugs.

The model was 'kiosk' based. The idea was to have a computer centre in a village which would enable education, healthcare and a host of other benefits. Several organisations were trying to make this happen in Karnataka, Maharashtra and Tamil Nadu. In all, there were 7000-8000 kiosks spread across the country.

"The problem these kiosks were facing was, they were free for ten hours a day. That means over thousands of hours of computer time lying idle."

Saloni's idea was simple: get people to start working from these kiosks. To do this, she took the help of 'nLogue', a company started on the IIT Madras campus which had put up 3000 such kiosks.

"For the pilot program we identified 15 locations. Then, I began looking for 'work'!"

The team decided to start with publishing – DTP, data entry, formatting of documents. She tried selling services internally to IIT, to friends and to ex-IITians who were running companies.

* *Now known as Rural Technology and Business Incubator (RTBI).*

And work did come, but the model was just not scalable.

"In small numbers – like ten to fifteen or maximum twenty kiosks – you can make it happen. You can get seasonal work. But that's not a business, which you can sustain."

But at least there was proof of concept. There *are* educated people in villages who would rather stay back – if they could earn a decent living.

You just needed a better business model.

After much introspection, Saloni realised a couple of basic home truths. Asking people to 'work from home' would do no good. They didn't have enough discipline, exposure or infrastructure.

"We decided there should be four-five computers in one place – so small groups can come together. And each centre would be run as a franchise."

In Feb 2007, the project was formally registered as DesiCrew Solutions Pvt Ltd. The company now zeroed in on ten locations and identified franchisees. But there were a host of issues.

"Since computers are expensive, they would buy second hand machines and have a lot of problems like viruses. So we decided to provide the critical bits – the CPU, UPS and original software."

Each franchisee was free to decide how much to pay employees. But, he would have to comply with labour laws and requirements such as PF and ESI.

But, within three months Saloni realised, it was not going to work.

"The franchisee will not invest in the business until he sees a steady revenue stream. A customer is not going to put work on the table till he sees stable infrastructure... So, it was like a chicken and egg story."

What's more, margins in the BPO industry are slim, especially for smaller companies. The model did not make economic sense. And that was important, because DesiCrew was not an NGO. It was a private limited company.

"We thought we could make money by getting work from the customer, keeping a small percentage of it and passing on the rest to the franchisees. But like I said, the franchisee had no interest in *building* the business."

Why train people – or retain them – if there was a lean period with little, or no work?

"Profit is important – but mainly as a measure of our efficiency. It tells us that everything is working fine."

"I remember, once we made a surprise visit and found that the franchisee had switched off the lights – to save on the electricity bill. So people were literally working in a dark room!"

The de-centralised model was clearly not working. DesiCrew would have to set up its own offices, to make things happen the way 'management' wanted. A decision was taken to buy out four of the existing franchisees and convert them to company-owned units.

"I said, 'Ok, *we* will make the investment in this setup – especially the infrastructure'. That way clients will be comfortable."

And if they ask, 'Is this a scalable model', Desicrew can say, "Yes! We can add on more PCs, more people, as required."

From the employee point of view, there would be the comfort of working in an 'office'. And not at the mercy of the franchisee.

"We took care of basic hygiene factors like small conference room, dining area, bathrooms. Apart from computers, we installed gensets to ensure there was no downtime due to electricity cut."

Expansion was not immediate, but over time, a unit with 3 computers has grown to a 65-seat facility. And the franchisee still works there – as an employee. The unit is located near Coimbatore, in a place called Palladam, with a population of 50,000.

"We tried different kinds of locations. So we set up two units in a panchayat village with a population of 10,000. And two others in smaller villages. Just to understand what kind of place works best for us."

This time, things fell in place. It was late 2007 – over three and a half years since Saloni had first conceived of the project.

But how did the company hold out, through tough times and slow revenues?

"We started with seed money of ₹ 5 lakhs from IIT. I put in my personal savings as well. All throughout, we made *some* money – but we kept searching for the right business model."

"Being part of the incubator, everyone really encouraged us by saying,'It is okay to fail – it's no big deal. You will learn something even out of that'."

That happened, and it led to other good things. In 2008, DesiCrew got its first 'investor'. And it was not someone out of the blue but a person who had been following the company closely. Rajiv Kuchhal, former COO of OnMobile.

"Rajiv was from the BPO space, so we used to go to him every quarter and ask for guidance. He had seen us grow over two years and he knew this was both a social and business venture."

That was, in fact, the reason *why* he chose to invest.

"Rajiv did not want to invest in pure business, or technology. In fact, he'd been running an NGO for some time so the social aspect of DesiCrew is what made us attractive."

Business with a social objective, or social operation with a business dimension – whichever way you look at it, makes a lot of sense.

As a BPO, DesiCrew offers three main lines of service. The first is documentation and digitisation – everything from data entry to scanning and indexing. Not very hi-tech, but high in volume.

"Insurance companies, a couple of banks and NGOs are the main clients for this service."

The second area DesiCrew works in is the content space, where it does everything from secondary research to content population and 'clean-up'.

"Someone has data running in tens of thousands; someone needs to make sure that everything is correct. Like if there is a picture of Abhishek Bachchan, it should not say Shahrukh!"

Among other things, DesiCrew also works with a local mobile search engine and undertakes feature testing for beta products on the web.

The third line of service is transcription and translation, especially from English to Indian languages, and vice versa.

In all, there are 250 employees on the payroll, which includes 2 business heads and 12 project managers. And this is where the social aspect comes in. There are people with ITI diplomas, with bachelor's degrees and even some post-graduates.

But, they are all people who've chosen to live and work in their native village. Or, move back from cities.

"Rural area does not mean that the salary is low. But yes, the cost of living is far less so they can save a large chunk of what they earn!"

Entry level workers at DesiCrew – known as 'crewmates' draw between ₹ 5000-6000. With another ₹ 2000 coming in as performance incentives.

The advantage to the customer is quality work, at competitive rates.

"Our rental expense is almost zero. We don't have transport cost, food is cheap – so the overheads are definitely lower. The other advantage is that the cost of attrition is very high in the cities."

At DesiCrew, employees are far more rooted, more loyal. Until recently, 70% were, in fact, women.

"Recent projects required evening and night shifts, so we hired male staff," explains Saloni.

Although reluctant to disclose revenue figures, Saloni does tell me – with considerable pride – that over the last couple of years, DesiCrew has become 'profitable'.

"That was very critical for us because we wanted to show this model is commercially viable before scaling it up and asking other people to put in their money!"

In July 2008, DesiCrew also did a very large project for the Government of Rajasthan.

"The government had launched a scheme which involved opening bank accounts, giving health insurance and giving ₹ 1500 to every below poverty line home in the state. But, the idea was to give these benefits only to the women of the house."

Now this posed a problem, as traditionally data about the woman of the household is not captured in any kind of survey. A massive exercise was undertaken to collect the names and details of women, and get them to sign the insurance forms.

"All that data would come to us, we would digitise it, separate it and send the details to the bank, to the smart card vendor and so on. We also alerted the concerned authorities when we detected fraud cases."

The work was completed over a period of just two months – to handle it, DesiCrew employed close to 1500 people. And if things go as per plan, such numbers may soon become a permanent reality.

"We are looking at 500 employees by March 2011."

Sounds ambitious, I think to myself. But this young woman is confident – it can be done.

"We have made a lot of progress. Till last year, our project managers were based in Chennai, or Bangalore or Bombay – wherever the customer was located. This year we felt people were ready to move to the next level."

Project managers do come to Bangalore or Bombay to interact with the client, but they are based on-site.

"In terms of growing the model that was another thing we had to validate. Because middle management was the biggest concern our customers had."

The quality of resumes DesiCrew is attracting is also evolving. One recent hire is an Air force officer, who took VRS after 20 years of service. The 'head office' is based in Chennai, and that team travels to different centres for training and monitoring.

"We have very structured monthly reviews, so everybody turns up for that."

Business is steady – with 8 main clients. Who, for obvious reasons, cannot be named here. Interestingly, one of them in an insurance company which came on board after reading about DesiCrew – in *The Economic Times*.

"The head of the organisation called and left a note on our website, that's how we landed the contract."

DesiCrew's second big customer is a well-known internet company. Their head of research was visiting IIT and on hearing about a 'rural BPO', expressed the desire to 'go see what was happening'.

"We started with one small project for them and today they're one one of our biggest customers!"

When it comes to the question of scale the question clients have is 'how many locations' and 'what's your management bandwidth'.

"Well I feel it is possible because firstly, we have answers to every concern that they have. And secondly, there is competition. A lot of other people have started similar 'distributed' models – so that validates our idea in a sense!"

In fact, more and more BPOs are looking at Indian customers. And they find, the 'global delivery model' doesn't always work.

"If a foreign company was willing to pay, an Indian company will pay 1/3rd of that. So many people are experimenting with our model – the Tatas, Infosys, Wipro, Aditya Birla Group..."

In time, some of these companies may even outsource *their* outsourced work to DesiCrew.

"We are open to it... our main objective is to create more employment and infuse more money into rural India. If that objective is met – why not!"

The social objective is also the gas which keeps the DesiCrew engine running – at the level of top management. It's what attracts top quality minds, committed to making a difference.

"We have Manivannan, who is our President and CEO. He was also one of the founding team members of GramIT which was Satyam's rural BPO."

Also part of the start-up team are Ashwant and Thiru.

"Ashwant is an MBA from UK who came back to try for civil services but joined DesiCrew instead. Thiru, is an entrepreneur, a lecturer, a hardware engineer – among many other things."

All people who could have been working elsewhere, making more money. But chose to be here instead.

"I think the drive of creating something that is valuable, that does good, but in a new and interesting way, is why we are all here."

The profit motive remains, but more as a measure of efficiency, than an end in itself.

"So, if an insurance company says, 'I can give you work but I want 100 people in Bombay', we will not take that up. Because it does not comply with our overall objective of setting up in a smaller town and providing local employment."

Or for example, an offer from an internet company, related to search engines and classification work.

"We turned down a very large business because we didn't know how much porn we would have been exposed to. It was difficult to say 'no' because the project would have employed 300 people – it could have been a big leap for the company."

But look before you leap, as they say...

Yet, sometimes, you simply have to take that leap of faith – as Saloni did – when she decided to stay back in Chennai.

It took two years to first set up the company. Longer, to find a model which worked. But then DesiCrew became a 'success story', the first incubatee at IIT Madras, to actually start laying eggs.

"The incubator is now called 'Rural Technology and Business Incubator' – so it has to have a rural component, a technology component and a business component. 12 companies have come into the fold over the last 2 years."

And finally, the question of 'social impact'. How do we ever really *know*? Well, a dipstick study undertaken recently threw up some heartening facts.

"With people earning more money, more money is available in the economy. Let's take one of our typical villages – Kollur – where around 25 people work. Each of them earns an average of ₹ 5000, so that's substantial purchasing power."

Then there are the intangible effects. Like DesiCrew brought broadband connectivity to the village. Now 60 people have taken connections, through that same exchange.

Most important of all is the impact on the local youth, especially girls.

"A lot of parents said if not for DesiCrew their daughters would have been sitting at home. Now they are earning, they are more confident and hopeful about their future."

Many girls are saving up for their weddings; some enrol in distance learning programs. Even the boys – reluctant to work in the fields – are happy to be gainfully employed.

Ultimately *jo socha, wahi hua*. DesiCrew is bringing opportunities, and income, to rural India.

And all because a petite girl, all of 23, decided it needed to be done. Despite all odds and obstacles.

"Sometimes things would not move or even go horribly wrong... I recall an episode where a franchisee walked away with our customer. We had trained the team and provided the equipment! I had to go the police station to get it all back!"

That was one time I really questioned, "What am I doing?"

But the moment passed.

"Fortunately, I have parents who are very supportive."

Matlab shaadi karne ke liye hassle nahin kar rahe hain.

"Yes, they have given me the space and told me that I can plan things, do things when I want, as I want."

If only more parents said such words, we would have more Salonis.

More rebels, with a wonderful cause.

ADVICE TO YOUNG ENTREPRENEURS

The only thing I can say from my experience is that it took us 5 years to 'break even' and we are still going through peaks and troughs.

DesiCrew wouldn't be there if not for the dedicated team.

You just have to hang in there. If you are really passionate about it, just hang on, and do whatever it takes. You can't do it half-heartedly as it won't take you anywhere. So don't put in half-hearted attempts.

If you want to contribute to some kind of cause or organisation – but still retain your regular job – fine.

You can do part-time, even one hour a week, but you should really feel for whatever cause you are working, not just go for the sake of it. Like before I started, I was not sure what I wanted to do exactly. So I did a lot of part-time and temporary work and I associated with NGOs.

You can contribute your expertise like co-ordinating or recruitment or whatever. There would be a thousand things to see to – NGOs will always be short on resources. So that will give you a taste of what it really takes.

When I worked in Webchutney in Delhi, it was very clear that you had to work 18 to 20 hours a day to get it off the ground. Be prepared to work really hard, whatever kind of enterprise you set up!

MOVING
MOUNTAINS

**Ishita Khanna,
Spiti Ecosphere**

Ishita is young, idealistic and passionate about conservation. But, she believes it must go hand in hand with development. Through Ecosphere, Ishita promotes eco-tourism and berry processing – economic incentives to mountain folk to preserve their majestic heritage.

Every time I go up to the mountains, I wonder what it would be like – to live there.

Which is why I am fascinated by Ishita Khanna. A young woman who lost her heart to the Spiti valley and made it her home *and* workplace.

Since 2002, Ishita has been running 'Spiti Ecosphere', a social enterprise dedicated to issues of livelihood and conservation. Lofty goals that many talk about, but few manage to achieve.

And yet, this petite young woman has shown that it can be done. That no matter where you are, there are resources which can be harnessed.

Who knows what magic lies in a delicate orange berry; in a hardy villager's hands.

In the steely determination of a young woman who always loved geography.

Because mountains must continue to stand proud, stand tall.

MOVING
MOUNTAINS

Ishita Khanna,
Spiti Ecosphere

Ishita Khanna was born and raised in Dehradun.

"I went to Welham Girls School. My father was in the merchant navy and my mother was a housewife."

Ishita was a complete backbencher, with little interest in studies. The only subject she really liked was geography.

"From a young age I always wanted to know about the environment, animals, wildlife and things like that. My mother took my sister and me on a lot of treks, so that's how my love for nature – especially mountains – grew."

Ishita went to study at Delhi University and went on to study geography – the only subject she truly enjoyed.

"In fact, I got into St Stephen's College, but for English honours. And I was not willing to compromise..."

After graduating, Ishita joined TISS (Tata Institute of Social Sciences) for a Masters in Sociology. She had a vague plan to work in the area of environmental planning. But TISS offered a course in urban and rural community development, and she opted for that instead.

"I did my masters dissertation on the socio-cultural and ecological impact of tourism. I chose to study Gangotri, which attracts a lot of pilgrims."

The project included fieldwork – meeting temple authorities, sadhus, travellers and those in the travel industry. Ishita's conclusion was that the impact on the ecosystem had largely been negative.

"There was a huge problem of drainage and garbage disposal. You need proper planning, and you need to involve the local community to handle these issues. That was my finding."

After completing her MA Ishita had no particular goal in life, except to get a job in the area of environment. Thus she joined a central government agency called CAPART, which disbursed funds to various NGOs. Keen to work in rural areas, Ishita asked for a transfer to the state government of Himachal Pradesh.

And that's when she first visited Spiti, and fell in love. With the place, the people, the ecosphere. Pristine, untouched by tourism – but how long before it succumbed to the lure of haphazard 'development'?

"There's got to be a better way," thought Ishita. "A way for economic development and conservation to co-exist."

The path to change is paved with ideas. And big ideas have small beginnings – in this case a lowly shrub with pretty orange berries, known as seabuckthorn.

"Seabuckthorn grows in dry, high altitude areas and these little berries are the richest known source of vitamin C in the world. So there is a huge commercial value!"

What's more, the shrub itself binds the soil and prevents erosion. It also 'fixes' nitrogen, thus improving the fertility of the soil.

"I tried to push it with the government but they had done some research ten years ago which concluded that the seabuckthorn growing in Spiti valley was the wrong species. They had no interest in making the project work."

But Ishita believed something *could* be done. Seabuckthorn was being harvested in neighbouring Ladakh by a private party, with good results. In 2002, she quit her job and along with two friends – Parikshat* and Sunil – started an NGO called Muse.

* *Parikshat died in the winter of 2003 in a tragic road accident*

"We were all passionate about the mountains and wanted to work towards sustainable development in Spiti valley."

The first person Ishita enlisted to her cause was Nono Sonam Angdui, the 'King' of Spiti. A man who no longer enjoys royal powers but is greatly respected by the local community.

"He is a very progressive person, who really wants to do something for the people of Spiti. He too had heard about the potential of seabuckthorn and agreed to extend every possible support."

An endorsement which helped the 'outsider' – with her newfangled ideas – get quickly accepted.

Ishita organised local women into groups for harvesting, and trained them to clean and process the berries.

"It would have been much easier to hire a contractor to do the job but the idea was to benefit the local population. We tied up with 'Leh Berry' to buy the pulp from us, so we could focus on production."

In the first year, two tons of pulp was harvested and processed; the next year that jumped to five tons. The berries were harvested in the month of September, over a two week period. Meanwhile, the German agency GTZ agreed to fund a small processing unit.

"We were not even properly registered at that point of time. I guess we were just lucky! We went with a proposal and they gave us ₹ 11 lakhs."

Most of that money went into machinery, as well as barrels, crates, a pulper and generators – standard equipment for any fruit juice production unit. Locals – mostly women – were employed in cleaning and processing. On average, they earned* ₹ 500-800 per day.

So far so good. But the enterprise was not *sustainable*. The problem was the purchase price of the berries – there was just one buyer and he could be unreasonable.

In 2008, seabuckthorn harvesters were paid ₹ 30 per kg; the activity benefits approximately 500 families across 30 villages.

"You learn a lot from the mountains. You learn that you are actually controlled by nature, and it makes you humble."

"We had to constantly struggle with Leh Berry to get a fair price. So in 2004 we decided to launch our own brand under the name 'Tsering'."

The venture makes a nominal profit.

Meanwhile, Ishita realised that there were other important issues, such as the rapid and unfettered growth of tourism. Till the early 1990s, even Indians needed permission to enter Spiti. But as the area was opened up, it began developing haphazardly, like a typical hill station.

"Guest houses were coming up everywhere, but there was no proper sewage or drainage system. And these guest houses benefitted the rich, helping them to get richer. We decided to change that by introducing eco-tourism."

The tourism business was mostly handled by operators from Delhi and Manali. Travellers rarely experienced the local culture, apart from visiting a monastery.

"I knew there was a market for a different kind of experience. We introduced homestays, so that anyone with an extra room could earn some money. And travellers got to stay with locals, eat with them, even learn to cook at times."

Apart from homestays, Ecosphere has trained local youth to take visitors on treks and jeep safaris. From how to set up camp, guide groups up the mountain and even basic first aid – they now know and handle it all.

Meanwhile, marketing is Ishita's baby. And the medium she uses primarily is the internet.

"Travel agents and hotels felt threatened, so we had to do the selling ourselves. Last year we brought in 30 groups – mainly foreigners. Some of them are even volunteers who are keen to work on our development projects."

These projects include putting up greenhouses to grow vegetables, and helping communities build energy efficient housing. These efforts have reduced the consumption of firewood by 50-60% per household!

"We ensure our trips are eco-friendly by reducing use of plastic. Our tour groups don't need to buy mineral water bottles – we provide them with Aquaguard water."

The tourism project generates revenues of ₹ 35-40 lakhs per annum and is profitable. The seabuckthorn unit just about manages to break even.

"We processed 17 tons of berries last year, but building a new brand is a slow process. We're getting there slowly!"

Ecosphere generates around 50% of its revenues – the balance still comes from funding agencies. But the fact that she can run a profitable social enterprise gives Ishita a big kick.

"If you are fully dependent on agencies for funds you have to constantly go around with a begging bowl. And often, their focus is different from yours. Since Ecosphere is self-sustaining, we have the freedom to do what we really think needs to be done."

Every year Ishita spends eight months – from April to November – in Spiti. There is also a small support team based in Delhi.

The Ecosphere local office is in Kaza, the headquarters of Spiti valley. A bustling township – kind of like the Shimla of Spiti.

"I live in a room right next to the office – a typical day at work starts at 9 in the morning and ends at around 6 or 7. Of course, everything has to happen in the summer because in winter, the temperature plunges to minus 35 degrees!"

Back in 2002, there wasn't even an STD facility, now there are mobile phones and even a cyber cafe.

"Electricity is not a big issue in summer but there is no running water. As it gets colder, you have to light a fire around the hand pump to warm it up and draw the *paani* out."

The culture of Spiti – its language, and its food, is heavily influenced by Tibet. People are simple and friendly, and women are strong willed.

"I have never faced any problems as far as being a woman goes. And my family has always been supportive," says Ishita.

So what lies ahead? Already, Ecosphere has started development initiatives in the neighbouring valley of Lahaul. Ishita also plans to do something about the mounting garbage problem.

"Ultimately we want to work with the government at a policy level. The number of visitors that Spiti valley can accommodate needs to be restricted to some extent, like Bhutan. This region is ecologically fragile and cannot take the strain."

Much as she loves the majestic mountains of Spiti, Ishita knows she has to focus on building local capacities. In a couple of years she might even withdraw completely – keeping only an advisory role.

The lessons from the Ecosphere experiment are many.

"I learnt that it is difficult to get everyone to work together. In seabuckthorn, we took the community approach. But with tourism we decided to focus on enterprising individuals."

And of course, working in villages, with simple mountain folk needs a lot of patience.

"In the city, life is fast and things move quickly. Here it takes two years to get anything off the ground!"

So what keeps Ishita going?

"I am not ambitious in the monetary sense – that I want to earn a particular figure or drive a certain brand of car. I just want to do some meaningful work, which can make a difference to people, and to the environment."

Yes, it has meant a different kind of lifestyle, but it never felt like a sacrifice.

"My parents constantly grumble that I don't spend enough time with them – which is true. I think someday I might want to settle down – go back to Dehradun."

For now, there are mountains to climb. And ecospheres to embrace.

For this child of nature, citizen of the world.

———————————

ADVICE TO YOUNG ENTREPRENEURS

If you have an idea, you just have to do it – that's what we did. There was no money, no roadmap but I think that is the way it works. You just have to jump into it. If you plan too much then sometimes you lose your nerve.

The more you give, the more you get back. Small changes you make in your own life can make a difference to the environment. You know what they say about closing your tap while brushing...

Well, every little drop does count. Since I started living in Spiti, I've experienced that personally! I know what it means to pump a bucket of water from the hand pump at high altitude. It is torture!

We take people upto Spiti and show them that these are the tough conditions people live in. Every little change in your life can make an impact on theirs as well.

PRODIGAL SUN

Harish Hande,
Selco

Harish Hande is a 'mad' scientist. As a PhD student, he spent two years living in rural Sri Lanka and India, before starting Selco, a company which makes solar lighting suitable – and affordable – for villagers. Selco has installed 120,000 systems in Karnataka, and plans to take the mission national, in the near future.

With his curly hair, crumpled shirt and crooked smile, Harish Hande looks every bit the young scientist.

But long ago – as a PhD student – he stepped out of the laboratory.

To solve energy problems of people – in the real world.

"I realised that equations are meaningless, the real challenge is taking technology to poor people – the ones who need it the most!"

But before you create a solution, you need to study the problem. And so, Harish spent two years actually living in the villages. At the end of which he knew one thing for sure.

Poor people can and will pay for solar energy.

But, there is no one-size-fits-all technology. You have to customise, create products people need.

Thus, in 1995, a company called Selco came into being. With its mix of practical insight and financial acumen, Selco has achieved what others have only talked about at conferences and seminars. Solar energy systems on a mass scale.

Systems bought by peanut farmers, *pani puri* vendors, midwives and even daily wage labourers. Because, it makes sound economic sense.

"Link energy with income generation and the poorest of the poor can afford solar lighting," shrugs Harish.

On a Sunday morning, in the stillness of Selco's Bangalore headquarters, Harish speaks with passion. About his ideals, his inspirations and the road ahead.

A road so different from the one most have taken. But so illuminated, so bright.

PRODIGAL SUN

Harish Hande,
Selco

Harish Hande was born in Bangalore but brought up in Rourkela.

"My father worked with the steel plant. Rourkela is a very closed society where you get all facilities, education was one of the best."

Thanks to peer pressure, Harish took a shot at IIT and got a decent JEE rank. The choice was between Computer Science in IT BHU and Chemical Engineering or Metallurgy at IIT Kharagpur.

Harish eventually joined Kharagpur, but opted for an unusual branch.

"I decided to do my Bachelor's in Energy Engineering – it was a small department, with just seven students!"

People warned him, jobs would be difficult. But Harish countered, "How do we know exactly what will happen after 4 years?"

Besides, 'job' was not on his mind at the time. He enjoyed the course – a mix of electrical, chemical and mechanical engineering.

"On the 'energy' front, it was a *khichdi* of everything from biogas to biomass to nuclear. But in my second year, I became fascinated by solar energy and decided to do my Master's in the US."

So in his final year, Harish looked hard for universities offering a program in sustainable energy. The University of Massachussetts (UMass) was one of the very few which did, and he was accepted for an MS.

At UMass, Harish started working on the 'thermal' side.

"I was researching how molten salts react when sun falls on steel."

Harish's advisor at the university was Jose Martin – a Cuban American.

"One fine day – about a year into my MS – he asked me to go to the Dominican Republic. There, for the first time, I saw how solar lighting was used by people, in their homes."

The experience changed his entire thought process.

Harish spent two months with his advisor's good friend Richard Ansen, a pioneer in the field of rural electrification. Richard had begun experimenting with the idea of 'decentralised energy' as early as 1984.

"I went there and saw his work in rural areas. Very poor people were using solar power and paying for it! That's when I realised I had to go beyond equations and 'technology'."

In 1991, Harish returned to UMass and asked his professors if he could shift his focus to the socio-economic side of energy. The department objected.

They said, "This is an engineering department, so you have to do a PhD related to engineering!"

But Harish's advisor stood by him. And allowed him to come back to India to begin field work. The question Harish wanted an answer to was simple.

"Let us assume technology is there, and it is usable. But what does it take to actually make it work? To get people to embrace it?"

Harish first went to Sri Lanka. because he wanted to blend in with the locals and get real answers. Not be treated like a *sahib*, or a 'better educated' person.

"That was my perception – right or wrong!" he exclaims with boyish delight.

Another, more practical reason was the presence of a friend in Sri Lanka, working in the NGO sector.

Harish contacted him and asked, "Can you put me in this village here you are working?"

It was tough – tougher than expected.

"But also fun in many ways – and then you get used to it."

There was the language problem, the LTTE problem, and the usual problems of rural areas. Say you want to go to Colombo – you go to the bus stand. And they say, "The next bus will come in 3 days."

"I learnt to say, 'Ok! No problem. This is life'!"

You are prepared to face anything.

After 6 months in that Lankan village, Harish shifted to India. He spent a year and a half in rural Karnataka, again simply immersing himself into life in the village.

"I discovered that what I had learnt over the years... boiled down to nothing."

The way people live their life or look at things is completely different. So are their 'needs'.

"For example, I was taught about 'efficiency' of solar home lighting. But in rural India it was hardly a concern."

After all, there is no issue of 'roof space'!

Then there are studies which say that the average rural household's needs are 500 watts. But Harish found this was absolutely not the case.

"Many villagers want just one light for 2 hours in the morning, to help milk the cows. And this consumes just 20 watts."

These were things Harish would never have discovered – sitting in Bangalore. And with these many different insights, came the idea of Selco.

"After the Sri Lanka experience, 'rural' became a part of me. I mean no water for 10 days, ok – I can live with it. And all the while, my parents had no idea what I was doing...!"

> **"If we look at the poor as a monolithic structure we come up with standardised solutions, that is why we are not able to succeed in removing poverty in this country or for that matter in South America, or elsewhere."**

In 1994, Harish was in Washington DC, where he met Neville Williams. Neville was running a non-profit called SELF – 'Solar Electric Light Fund'.

He said, "Harish, would you be interested in implementing a solar lighting project in India?"

"Of course!" replied Harish.

But within a week, he called Neville and said, "Your project does not make sense in India."

What happens after 100 systems are installed? Who will provide after-sales support? Are we merely doing these installations to take some pretty pictures and show the donors that 'good work is being done'?

Instead, Harish proposed, "Let us start a company."

Why a company and not an NGO? Because a company is more transparent, more accountable and more responsible to customers.

"If a company installs a system and it doesn't work, it will send an engineer to service it!"

That's unlikely to happen in a 'charity' model.

And so in 1994, Selco came into being. The name was inspired by Edison's Electric Light Company and the aim was to establish two Big Ideas.*

"Poor people can pay, and they can maintain technology."

Well and good, but starting a company – in 1994 – was not that easy. A social investor called e + Co agreed to take a small equity stake. But, that required permission from the FIPB (Foreign Investment Promotion Board).

* 60% of Selco customers had no access to electricity, rest had erratic supply.

"I had no idea how to handle the paperwork. Besides, you had to go to Delhi for FIPB – and that was expensive. So, for the first two years, I somehow pulled along with my own savings."

It took over a year to get the money – a princely sum of ₹ 4 lakhs. In 1995, Selco was formally registered, and the following year, received a working capital loan from USAID.

All the while, Harish ran a very tight ship, with a tiny budget of ₹ 1000-1500 per month.

"But it was fortunate I would say. Because we did not have money in the early years, we became innovative in our thought process."

Selco did not 'invent' any new technology. A solar panel is fairly standard – it consists of a rooftop panel, a battery which gets charged daily and lights.

"The battery can dry off so someone needs to top it up once in 6-8 months!"

You also need to wash the panel every now and then and watch against cockroaches or rats eating up the wire.

"Solar panels are made in India by companies like Tata BP – we have only improved the technology slightly, over a period of time," adds Harish.

So, where was the innovation? Well, the main issue with solar lighting is the cost. When Selco started up, the system it was trying to sell had a price tag of ₹ 15,000. Even rich farmers were unconvinced.

"But one of the farmers – his mother was keen. So one day when he was not at home, I quietly went and installed the first system."

"For us, profit was never a bad word. If we have to cater to a street vendor, for her to survive she had to make money. If she has to make profit and we will survive on grants... it won't work in the long run."

"Today we glorify articulate speakers and people who leave lucrative careers to become 'social entrepreneurs'. But it's the guys with no polish or education, only complete faith in the idea who've made Selco what it is today."

When Harish nervously went back a week later, the farmer was ready to pay the full amount.

"We are all thrilled with this!" he beamed.

Selco's first system was installed in Mulleri – a village on the Karnataka-Kerala border. In its first year of operations – 1995-96 – Harish installed close to 150 such systems. All with his own hands.

"I installed the first 400 systems myself. I used to go at 5:30-6:00 in the morning so I could finish by 10 o'clock and catch the last bus back."

Basically, Harish had no money to hire someone to work for him. But having done it himself was a huge advantage, when technicians did join.

"I learnt exactly how many hours is took to install a system in a 4room house. No one could fool around or bullshit me," he grins.

Selco's first 'employee' joined in early 1996. By the end of that year there were three of them – Shridhar Rao, Guruprakash and Umesh.

"My first 2-3 technicians were incredible. I had a PhD to fall back on – they were the ones who really took a risk, made a sacrifice."

Giving up their small time jobs repairing TVs and the like. For a company no one had heard of, and paid a pittance.

"I used to eat in their homes, and I could see how from vegetable and rice, it came down to just plain boiled rice at end of the year and a half!"

Wives and mothers were not pleased.

"Why are you tagging along with this guy who has some kind of crazy idea ? Go out and get a proper job!" they said.

"Don't worry, we will survive," they would laugh back.

Although it was no laughing matter. There were early adopters – well-to-do farmers, doctors, teachers. But, as Selco tried to expand its user base one thing became very clear. Solar lighting was simply out of the reach of most potential users.

People asked, "Can you provide some finance?"

Selco neither had the capital, nor the expertise to extend credit. So Harish turned to the local financial institutions.

"India has a fantastic network of RRBs or Regional Rural Banks. Why not we use that?"

But, when Harish approached bank managers, they had a stock response.

"Solar home lighting does not generate income. It is not agricultural finance, so we can't get into it!"

Harish refused to take 'no' as an answer.

"I kept meeting, kept pestering, it took me two years – but ultimately I managed to convince them!"

RRBs started extending credit to Selco customers with ₹ 5000-7000 income per month. By 1997-98, Selco was selling 300-350 systems a year. But – it was still not good enough.

"We wanted to sell to people earning ₹ 3000 p.m. and even lower. To do that, we had to think different."

And thus came the idea of user segments, each with its own

"Last month 30 families in Sonamhalli village, who earn around ₹ 1600 per month bought a ₹ 9500 solar lighting system. Earlier, they spent ₹ 210 on candles and kerosone every month!"

unique product. One which met the customer's exact need in terms of usage, as well as finance.

"For example, a *pani puri* vendor needs one light for 4 hrs and it should not cast a shadow. I can easily design that product. But her cash flow is on a daily basis, so can her 'finance' also be on a daily basis?"

Now that was a real innovation.

Similarly, a paddy farmer might need two lights – one for his wife to cook in the evenings, and another to thrash paddy after dark.

"However he sells his harvest in January, so the payment schedule should be on an annual basis – say over 5 years."

Remove the 'M' from EMI and all of a sudden, even an 'expensive' technology comes within the reach of the 'poor'.

"In fact poor people pay more than you or me for energy. On average, a street vendor in Bangalore spends ₹ 15 a day – on kerosene."

That's ₹ 450 a month, enough to pay for a 6 light solar system over 5 years!

"However, Selco will actually recommend a single light system, costing just ₹ 6 per day," he adds.

A skilled technician can assess – within 5-10 minutes – the 'right size' of technology and the 'right size' of finance. Whether it was a midwife, a *pani puri* vendor, a paddy farmer, peanut farmer or sugarcane farmer.

The customer might say, "I need 4 lights."

But the technician knows, he cannot afford it.

So he will advise, "You don't need light in 4 rooms at the same time. I will provide you with 2 lights – when you are done with the cooking, shift it to the room where your child studies."

With this kind of out-of-the box approach, Selco solar lighting is now reaching more and more people. In 2009-10, the company installed 12,500 systems in rural Karnataka. And among its customers are daily wage labourers – who are quite literally at the bottom of the famous C K Prahalad pyramid.

To make all this possible, Selco now has a 170 strong workforce. This include 140 employees spread across 21 branch offices; each office has 2 technicians, 2 sales staff, an office assistant and manager. Many have moved up the ranks, from technical to management positions.

"Our deputy operations manager started as an office assistant in a village in 1999. Now he sits here in Bangalore and oversees all 21 branches."

And no, he does not have any formal management education.

"Philosophically if you look at Selco that is what we wanted to do. Cut the hierarchy, look at individuals and see how you can bring out their potential.".

In keeping with that philosophy, Selco does not have a cubicle structure.

"Any techinican has the right to walk into my room and say, 'Harish you made a stupid mistake'."

Technicians don't merely install and maintain the systems.

"We always say to the technician in training that the system you install 'belongs' to you 50%".

Client or staff member, you become part of the Selco 'family'.

"5 years ago when our technician got married, 250 clients came for the wedding!"

The first 500 clients – for whom Harish installed systems – still ask for him by name. The manager who takes the call offers to send a technician but they're not satisfied.

"Where is he – *kya wo itna bada ho gaya hai*?"

"Aisa nahin hai."

Harish apologises, and goes down to their homes.

Over fifteen years, Selco has brought solar lighting to 120,000 homes. The target for the next 4 years is to reach 2 lakh households. But, it's not just about numbers.

"Our priority is that by 2012, 40% of our clientele should be from the poorest section of society – earning less than ₹ 2000 per month."

"There are managers who have torn their salary increases in front of me and put it in the waste basket saying, "You are crazy. We have not done well so I can't take this!"

Currently, close to 35% of Selco's clients are in the ₹ 3000-3500 per month bracket. To reach out to the next, lower income group, Selco has to go that step further.

For example, banks are usually reluctant to extend credit. The margin money for a ten thousand rupee solar lighting system is ₹ 1500. A princely sum for a daily wage labourer.

"Selco will put down the margin money. We don't subsidise it, just increase the installment slightly."

After a year, the 'down payment' has been made, Selco withdraws the money and uses it to help out a new customer. And so the cycle continues.*

Of course, there are cases of bad debt; in such cases Selco helps out the bank by buying back the system.

"NPAs are natural – 8-10% is the norm. I absolutely don't believe microfinance instititutions (MFIs) who claim they have zero default!".

From time to time Selco has been advised to 'scale up' like MFIs. Or, use microfinance as a means to make systems accessible to the poor. But Selco is not going that route.

"MFIs charge high interest rates, that makes my product more expensive. Also they want to recover their money over 15 months, not 5 years!"

However, Selco does work with some MFI, such as SEWA Bank. And has, in fact, learnt a great deal from them.

"SEWA has 35 years of solid field experience. SEWA Bank uses that to create new and innovative finanical products."

* Lemelson foundation, E & Co and Good Energies own over 99% of Selco's equity; there is also some debt from IFC

"We don't have a cubicle structure. Any techinican has the right to walk into my room and say, 'Harish you made a stupid mistake'."

For example, SEWA knows that a ragpicker's cashflow comes on Monday, Wednesday and Friday. So the bank designs her payback schedule accordingly.

Studying the minutes of SEWA Bank's meetings helped Selco to design 'products', on similar lines.

At the crux of Selco's entire operations is the idea of sustainability. From day one, Harish knew the company had to be 'profitable'. But how do you run a commercial enterprise while trying to meet social objectives?

"Today you have a buzzword – 'social entrepreneurship'. But it didn't exist at that point of time. We somehow figured it out!"

The basic philosophy is simple: "Make a profit and re-invest it, to grow the company".

Thus in 2009-10, Selco earned ₹ 14.5 crores in revenues, and made a surplus of ₹ 40 lakhs. This money was used to open new centres, improve salaries for employees.

There is no concept of 'shareholder' returns. Selco is owned by 3 non-profits and even Harish has only a notional stake. But a sense of ownership – and mission to accomplish – runs through the organisation.

"Quite a few in our top management team could earn 10 times what we pay – elsewhere!"

One such person is T Revathi, CFO and Vice-President. Professionals like Revathi brings in systems and financial discipline. And yet, Selco never loses sight of its social focus.

"It's important for each centre to break even. But, they can't do it just by selling a system costing ₹ 1 lakh each to two hospitals!"

There are pulls and pushes in the model, and naturally there are disagreements.

"You have to come to one of our operations meetings to see the fireworks. The management is a mix of treehuggers and commercially savvy people... Which is – touchwood – what has kept Selco alive!".

And attracted a motley bunch of mavericks. Like Anand Narayan.

In 1998, Harish was demonstrating his solar panel in a village when one chap stood up and asked, "Which IIT are you from?"

This, was Anand Narayan – an IIT Chennai grad himself. Master's and PhD from University of Colorado, but living in rural Karnataka. Growing organic coconuts.

"Anand had no electricity, so he became a Selco client – and a good friend."

Two years later Anand returned to Colorado, to help his girlfriend complete her PhD. Then he got married, had a baby and shifted back – to rural Karnataka. This time, to start an incubation laboratory for Selco.

"Our idea is to examine problems and find solutions. Rather than take existing solutions and fit them to a problem!"

Since 2008, this 'laboratory' in Ujjire village – 5 hours from Bangalore – has attracted talent from all over the world.

"Our summer internships get filled up in less than a week. We have students from MIT and Imperial College, London".

Interns work on a variety of problems – from designing longer lasting batteries to how to use solar panels in monsoons. Many return to their colleges and continue these projects.

The work that Selco does is truly amazing. The question you cannot help asking is, why not do more. Why not take this successful solar model – to the rest of India?

"Selco is an open source organisation. We have nothing known as 'confidentiality', we want people to replicate whatever we have learnt."

"We do want to scale up Selco, but we need to find the right person to make it happen in each state. With our support, of course."

Selco has now partnered with E & Co and Grameen Foundation in Seattle, to help in this process.

"We have shortlisted 4-5 entrepreneurs now and put them through a 3-month program. Hopefully, they will do in 5 years what Selco achieved in 15!"

Government support – at a policy level – would certainly help.

"We have a wonderful system called as 'financial inclusion'. Why not also have 'energy inclusion'!"

Give RRBs a mandate to finance not just agriculture, but energy needs.

"If the local manager has a target of 5%, only for solar lighting, things will rapidly change!"

Side by side, we need more efficient everyday equipment.

"A lady in Ahmedabad – a seamstress – wanted to run her sewing machine on solar power. But it wasn't possible as no manufacturer has a machine which can work at 40 W".

To make such machines you need to recognise, and to 'buy in' to the solar revolution.

"It took years and years to accept – for my own father," grins Harish.

A hardcore 'coal' guy, Hande Sr is now a passionate supporter of solar energy.

Another passionate supporter is wife Rupal, who lives and works in Boston. The couple met in Boston, and got married.

"We've had a long distance marriage – for 11 years."

The couple has an eight year old daughter – Adishree – who comes every to India every summer and goes with Harish, to the villages. Experiencing the world where her father's heart resides.

"The Karnataka state board topper for 10th class this year is the daughter of a client," beams Harish.

When she got the result, the first phone call her parents made was to Selco.

"Because of your lights, our daughter could study at night," they said.

It is such stories which make up the intangible bottomline.

Which keep Selco dedicated to their mission.

Of taming the sun.

To harvest hope, happiness and light.

ADVICE TO YOUNG ENTREPRENEURS

Spend time with what you want to do, without looking at economic benefits from day 1, day 2. For example, if you want to do solar business you should go know what it is yourself. You should first be a technician!

Go through the process – there is a lot of fun in doing that. It will take 2-3 years. Ask yourself if you are willing to invest that time. In future, it will be extremely valuable.

Don't start with a fancy business plan. If you go around with a PPT, trying to raise money, you will only become what I call a 'loose rubber band'.

You can never design a system based on Excel sheet economics.

Even when you grow big, keep your ear to the ground. Before a board meeting I usually call up 2-3 technicians and ask, "Boss, *kya hai* – what is happening out there".

Listen to every person in your organisation, no matter how little his 'education' might be. At Selco, we don't even look at resumes for hiring or promoting people. We evaluate people for who they are, not that piece of paper called as 'degree'.

Finally, it's not technology, it's not process. You need the right people, who believe in the mission, the goal of the organisation. Everything else is then easy.

TREE OF
LIFE

Santosh Parulekar,
Pipal Tree

Santosh was a well-settled IT professional until one fine day the job demanded he go out and learn all there was to know – about microfinance. Today, he runs a unique social enterprise which transforms poorly educated rural youth into highly skilled construction workers.

Santosh Parulekar is a very polite, very precise, very level-headed man. I am sure his clients swore by him, in the IT business.

Even when Santosh complains, it doesn't sound like a complaint.

"See, we are doing this work, it is changing the life of many boys. But we cannot expect them to come and say 'thank you'. That is not going to happen."

Indeed, but Santosh is one of those who has always made things happen. After working with Citibank and an American IT consulting firm, this young man could have put his career on auto-pilot.

Instead, he stepped out of the IT parks with steel and glass buildings which protect 'our India' from 'their India'. And discovered he was drawn to a different kind of challenge.

Carefully, logically, he studied different models – microfinance institutions, self help groups and actual conditions in villages. He then came up with a unique solution to one issue which was very dear to his heart: creating livelihood.

As I sit in his tiny office in a nondescript building in the suburb of Goregaon, I am transfixed. The man in front of me speaks matter-of-factly, objectively.

But what lies beneath is a throbbing conscience, a thumping heart.

For having the courage – and the commitment – to take up this cause.

I thank you, on behalf of my fellow Indians.

TREE OF
LIFE

Santosh Parulekar,
Pipal Tree

Santosh Parulekar was born and brought up in Mumbai, son of a municipal contractor.

"I grew up in Mahim and attended a local vernacular medium school – Saraswati Vidya Mandir."

That did not stop him from getting into VJTI – the top engineering school in Mumbai after the IIT.

"I was always inclined towards academics, engineering being a technical subject knowledge of English was not so important."

After graduating, Santosh joined the Tatas. After working for two years, he decided to go for a master's at the Indian Computer Academy, an offshoot of the Indian Institute of Science, Bangalore.

"I did my post-graduation in computer science. It was a one year course in collaboration with Harvard University, so I even studied for some time in the US."

After completing his master's in 1990, Santosh joined Citicorp, where he worked in the technology end of corporate banking. After some time, he was sent abroad – first to UK, and then to Poland.

"I was mainly on the technical side but you know in Citibank, there is nothing like 'pure technology'. Automatically, business comes into picture!'

After 6 years with the organisation, Santosh decided to move on. He joined a company called 'THINK' Systems, started by India-born entrepreneurs Sandy Tungare and Ravi Reddy. Santosh moved to the US.

"THINK Systems had a very niche product – a 'Demand Planner'. When I joined, we had only a handful of customers. In a short span I was able to take that number up to 200 customers."

In 1997, the company was sold to i2 Technologies for $150 million. However Santosh stuck on with Sandy and Ravi, and joined the new company they were starting – 'Vistaar'.

"I joined as one of directors, with some stake in the organisation. Vistaar was based in the US but we had backend operations in India as well."

What exactly did Vistaar do? Well, without getting into details, the company – rather the group of companies – provided 'solutions'. However these were not pure technology solutions.

"For example, there is a company called ROW2 which I have been closely associated with. It provides the complete cheminformatic solution – not drug discovery – but drug 'route' design."

Aided by a team of scientists based in India, and a very strong technology backend, ROW2 helps a drug company find all the ways possible to make a particular formulation. This is important from the IP and patents angle.

There are similar products for other industries – for example, shipping.

All was going well but in 2002 Santosh's father became critically ill. Prompting him to move back to India.

At the same time, the IT industry experienced a severe downturn. Thus it fell on Santosh to take stock of various operations of Vistaar which were bleeding. And nurse them back to financial health.

A tough task, but he was successful. Without ever having studied 'management', Santosh became a business manager.

"Microfinance should not be mere 'financial aid' – or a cheaper alternative to moneylenders. It must create livelihood."

"That's true... in fact at this point, in 2005, I did my EMBA from S P Jain. Because I sometimes felt I may be missing something – a qualification might help."

Around the same time, a micro finance institution (MFI) by the name of SKS approached Vistaar.

"The founders of Vistaar also run some trusts. SKS approached these trusts for funding."

Santosh wanted to understand what 'microfinance' was all about, techonologically and operationally. After all, people make all kinds of claims when they come to you. But did the ground reality match up?

To find out, Santosh travelled across the length and breadth of Andhra Pradesh, along with teams from SKS and other, smaller MFIs...

"I did not get involved with top people, rather I interacted with people at the grassroots. I spent some time in their branches, in the villages. And I was impressed."

This was Santosh's first exposure to the concept of 'social entrepreneurship'. Of being able to achieve social objectives with a 'business' approach. He decided to delve deeper.

"I was intrigued by Grameen Bank in Bangladesh. I interacted with them, studied their models and in fact, was all set to go to Bangladesh and see their operations."

But violence erupted between political factions supporting Khaleda Zia and Sheikh Hasina. The trip was cancelled.

Santosh then turned his focus on MAVIM – the Mahila Arthik Vikas Mandal run by the Maharashtra government. MAVIM supports Self Help Groups (SHGs) engaged in small-scale economic activities, with the help of the banking system.

"I spent lot of time with their teams in Bandra and in Bhiwandi. I wanted to understand how they work, and whether our trust could be of help to them."

Similarly, Santosh spent time with Veena Mankar, founder of Swadhaar. The pioneers of urban micro-finance in India.

"I also interacted closely with people at ICICI and SIDBI," recalls Santosh.

ICICI was keen that Santosh start his own MFI (Micro Finance Institution). And for some time, he seriously weighed that option. A close friend and classmate from VJTI – Shailendra Ghaste – was also keenly interested.

"We met another friend who was a banker and considered opening an NBFC (Non Banking Financial Institution)."

Why NBFC? Because at that time most MFIs were struggling, and very small in scale. Santosh felt there was a need for a bigger initiative, along the lines of Grameen Bank.

"For example, Grameen Bank used to run mobile assembling plans in the villages of Bangladesh. That created real jobs and livelihood. We wanted to do something similar in India."

Another issue was the MFI lending pattern – loans were given almost exclusively to women. That made sense – the default rates were extremely low – but Santosh wanted to expand the canvas of customers.

"I wanted to do something with the young boys – the youth – which would give them a livelihood option. Perhaps a 'joint liability' loan scheme."

Even as he was pondering these questions, there was a earthshaking piece of news in the world of micro-finance. In December 2006, Mohammed Yunus of Grameen Bank won the Nobel Prize.

"Before Yunus won the Nobel prize, no one knew what is micro-finance. After he got the Prize, everyone wanted to jump into micro-finance."

And they did. Companies like Reliance and Bharti, venture capital and adventure capital – all poured into MFIs.

"Even my father, who thought I was 'mad' to think about lending to the poor, suddenly thought it was a good idea," grins Santosh.

The long and short of it is, Santosh realised that MFIs were becoming more and more commercial. And that did not excite him.

Another technical issue was that unlike in Bangladesh, RBI did not allow NBFCs to open saving accounts.

"We wanted to offer loans at lower rates of interest. But that is not possible unless you can take deposits from customers."

The project was therefore shelved. But, by this time Santosh had visited dozens of villages, seen what the issues were. Somewhere, *somehow*, he wanted to do something to make a difference.

The question was 'what'.

Santosh felt that 'livelihood' was key. Even while he was trying to understand the MFI model, one question always concerned him. How does microfinance actually create livelihood?

"When I asked this question, I was told there are computer databases which will tell you which loan was given for what purpose. But, how do you know that a loan given to buy cattle has actually been *used* to buy cattle?"

You don't.

And microfinance lenders really don't care. As long as they were disbursing money, and collecting the sums due, the money could well be used – for anything.

"You see then, microfinance is actually nothing more than a sophisticated form of *sahukaari*..."

The second point which bothered Santosh was that microfinance companies lent only to women. What about the young boys, the unemployed youth? They simply could not be trusted with a loan!

"When I visited the villages many young boys would come, surround me and ask me,'Sahab, can you get us a job'?"

Some would be eight standard pass, some fifth standard pass, a few would even be matriculate. They had no interest in working in the fields and there were no jobs – in the village.

One fine day, Santosh and his partners Shailendra and Vikram reached a conclusion.

"Let us focus on creating livelihood – by forming a charitable trust."

Thus was born Pipal Tree.

Now came the question, do you aim for self-employment or do you focus on making people 'employable'.

"Everyone is very comfortable creating self-employed boys,

entrepreneurs. But we had our doubts. To become self-employed you need capital, you need willingness and it is not easy to sustain."

Hence, Pipal Tree decided to train the boys to take up jobs. But what kind of jobs, what kind of skills? The idea was not to become a human pipeline for low wage, dead-end jobs. Like the ubiquitous security guard.

"Security guards have no skills as such, so they get the same salary – around ₹ 3500 per month – no matter how long they work."

So, how do they survive? By taking up a second job, by drowning themselves in drink.

"By the time he reaches 40 either his habits kill him or he goes back and sends his son to take his place."

And thus the cycle continues.

This was not acceptable to Santosh. He started looking into different sectors – where was the demand more than the supply?

"Retail came to our mind but the profile of our boys was not suitable. They are not well groomed, cannot speak English and moulding them – changing them – is not easy."

Same was the case with the IT sector.

But one industry which looked promising was construction., for several reasons.

"Construction offers the second largest employment opportunity in the country, and the profile of our boys matched. What's more, most of the construction companies were facing shortage of skilled manpower."

Few companies want to train labour – only to see them jump to another employer as soon as they get a better offer. But one man's problem can be another man's opportunity.

"We know that this is not the traditional business where one makes money. Yes, you will eventually make a little money so that the growth is sustained."

"People expect a business should break even in three years but with a social venture you need a five year timeframe."

Now came the question of *how* to open that door...

"Intially we had talked about forming a trust but we realised that attracting professionals to work for us would be difficult, sustaining growth would be difficult."

And therefore, it was decided to run Pipal Tree as a private limited company.

"In the worst case, we would lose all our money. But that was a risk we were willing to take."

The advantage of forming a company was, its ability to attract outside investors.

And therefore operate at a much higher scale.

Santosh and his two partners put in ₹ 50 lakhs each. Two strategic investors* and a venture capitalist – in his personal capacity – put in additional funds.

Thus, Pipal Tree was formally registered in November 2007, with ₹ 8 crores of equity.

Why was so much money needed, I wonder.

"Because we wanted to have one training centre – of our own."

This went completely against conventional wisdom. Training could be imparted at rented locations, after all. Why invest so much in an activity which will never generate substantial financial returns?

Because that is the way Santosh thinks.

He thinks big.

"People feel comfortable doing business with less assets, that way there is no exit barrier. But a slightly asset-heavy model creates more confidence in the eyes of all the stakeholders – the students, the construction companies, the investors."

* KMC Constructions and BSCPL Infrastructure, both construction companies based in Hyderabad.

It indicates 'I am here to stay'.

Secondly – practically speaking – you need to invest in space and equipment, in order to teach effectively.

"To operate heavy machinery you need land, you need equipment which is very costly."

A 'grader' costs between ₹ 40-60 lakhs, while a single paver costs ₹ 2-5 crores. Some of these machines have been lent, or donated, by construction companies. Others had to be bought.

A full fledged campus was also set up in Hyderabad, at a cost of ₹ 4 crores.

"It is a 25 acre campus, on a 29 year lease. We have constructed a residential facility where 200 boys can be trained at one time."

Pipal Tree also tied up with TAFE – a leading technical university in Australia.

"We pay them service and royalty fee to come and train our people. Similarly, we have a tie-up with some German companies and experts."

It really would have been much easier to focus at the lower end of the market. But Santosh knew that with more specialised training, his boys would have better growth prospects.

"We offer courses in relatively low tech areas like steel fixing and bar-bending, as well as heavy machinery and surveying – which are more complex."

Crucial to the success of the program was linkage to jobs. Santosh and his team did meet several construction companies to understand their requirements. But there was a major difference of opinion, on course content.

"You go to any construction company, they will give you readymade content. Unfortunately, if you use that to teach, the boys will still not be employable. That is, ready to start working from day one."

What every employer wants...!

And so Pipal Tree has designed its own unique program, to be completed in six weeks. Because that is the attention span of its students.

"The boys have left school in sixth standard and eight standard because they were not interested in studying. They don't have the patience to attend a one year program!"

So the issue is, what should you do in six weeks so that they can deliver reasonable output, from the day they join.

"I always told my people, course content is only reference material. I want the boys to get trained on the skill which they need to use day in and day out."

What is important is quality of work, and productivity.

"So I will teach the boy only five things but I will make him excellent in that because that forms 80% of his work content."

The remaining 20% can be taught over the next year, because the trainer will be with the boys for that duration.

Why this is necessary is another, fascinating story.

Initially, Santosh met the owners of various construction companies; they agreed to absorb the boys after training. But getting this commitment was the easy part. Getting the site manager's co-operation was quite another thing!

"When you meet the owners and senior managers, you get a different picture. When you go on the site, you get the real picture."

And it is not pretty.

Most companies do not want to take workers on their payroll. For many kinds of jobs, they prefer sub-contractors. And they treat the people working for them 'like dirt'.

"The sub-contractors won't pay on time, won't give proper food – we did not want that kind of job for our boys!"

Some companies agreed to take Pipal Tree boys on on NMR roll ie 'project roll'. But when the boys reported on the site, they were given no work to do. Or harassed, in the hope *ki aath-dus din mein dukhi hokar bhag jayenge*.

"You see, the site manager has his own equations with the sub-contractors and people who supply labour. He does not want to co-operate."

The first batch of 40 students from Pipal Tree passed out in December 2008. After 2-3 batches struggled with these issues, Santosh took a bold decision.

"Pipal Tree will work as a sub-contractor, we will take responsibility for the work, We will take money from the construction companies and pay our boys. And this way we will satisfy both our students and the companies."

Of course, there are issues. You have to deliver – on more than one front. A trainer from Pipal Tree is with the boys at all times. And an operations person has to be deputed on site as well.

"This increases our cost structure. We have 30-35 trainers on the payroll but the important thing is we have to make this model work."

And certainly, it is working.

From the student point of view, there is a steady income, with a chance to climb higher.

"At the lower end – what is called as the labour class – the boys get ₹ 6000 per month. Accommodation is free."

On average, a boy might spend ₹ 1000 per month on food, while ₹ 1000 is deducted by Pipal Tree towards training cost.

"So in hand they get ₹ 4000 and they are very happy."

At the higher end. Boys trained in operating heavy machinery start at ₹ 7000 per month and Pipal Tree insists that they are taken on the construction company's payroll.

"Heavy machinery course is costly due to expensive equipment, so we deduct ₹ 2000 from their salary towards training for one year."

Thus for the first year a Pipal Tree student would get ₹ 5000 in hand, but from the second year onwards he can expect to get ₹ 8000. These boys can potentially rise upto the level of 'grader operator'. At which point they will earn ₹ 25,000 per month.

"It takes time to change people's mindset and gain their trust. When you start a training center in a particular area most people assume you will run away in a few months. They wait and watch."

"If I take government support and train 20,000 boys but I don't give them a job... it serves no purpose. All I have done is shown utilisation of funds."

Some of the boys also stick on with Pipal Tree and become supervisors.

"Even if they remain as labour, if their productivity in steel-fixing and bar-bending goes up, they can easily earn ₹ 8-10 thousand per month."

The foreman at a construction site draws ₹ 18-20,000 per month. To rise further, the boys would require additional training. And Santosh is planning – at the back of his mind – even for that.

The commitment of Pipal Tree towards its students is amazing. Keep in mind the fact that the fee for the course – at the star-t – is a mere ₹ 1500. The rest is deducted from each boy's salary, so he does not feel the pinch.

But the amount is small – compared to the efforts. How does this then become a sustainable business model, and not mere social service?

"You need volume of students. Our main campus is in Hyderabad, the spokes are in Rai Bareli, Nasik, Bihar and just recently we have started in Rajasthan."

Each spoke can take in 25-50 students at a time, and two programs can be run concurrently. Even then, current operations are modest; Pipal Tree produces 300-400 'graduates' a year.

That number is expected to grow to 1500 over the next one year, and 5000 the year after that.

"Our model will be sustainable when we train 5000 boys a year. Pipal Tree will then make a small operating profit."

And that would be enough – for the promoters, for the investors*.

* In October 2010, IDFC Foundation – a not-for-profit division of IDFC – took a stake in Pipal Tree

"We could have gone only for the numbers, but we want to develop our value proposition, resolve all the issues. Then, growth will automatically follow."

Pipal Tree can easily get a grant of ₹ 5-10 crores from the government. Train 20,000 boys. But, then what?

"If we go for numbers, we will lose the faith of these boys. On paper we will 'train' 20,000 people but we will not be able to find them steady employment."

Which means that after the initial 20,000, not even 20 boys will enrol for the next program. And Santosh is not in it, to make a quick buck. In fact, he will probably devote the rest of his working life to this cause.

"Initially we thought of hiring a professional, but then we realised that at least one of us has to be in this full time. Because unless there is a passion and commitment, you will find it difficult to stick through the tough times."

That is the case with any kind of entrepreneurship, but even more so with social entrepreneurship.

"Companies have cracked how to sell mobile phones – or Lux soap. Even microfinance model has been successful. But our job is tougher!"

While microfinance is about disbursing money, Pipal Tree charges money. No doubt, a very small sum, but it takes time to win the trust of villagers.

"When we started in Bihar, initially the boys said, '*Hum paanch sau rupya bhi nahin denge*'. Slowly they are coming, and now they are willing to pay ₹ 1500."

For every good intention, there is a question. From finding boys to train, to delivering upto company expectations, it is a long chain of value which Pipal Tree must deliver.

And it has its own unique challenges.

While on the road from Lucknow to Rae Bareli recently, Pipal Tree's training AVP Sachin remarked to Santosh, "You told me this business is different, that we will have issues, we will have surprises. But if there are surprises everyday, how do you think we should work?"

One small example – Pipal Tree sent a batch of boys to Chennai. They came back within a week saying, "*Peene ka paani baraabar nahin tha.*"

The real reason was completely different.

"The boys wanted to come home for Holi, so they made up this excuse. Same boys are now working in Rajasthan and doing very well."

That they left their job midway was one problem. On top of that, they came back and created a lot hungama at Pipal Tree's training centre.

The boys went on dharna outside the centre and said, 'Give us a job or we will tell everyone you are cheating'."

In fact, they kept knocking on the door – all night.

"That day we really got frustrated although eventually we did get them jobs elsewhere."

Santosh shares a trade secret.

"Internally you should be very soft, but externally you should never show that you are soft. Otherwise the boys will exploit you."

And sometimes you *will* wonder, is it really worth it?

"Initially boys would call me in the middle of the night. Someone will get drunk and then abuse you because he did not get roti on the site."

With time and patience, Santosh found a way to handle the issue.

"Now I freely give my phone number but there are two rules. First is that if you have any problem. you first sms me and then I will call back. And secondly, I will call you between 11 in the morning and 7 at night only."

At other times – and Sundays – Santosh will simply not pick up.

But despite these irritations, he is keen to retain a personal touch.

"Even my operations people are fully hands-on, on the site. Nowadays they sort out 90% of the issues themselves. But I want to remain accessible, in touch with the boys."

This level of passion and commitment means some compromise – in personal life.

"My wife has been supportive but initially I used to travel a lot – I was out 20-25 days a month."

The moment his five year old son saw papa at home he would ask, "When are you going back?"

Things are better now but even today, Santosh is on the road for more than two weeks every month.

Apart from that, Santosh has scaled back on his lifestyle, to an extent.

"I am driving a car which I bought 8 years ago. I don't want to waste money, or splurge unnecessarily."

Santosh does draw a salary from Pipal Tree, but he puts it all back into the venture.

He is the caretaker of a seedling, which has grown into a plant, and will one day be a mighty tree.

"Like Buddha got his enlightenment under a Pipal tree, our students are discovering new skills in their life."

May this Pipal spread light, spread love.

Bring shade into the lives of those who have toiled under many suns.

ADVICE TO YOUNG ENTREPRENEURS

The country needs social entrepreneurs. I don't think the politicians have been successful in development efforts.

But only people who really have the passion should get into it.

You should be willing to take disappointments. You should be willing to accept that the people you help may will never say 'thank you' to you although they are grateful and will express it in their own way.

You have to have a soft heart, but act tough. Only then you will earn trust and respect.

I advise people to have some savings as a back-up. Enough to take care of your day to day life. Otherwise, in the initial years you will find it difficult to sustain, especially if you have a family.

TEACH A MAN
TO FISH

Dinabandhu Sahoo,
Project Chilika

Dinabandhu Sahoo is a marine biologist who's stepped out of his laboratory, into the real world. Through Project Chilika Sahoo has trained villagers in Orissa to 'farm the ocean'. Sowing the seeds of a 'Blue Revolution', a new hope for millions across the world.

I grew up in a colony of scientists. Badly dressed, moody, middle-aged men in thick spectacles were a common sight on the campus.

I always wondered what they actually did.

"So you conduct research in a laboratory," I once told my dad. "But what use is it to anyone?"

I'm afraid he really did not have an answer that satisfied me.

Over the years, I have come to realise the importance of fundamental research; I accept the premise that a tiny fraction of people must dedicate their lives to expanding the frontiers of knowledge.

But still. It is refreshing to meet a man of science who takes it upon himself – for no particular reason – to apply his knowledge in the real world.

Dinabandhu Sahoo has devoted his life to the esoteric area of seaweed. He could have spent his life like any other academic. Quietly working away in his lab, making the occasional splash in an international journal.

But that was not enough for him.

Sahoo wanted his technology to impact people, improve their lives. And that is exactly what he is doing through the 'Chilika project'. Teaching villagers how to 'farm the ocean' and make a sustainable livelihood through the cultivation of seaweed.

Sahoo never thought of himself as a 'social entrepreneur', but he is one. I sit cross-legged on freshly mowed grass – distracted by the occasional mosquito – listening to him.

And I think, "You don't have to give up 'everything' to do something."

Start by doing your job. Then, do *more* than your job. Finally, forget that you are even *doing* a job.

See the magic.

TEACH A MAN
TO FISH

Dinabandhu Sahoo,
Project Chilika

Dinabandhu Sahoo was born and brought up in the temple town of Puri.

"Nobody in my family had a proper education – I am the first to graduate from college."

To pay his fees, Sahoo took tuitions for children. The perspiration paid off when he stood first in the university. But, due to a technical error, he was actually listed as 'second'.

"That's when I decided, if I have to make something of my life I better leave this small town. I applied to Delhi University for my post-graduation."

With difficulty, Sahoo collected ₹ 800 to make the journey. His first, outside the state.

"I came to Delhi without reservation. In fact, I spent my first night sleeping at the station."

Sahoo secured admission for an MSc in Botany and even received a national scholarship. But at the end of the course, he was once again lost.

"There was no direction what to do next!"

Sahoo's Japanese roommate Shunji Hosaka got him a job with a newspaper in Tokyo – the *Asahi Shimbun*. But, it did not excite him.

"I joined Delhi University as a researcher. Like most of the students, I was also preparing for my civil service exam."

And this story is no different from a thousand others, but for a twist of fate. Dinabandhu Sahoo was selected as the first Indian student to go to Antarctica in 1987, as part of the 7th Indian Scientific Expedition to the icy continent. It was an offer he could not refuse.

"I left everything else, and went to Antarctica. That is when I saw the 'real world'."

Sahoo travelled extensively – to many countries – and it opened up his eyes. It was the 1980s, and the difference between India and the developed world was stark.

After completing his PhD in Botany from Delhi University in 1989, Sahoo migrated to the US. But although he did well professionally – and enjoyed the many comforts of living abroad – his heart was still in India.

"I had a car, an air conditioner, a big house. But there was this feeling that I should come back to my own country – and do something."

Something 'different'.

Sahoo returned to Delhi University – this time, as an academic. Not the ideal location for a marine biologist, but he worked around it.

"When I started my research career I decided to work on the Chilika lake because I have been seeing it since childhood."

Not just the lake, but the human and marine ecosystem around it.

As a researcher, Sahoo had a special interest in marine algae – or seaweed.

There is very little awareness of the utility, and the nutritive value of these plants in India. Unlike Southeast Asian countries where seaweed is part of the staple diet.

"Marine algae have a large number of applications* in day to day life," adds Sahoo. "Be it in toothpaste, ice cream, tomato ketchup, chocolates, dye industry, textile printing – even pharmaceuticals."

* Value of seaweed extract (agar agar) used in industry is estimated to be ₹ 50,000 crore per annum.

Of course, there are many different kinds of seaweed. Red algae – 'Gracilaria verrucosa' – is an important commercial variety which grows in Chilika Lake. But, not in quantities sufficient for the needs of industry.

"Can scientific method be applied to change that?" wondered Sahoo.

In the Phillipines, more than 10,000 families earn their living through seaweed farming. The coastal areas of Ganjam district had the same potential. To spread awareness about this potential, Sahoo had authored a book called 'Farming the Ocean' in the year 2000.

But the focus in India was hardly on seaweed – it was on aquaculture. And unfortunately, harvesting prawns, shrimps and other such marine animals was actually destroying the lake ecosystem.

"Seaweed cultivation on the other hand is eco-friendly, it is sustainable. I decided to develop a model where seaweed can become a source of income for the local population."

A model which could then be replicated in other parts of the country.

The model was simple – teach locals how to cultivate commercially viable seaweed and simultaneously tie up with the industry for a 'buy back' arrangement at a pre-determined price, so that the farmers get a guaranteed income.

"Over a period of time when enough seaweed is being produced, then you can set up your own small scale industry*."

Sounds like a simple, workable model; industry appeared to be interested. But how do you kickstart the cultivation? Sahoo was a scientist, not a businessman. So, he decided to first approach various government departments.

"I met many senior bureaucrats and ministers – all of them said it is a good idea but did nothing to take things forward."

Finally, Sahoo approached the Department of Science and Technology (DST). DST's 'Science and Society' division specifically sanctions funds for applied research, where society in general reaps the benefits.

A committee examined Sahoo's project and disbursed ₹ 20 lakhs for a pilot project spread over 3 years.

> **"The socio-economic dynamic in the coastal area is very different from other parts of the country. In a big city one rupee has no value, but in Orissa even ten paise has value."**

"I developed a uniform module for the training of villagers, in different parts of India. Since the idea originated from here, we call it the 'Chilika' model."

The beauty of seaweed is, it multiplies on its own. You just take the seedling, leave it to grow and then harvest it after 45 days. The investment is extremely low; unlike farming on land you don't require ploughing, watering, pesticide or fertiliser.

"The water body is a common resource – it does not belong to any one person but to the entire community."

Having said that, there is a 'science' of seaweed.

"We identified four different seaweed having both national and international markets. In fact, demand has been increasing – at the rate of ten percent every year."

Then came the important task of identifying which species to grow where. Because parameters like climate and quality of water make all the difference.

"Our job is to scientifically survey Chilika. Based on the salinity, the pH and turbidity, we recommended species which would grow abundantly."

The key is to communicate this information to the local community in a simple and succinct manner. The information is translated into various languages – Oriya, Tamil, Telugu, Marathi. And, there is a training-cum-demonstration workshop.

The first such program on cultivation of Gracilaria species was held at Satapada site of Chilika lake in February 2009.

The entire activity is handled – at the grassroots – by NGOs and Self Help Groups (SHGs). Sahoo himself plays the role of trainer, co-ordinator, disseminator of knowledge*.

* In Tamil Nadu, 5000 families cultivating seaweed are now setting up a factory

"The beauty of seaweed cultivation is its simplicity. The only equipment you need are common items like bamboo, nylon rope, torn fishing nets and hammers!"

The method used is 'raft culture'. After receiving training, four women SHG groups at Langaleswara site of Chilika lake cultivated G. Verrucosa species of seaweed .

"Within 15 days of cultivation we could see excellent results!" exults Sahoo.

The purchase price of the seaweed has been fixed at ₹ 10 per kg. On an average, a cultivator can earn ₹ 5000 per month – a large sum of money for a village in Orissa.

"The only alternative is NREGA – where you dig roads or do construction work on daily wages. That too, only for a certain number of days."

Seaweed cultivation, on the other hand, is a continuous cycle.

"Let us say three people from one family work in a water area of five acres – they start planting from one side and keep going that way... At the end of 45 days their first crop is ready to be harvested."

Along with harvesting, seeds are sown for the next cycle of crops. So in a sense, you have a perennial, daily income.

'Give a man a fish and you have fed him for a day' goes the old Chinese proverb. To that, I am tempted to say, 'Teach a man to grow seaweed, and you feed him for a lifetime'.

Of course, it is a slow process. Several villages in different pockets around Chilika lake have been brought into the fold, but it is taking time.

"The program is spreading slowly because we are not taking any help from the government," he adds.

"As a scientist you publish a paper and get credit – that is one thing. But the real challenge is when you transfer a technology to the field, where 99% of efforts fail."

Livelihood is one aspect of the Chilika project, but closely linked to it is conservation. Seaweed farming is a sustainable alternative to the more popular – but poisonous – fish farming.

"Aquaculture is an enclosed system where you add the artificial fertiliser whereas seaweed cultivation is a photosynthetic process. It actually restores the carbon absorption capacity of the water."

The removal of CO_2 from the sea is going to be a huge project in the future, believes Sahoo. He is part of an Asia Pacific network of 11 nations, deliberating on this issue.

But how does the *rickshawwallah*, or tea stall owner care about 'acidification' of the ocean? How do you bring alive the importance of preserving the coastal ecology to the common man?

In his training module Sahoo does not talk only about technicalities; beyond a mere natural resource, Chilika is a cultural icon.

"I talk about how Chilika is the lifeline of the people, the pride of Orissa and an inspiration for writers and poets."

And from this line of thought came the idea of making a documentary film *'Chilika – the untold story'*. An entirely self-funded, self-driven effort, the film focused not just on the 'nature' aspect of the lake, but the human beings who depend on it.

"I had seen a documentary on Sunderbans by an NGO, I invited them to come for one of my training workshops and film it. From there I got the idea of doing an entire film, with a 'story' of some kind."

Sahoo put down a 3 page outline, this was refined into a script. He then hired a camera crew hired and began shooting; but it was not that simple.

"We came back and found the picture quality was poor, some shots were missing. So we had to go and come back 3-4 times, to fill up the gaps. But at the end of all the effort we had a nice picturisation."

While Sahoo bore most of the cost, he insisted on sharing credits with the NGO Nature Environment Wildlife Society (NEWS).

"They gave a lot of logistics support, including use of their studio in Kolkata. I am especially grateful to Biswajit Roychoudhry, co-director of the film."

Ultimately it was a team project, with one door literally opening to lead into the next. And the result was much appreciated.

"When I showed this film to the Swedish International Development Agency (SIDA), they liked it and took it up as a 'Project for Change'."

Sahoo is hopeful that Project Chilika will be able to impact not just Orissa, or India, but also nearby countries like Thailand and Maldives.

The question I cannot help asking is: "Why?" It would be enough to do research, publish papers and attend international conferences. Why would an academic actually want to step out of the laboratory, roll up his sleeves and make things happen in the *real* world?

"Because when I look back, after thirty years, I will find some small contribution I have made to the society. If you don't have that type of thinking, then why do you live?"

And no, there is no monetary reward in all this, for Sahoo. There is no company formed in which he has a stake, no extra payment for extra work done.

"In fact, if you come to do fieldwork and training, the university will ask you to apply for leave!" he says, shaking his head at the absurdity of the situation.

Sahoo does not keep track of the 'turnover' from each micro enterprise, he prefers that the SHG or village co-operative manage it themselves.

"I am not a businessman." he says, very simply.

If a company wants his technology someday, he will charge them. But he *cannot* think of charging the poor.

"Goodwill is very important in life. Whatever amount of money you may earn, your stomach is only this much! Both my wife and I work – we have a house in Delhi – what more can we ask for?"

The one small regret is, less time for family life. Travelling and fieldwork consume a lot of his time. But Sahoo is lucky to have a strong group of PhD students, as passionate about this project as he is.

"We have seen Green Revolution, and White Revolution. My dream is to see a 'Blue Revolution'. To harness the vast potential of the sea."

In a state like Orissa, where malnutrition is a chronic issue, Sahoo believes that seaweed can be a potent weapon.

"Did you know that 100 grams of seaweed has nutrition equal to one kg of vegetables?" he asks.

Hmm, not really.

But I do know that one scientist who decided to make the world a better place is better than a hundred IAS officers keeping the status quo.

Let us weed out old ideas and plant new seeds.

Seeds with the power to do as much good, as the humble seaweed.

ADVICE TO YOUNG ENTREPRENEURS

Society has given us many things, it is high time to give something back to society in whatever way possible. Each one has a role to play and I think every individual, if he tries, can do something.

If every individual thinks "I am doing only my job" – if everything is 'I' – then where will society go. There are many people who have sacrificed their career to serve society. I am not in a position to quit my job but feel I can do a great deal, even staying in the job.

I am helping people to the best of my ability and that is a great source of satisfaction in my life.

THE HUNGRY
TIDE

Anand Kumar,
Super 30

Anand Kumar is a mathematics teacher who ran his own coaching classes. But in 2002, his classroom turned into a unique social experiment, tutoring poor but meritorious students for IIT JEE. In 2008, all the students of 'Super 30' cracked the exam, igniting hope in the heart of darkness. A hunger to succeed, in gaons and gullies across India.

I am fascinated by billboards. They tell you so much about a city, and its inhabitants.

In Patna, wherever you turn, you will see an advertisement for "IIT Coaching".

A seat in IIT is coveted by any student, anywhere in India. But in Bihar, it is a matter of life and death – academically speaking.

Study hard, join IIT – your life is made. Fail and you will be stuck in a state where nothing much happens.

Into this scenario stepped Anand Kumar. A mathematics lover who ran a coaching class – like many others. Until one fine day, he started an experiment.

He took in a batch of 30 poor but talented students and decided to train them – free of cost – to crack the JEE. This experiment came to be known as 'Super 30'.

A program which has succeeded in opening the doors of the hallowed IIT – to a whole new class of aspirants.

If reservation is about lowering the bar, Super 30 is about raising it.

The phenomenal success of Super 30 is testimony to the fact that talent is important. But hunger to achieve, to make something of yourself is an equally powerful force.

A good teacher can unleash that force in a willing student.

Thousands of such students will create a hungry tide, carrying a new generation of Indians into the New India.

THE HUNGRY
TIDE

Anand Kumar,
Super 30

Anand Kumar was born in Patna in a lower middle class family.

"My father was a clerk in the postal department. We were a large family – a joint family – so money was always scarce."

Anand studied in Patna high school – a government school – but right from childhood, he thought differently.

"Mera sapna tha ki main scientist banoon. Other children would be playing cricket while I would be on my own, making science models or reading biographies of great scientists."

By the time he reached class 9, Anand realised one important thing. To become a good scientist, making 'models' was not going to be enough. He would need to be an expert in mathematics.

"*Yehi samajh kar maine apne aap ko Mathematics mein poori tarah involve kiya*. I became very serious about studying mathematics."

After class 10, Anand joined Bihar National College (B N College), affiliated to Patna University.

"Plus 2 *ke baad*, I was confused. Because in a poor state like Bihar, most people go only for medicine or engineering. Or they try for IAS. But I only wanted to do one thing – to become a mathematician."

Anand spent much of his free time devising mathematical problems, and then solving each one in many different ways. Around this time, he came to know Dr Devi Prasad Verma, the head of the science college in Patna University.

"Dr Verma is a very learned, very respected professor even today. I used to go to him and share my new ideas, new formulas."

Dr Verma encouraged the young man. He polished the presentation and sent some of Anand's work to mathematical journals in India and abroad. Among them, the prestigious British journal 'Mathematical Agent', whose editor had once been G H Hardy (also famous as the teacher of S. Ramanujan).

"When my formulas were published in such journals, my enthusiasm increased. I applied to Cambridge University for a Master's degree in 1994."

Sadly, Anand got admission, but only a partial scholarship. The family had no money, to spare. But Anand's father appealed to the Postal department for assistance. The department approved a scholarship of ₹ 50,000. But before the money could be disbursed, there was a tragedy. On August 23, 1994, Anand's father suddenly passed away.

"He was absolutely normal, had no history of any disease. He came home, had his dinner, went to sleep. Ten minutes later – he was gone."

Everything changed overnight.

"Hamare upar dukhon ka pahaad toot pada. Aisa laga jeevan mein kuch bacha nahin."

The responsibility of the entire household fell on young Anand's shoulders.

"First thing, I decided I will not go to Cambridge. I would have to stay in Patna and support the family."

His father's colleagues advised, "*Bete*, take the job that the postal department provides to next of kin."

Anand argued, "Uncle, I am a student and I am a lover of mathematics. If I start a job now, I will have to leave my studies altogether."

Yes, he had to earn money at any cost. But could he do it, without losing the only thing he loved in life? Anand's mother sensed her son's dilemma.

> *"Ek sawaal ko kai tarah se banana,*
> *naye naye forumule se dekhna,*
> *yeh sab karte rehte the hum."*

She said, "*Koi aur raasta nikalte hain.*"

With her help, Anand started a business selling *papad*. "My mother and some of the ladies in the mohalla got together and made papad. We called it 'Anand Papad'. Every evening between 4pm and 7 pm I went door to door – selling it."

The money generated was just about enough, to run the home, and send some money to Anand's younger brother, studying at Benaras Hindu University.

Meanwhile, Anand decided to try earning a living by teaching mathematics.

"I started taking tuitions for children of rich businessmen. But in less than a week, they ran away saying, 'We don't like your teaching'."

Anand felt embarassed – was he so poor a teacher? But, he did not lose heart. With ₹ 500 which he had saved up, he took a room in a nearby school on rent. Every evening between 5 and 8 pm, he would teach students mathematics.

"This was in 1995-96. It was not fixed that time that I will be preparing students for IIT – they simply learnt mathematics, and it was a great success."

The coaching centre started with two students. At the end of one year there were 100 students and within two and a half years, more than 1000 students.

"From the beginning I was famous for my fees – I used to charge only ₹ 500 per year, which was very low even by Bihar standards. People wondered why I charged so less for good quality teaching, and hundreds of students enrolled only on word of mouth."

But, there was more to come.

In 1998, Anand first met Abhayanand – Additional Director

General of Police – in the office of Uttam Sengupta, editor of *The Times of India* Patna edition.

"We talked about mathematics, and after that I kept in touch with him, and met him regularly."

By this time, Anand decided to make his classes more 'systematic'. Since most students were keen on engineering entrance exams, and most of all IIT JEE, why not prepare them to perform better?

"I developed a course for IIT entrance, but again with modest fees. I used to charge ₹ 1500 per year, inclusive of study material, tests and assignments."

500 students quickly enrolled, results were encouraging. But every now and then a student would come and say, "*Sir, pandrah sau rupye ka fee mere liye kuch zyada hai.*"

Such students Anand sir would admit, free of cost.

One day a boy, accompanied by his father came up to Anand and said, very politely, "Sir, I will pay you the fees in instalments. I will give you ₹ 500 right now, ₹ 500 after 3 months and the remaining amount when my father harvests the potatoes."

Anand said, "*Itne kasht se fees to bhar loge*, but where will you live?"

The boy replied that a lawyer from his village now lived in Patna. He would work as a guard and live below the staircase of his house.

Touched by the boy's sincerity, Anand admitted him. One day, on a whim, he decided to drop by and see for himself – *ki kya yeh ladka sachmuch seedi ke neeche rehta hai*?

"I found him exactly there – under the staircase – studying. I was reminded of my student days spent in poverty and the hardship. And how I could not go to Cambridge because of lack of funds."

Kuch karna chahiye aise bachchon ke liye, thought Anand. He shared these thoughts with Abhayanand, and found in him a willing support.

Although an IPS officer, Abhayanand had a love for teaching. When his son was studying at the Ramakrishna Mission school in Deoghar (now in Jharkhand), he got involved with the students.

In the very first class I tell students that we are studying mathematics only because we love it. *Hamare liye yeh ek tarah ka jadoo hai..."*

"I found myself happily asking the schoolchildren thought-provoking questions. The children learnt how to apply their knowledge to problems and I learnt the way children of generation next think."

Helping others think for themselves was *more* satisfying than thinking for oneself, found Abhyanand.

Now, his son and daughter had grown up and were preparing for the IIT entrance exam. While Anand helped them with Maths, Abhayanand straightened their fundas in Physics.

"Physics was the subject I loved most, but I also became fascinated with Mathematics. When both Richa and Shwetank got into IIT and left home, there was a void. I did not want to lose whatever I had learnt in the process of their development."

Thus, in 2002, Anand Kumar and Abhayanand came together to form 'Super 30'. The idea was to pick 30 poor but talented students who could not afford IIT coaching. 'Super 30' would groom these students, to crack the JEE.

The road map was clearly laid out, the mission statement clear. There was no financial backing but there was absolute conviction, that money would not be a stumbling block. All that was needed was the hunger to succeed and two dedicated souls who would feed those hungry minds.

Anand's mother volunteered to feed their hungry stomachs. 30 students were recruited by word of mouth and housed in 2s and 4s in rooms nearby. Classes began in a small room with a tin roof, creaking benches and a piece of wood painted black for a board.

Abhayanand jokes, "I had to boost my skills as a teacher so that I could present a more engrossing discussion in class than the playful display by the rats!"

But it did not matter. So passionate were the students, so eager to learn, that even in the short lunch break they would be discussing concepts and formulas.

The teachers quickly realised they were mere catalysts – their presence initiated a reaction within the student, but the momentum had to be maintained by the child himself.

"Luckily, all our students were extremely hard working and ready to slog it out. We used to hold regular mock tests and at the end of the year we were convinced that if we woke up these boys from deep sleep and handed them a JEE test paper, they would be able to solve it."

Early on, it became clear that self-confidence would be the key to success.

"The fear of the IIT JEE is the main source of trouble," says Abhayanand. "Even capable students are stumped by this fear and finally beaten in the race."

By the end of the year of coaching, 'Super 30' students were saying, "I am waiting to see my rank, Sir!" Yet, everyone was astounded when 18 of the 30 students actually made it to IIT, from that very first batch.

Building on this experience – making some mid-course corrections – a second batch was enrolled. This time, thanks to the local press, more than 1000 students applied to be part of 'Super 30'. A written entrance test was held.

Says Abhayanand, "In our management group we had a person without formal education, but who had excellent observation skills. He developed the uncanny knack of sighting confidence – or its lack – in students. To our surprise, his forecast of results was closer to reality than our mock test results predicted!"

"We do not get any financial return from this venture. Yet we do ask for a guru-dakshina from students: 'Give back to society what you have got, if not more'."

"The poor student has *taakat*. We instill this thought in their minds to such an extent that their blood boils and they wait for the exams to come."

And thus, it was tangible and intangible qualities that the teachers looked for, when admitting a student to 'Super 30'.

At JEE 2004 22 out of 30 students from 'Super 30' qualified for IIT, and with better ranks. It was heartening to see the son of a brick kiln worker, or a rickshaw puller making it to IIT. 'Super 30' got more media attention and even more applications from hopefuls.

"*Kuch logon ne ise gurukul kaha, kuch ne factory.* We continued our efforts, with even more resolve," says Anand.

Managing parents and their expectations also became a challenge. "We realised the amount of damage that doting parents can do to their children," says Abhayanand.

"Those who had faith in our group would leave us to our job, and their wards would do much better than the wards of those who tried to interfere... If one has faith in a process, it can give wondrous results!"

However, this success brought with it a dark shadow. The coaching mafia in the state decided '*inka kuch to karna padega*'.

In November 2004, Anand escaped a murderous attack – while he escaped with minor injuries, a non teaching staff member was grievously hurt. In February 2005, there was another another abortive bid on the Super 30 centre, but the heavily armed criminals were caught.

"The police department provided armed guards for my security. I am grateful to the state government for their support," says Anand.

Despite all this drama, the academic atmosphere at Super 30 remained unaffected. In 2005, 26 students made it to IIT. Would 'Super 30' hit bullseye the next year? Many people came forward offering financial help – for better infrastructure, to accommodate more students.

"A lot of thinking went and ultimately we decided not to accept money from anyone, whether an individual or an institution. We also decided to stick to 30 students."

Prompt replies were sent off to all those who had made the offer, saying, "Super 30 needs only your good wishes."

But now, came a new googly. In 2006, the IIT JEE pattern was changed. As if fear of the exam was not enough, fear of the 'unknown' added to it. But 'Super 30' students rose to the challenge. "28 out of 30 students made it to IIT, with one student securing All India Rank 10!" exults Anand.

Bihar Chief Minister Nitish Kumar felicitated the students and announced a cash prize of ₹ 50,000 each.

The following year, another 28 students achieved the IIT dream. Finally, in 2008, 'Super 30' received the ultimate feather in its cap. All 30 students were successful in clearing the JEE.

At this point, the teacher of mathematics and the police officer with a passion for teaching parted ways.

"Now that we have achieved 100 per cent results, there is nothing to prove to myself," felt Abhayanand. "It's time to move on and take this social laboratory to other sectors."

"What will happen to 'Super 30'?" wondered the skeptics. Well, it continues to flourish.

Two of Anand's former students – Praveen Kumar and Amit Kumar – have joined him as teachers. His brother Pramod, who lived in Mumbai and worked as a violinist, has also come back to Patna to manage the administration. In 2009, all 30 students once again made it to IIT.

"Our intention is not only restricted to earning money. Sometimes a 45 minute lecture will go on for 2 hours – until we find a solution to the problem."

The same year, 'Rahmani-30', ten students from the Muslim community who were coached along the same lines as the original 'Super 30' – and mentored by Abhayanand – also achieved cent per cent results.

There is now a competition, of sorts.

Anand has increased the 'Super 30' batch to 45. He plans to take that number up to 60, or even 90. The Abhyanand led effort is yet to find 30 students per group who make the cut. But, they are looking...

For as Anand puts it, "*Gareebi ka bachcha itihaas banaata hai.*"

It is the poor who make history. In fact, Anand uses two characters – Ricky and Bholu to illustrate this point.

"Ricky is a rich student, he comes on a bike, eats pizza and says 'hi'. Bholu is a poor student, he comes on a cycle, eats *chapati* and says 'namaste'."

Ricky is a good student, an attentive student but Bholu thinks smarter and more systematically..

"I give them a problem and we see how Ricky would complicate the problem while Bholu would solve it simply like a 9th or 10th class problem in 2-3 lines. I give a second problem and again we find that Ricky makes it confusing while Bholu solves it in a simple manner."

The difference is that Bholu first understands the problem, understands the objective, and then chooses a method to solve it.

"Once we solve the problem we do it again, using a different method. And again, and again."

Ultimately, Anand teaches the students to generalise the problem and even make up their own *milta julta* problems.

"*Lecture ko ek kaahaani ke zariye se batana, har mathematics ke problem ko ek nahin kai method se banana.. Usko generalise karna... Yehi hamara secret hai.*"

And it's about constantly raising the bar. Motivating a student to reach beyond what he believes he is capable of.

"I keep looking for tougher questions. At times I even take problems from the international Mathematics Olympiads!" says Anand.

All well and good, but how does he support this noble effort – without outside funding, without grants? Simple.

The 'Super 30' effort is subsidised by 'Ramanujan School of Mathematics', the coaching class for regular, middle class students which Anand still runs. He takes in a maximum of 500 students a year, charging a modest fee of ₹ 9000 for Physics, Chemistry and Mathematics.

"We prepare these students for IIT entrance tests but not like other coaching classes which charge upto a lakh."

Out of these earnings, the 'Super 30' are supported – given free food, accomodation and training.

"More work is remaining." says Anand. "But good teachers are difficult to find."

Anand himself has been offered big money by coaching institutes in Kota – to come and join them.

"I have been offered partnership by such training centres. The package they offer is not in lakhs but in crores. But I am not interested."

In his spare time, Anand continues writing papers on mathematics. And finding new and intriguing problems for his students to solve.

As for Abhayanand, apart from police-related duties, he is busy duplicating the 'Super 30' concept across Bihar.

Each 'Super 30' is a community-led effort. For example, a dozen businessmen and doctors pooled in ₹ 5 lakhs to start 'Magadh Super 30' at Dandibagh, Gaya. In Biharsharif, local doctors and school owner Arvind Kumar came forward to support 'Nalanda Super 30'. At Bhagalpur, two retired professors from the local engineering college are teaching mathematics and physics at 'Ang Super 30'.

Each centre is funded and managed by the community. Abhayanand remains the guiding light, in charge of academic activities. At Rehmani Super, he takes physics classes; the other centres he visits once a month.

"I also take classes on mobile phone for students of Bhagalpur, Nalanda and Gaya," he says.

What an idea, *sirjee*.

The original Super 30 is an amazing, and inspiring effort. The fact that this model can be replicated – with a high degree of success – makes it doubly so.

The challenge, then is to find more rough diamonds. To be polished and ground into revealing their natural brilliance. And may there be more teachers who dedicate their lives, to such a cause.

———————

<u>ADVICE TO YOUNG ENTREPRENEURS</u>

Sabse badi baat hai lagan ki. Kaam ke prati ek nasha ho jaana chahiye. Sote, jaagte, sapne mein – man mein kaam ke baare mein hi sochein.

You must have *deewangi* towards your aim.

Whether people at home are with you, or against you, if you are completely passionate and committed to what you are doing – nothing else will matter.

Lack of resources and circumstances are not barriers.

Yeh cheezein koi maayne nahin rakhti agar aapka hausla buland hai.

THE SOUND OF
SILENCE

**Dhruv Lakra,
Mirakle Couriers**

Dhruv Lakra could have become an investment banker. Instead, he invested in a very offbeat idea – a courier service employing the deaf. In a short span of two years, Mirakle Couriers is a robust business, competing with the best. And Dhruv dreams of making it as big as FedEx, but keeping that social edge.

It's a busy morning at Mirakle Couriers. A dozen young boys in bright orange uniforms; a girl typing away furiously on her computer.

But, there is something different about this place. You wonder what it is until you realise – it's the silence.

Mirakle is a company which exclusively employs the deaf. But why this special interest only in the deaf, I ask Dhruv.

"People buy *diyas* from mentally challenged children during Diwali. Or go to a blind school and distribute sweets," he replies. "But tell me, do you even notice people who cannot hear?"

Baat to sahi hai... but what can be done about it? Dhruv Lakra decided, *kuch to karna hai.*

Newly graduated from the Said Business School in Oxford, he hit upon the idea of a courier business.

A conventional, scalable business where there is literally no need for verbal communication.

Sealed, signed, delivered.

Mirakle Couriers was started with 'capital' of 200 pounds and 10 shipments. In just 18 months, it has grown to handle 60,000 deliveries a month. But the real story is not on an Excel sheet.

It is the light in the eyes of the employees.

The pride in their stride, the hope in their hearts.

Mirakle is indeed a miracle, it makes you believe. There is sadness, there is injustice but we human beings can do something about it.

Uparwala sun raha hai... pukaar ke to dekho.

THE SOUND OF
SILENCE

Dhruv Lakra,
Mirakle Couriers

Dhruv Lakra grew up in Jammu, in a business family.

"My dad is in the furniture and chemical business. My mother was also an entrepreneur, she ran her own boutique from home."

Dhruv attended a well known school in Jammu – MHAC. The same school his dad, brother and uncles had attended.

"It's a school with massive area, sports grounds and even a stream running right through it!"

As a child Dhruv had one burning ambition: to become a swimming champion. But he didn't receive much encouragement from the family for it. One good thing however, he was packed off to Bombay to study, right after class 10.

"My mom and dad both studied in Delhi so they wanted me to have exposure to a big town. I studied in HR college, attended lectures – also did a lot of partying – took in the whole big city experience."

And that included getting a taste of the real world, outside the classroom.

"I worked as a cashier in a bowling alley for two months and earned about nine thousand rupees.

And I really enjoyed blowing up that cash! But I also learnt a lot while on the job."

Dhruv then applied to the Tata Finance internship program. He was one of the few students selected. The job involved travelling all the way to Dahisar and Mira Road to sell Hero Honda bikes.

But, so what?

"To convince someone to buy a bike – I thought that would be a good challenge!" he grins.

And yet, after BCom Dhruv got into the usual rut of appearing for CAT. He did not make the cut.

What's more, he realised "this ain't for me".

"I cannot do 30 questions in 20 minutes – sorry, I just can't! So after the exam I took off to Uttaranchal, trekked around for a couple of months. Did some soul searching."

At one point his grandparents got rather worried and asked him,"Are you... on drugs??"

Eventually, Dhruv returned to Mumbai and joined Merrill Lynch, in the investment banking division. A job he hated, but which taught him a lot.

"I think investment bankers are evil, but when it comes to professionalism and discipline you just cannot beat them! When something needs to go out on a Monday, it simply has to!"

That result-oriented approach was something Dhruv deeply and completely imbibed.

"Secondly, within six months I realised this is all bullshit. Yes i-bankers get paid a lot of money but I don't want this life."

After nearly two years, Dhruv quit Merrill and decided to do what he really wanted to do: get into the social sector. He joined an NGO called Dasra in Mumbai and as fate would have it, the tsunami had just happened.

"They offered me a position on the condition that I spend 3-4 months with the fishermen in tsunami-hit areas of Tamil Nadu – Nagapattinam and Cuddalore. I readily accepted."

Dhruv spent two years at Dasra where he worked on a wide variety of projects. Apart from tsunami, he dealt with organisations for women, HIV AIDS, children and the disabled. The job exposed him to concepts like strategy, scale, impact measurement, donor reporting, fundraising – the works.

"A lot of people who join IIMs believe I-banking is 'it'. Absolutely not! It's bullshit."

"Actually, Dasra was started by former investment bankers, so it had the same professional rigour, discipline and emphasis on quality and content. I enjoyed every minute of it."

And, there was an unexpected bonus. When Dhruv applied to the SAID School of Business at Oxford University, he got a full scholarship from the Skoll foundation. Whose special area of interest is social enterprise.

The scholarship was worth 45,000 pounds and the only condition for Skoll Scholars was that they had to take the electives on social entrepreneurship. Courses included 'Social Enterprise and Design', 'Social Finance' and 'Social Innovation'.

"I would have taken the courses anyway but it felt good that someone paid me to do so!" says Dhruv.

The Oxford experience was amazing, and opened up many new doors. Access to so much academic knowledge and ideas led to the eureka moment when Dhruv realised,"I want to do something on my own".

What, exactly? He had no clue. During his summer project in August 2008, that's when it hit him. Sitting in a bus.

"There was a boy sitting next to me. He wrote to the conductor where he wanted to go and that's when it struck me. How come I've never noticed deaf people before?"

"Do you have a job?"Dhruv asked the boy.

"No," he replied.

Back home, Dhruv hit Google. The statistics were shocking, to say the least. India is second only to China when it comes to the number of deaf people.

"But what can I do about it?" was the question which haunted Dhruv.

As luck would have it, he was sitting at home one afternoon – having a cup of tea – when a courier arrived. As he signed for the shipment, Dhruv noticed there was no verbal communication.

And that's when it came to him – "I can run a courier company, with deaf people."

A bit of asking around revealed that courier boys were paid decent salaries, along with benefits.

It was a hard job to do, no doubt, but respectable.

In October 2008, Dhruv completed his course at Oxford and returned to India. The following month, he set up Mirakle Couriers with one deaf boy – Ganesh.

"I did not know sign language then, I did not know any deaf people. So I went to a club for deaf youth and convinced Ganesh to join."

The first order, procured through a friend, was for 10 shipments.

"Ganesh made five deliveries, and I made the other five," he recalls.

Business was extremely small but steady for the first six weeks. Then, through a reference, Mirakle bagged its first large order – 5000 deliveries!

Dhruv said to the client, "It will take me ten days to complete your order."

The client said, "No problem – my event is three weeks away. Take your time."

Quickly, Dhruv asked Ganesh to find two more deaf boys looking for work. And the order was completed.

"That guy simply loved our service and gave us another order of 5000. So revenues finally started coming in."

More orders, more employees – wonderful. But where was the space? Mirakle was operating from a friend's house and there was simply no room to expand. Luckily, Dhruv was able to meet with Anu Aga of Thermax, through Indu Shahani, principal of HR College as well as Sheriff of Mumbai.

"Mrs Indu Shahani has been so encouraging – she is phenomenal."

The space provided by Thermax was large enough to seat 6-7 people. So, Dhruv began hiring more staff. Now the deaf don't find it easy to get a job, but that doesn't mean it's easy to get them to work – for you.

"Deaf people are a tribe. For hearing people to get into the tribe is not easy!"

Of course, the boys on the team were the best recruiters – they brought in their friends. Then, in January 2009 Mirakle hired Reshma – a deaf girl. Dhruv had to first win over her parents.

"I had to convince them to let her travel all the way from Goregaon to Churchgate. And the salary wasn't all that much either!"

After all, Mirakle was set up on a capital of 200 pounds – money left over from the Skoll scholarship.

The company was generating some revenue but little cash.

"Working capital was very tight. When it comes to payment couriers are given last priority."

And sure, you will pay next month but workers want their salary this month. As an Act of Faith.

"In any case, deaf people do not trust hearing people. The logic is, 'We are deaf, we have always been discriminated against... ' So you really have to work hard to earn that trust. Make them believe in you."

Friends and family would chip in from time to time. Then, Dhruv found an angel investor who put in a lakh of rupees.

"We would not have been here today, if it weren't for him."

A growing business is like Oliver Twist – always hungry for more. More capital, to service more clients. And while there are many VCs out there, keen to fund social entrepreneurs, Dhruv did not approach them.

"Once an investor comes in the ball game changes. The only thing VCs care about is Excel sheet calculations!"

There is tremendous pressure, then, to deliver 'returns'.

And so Dhruv chose an unconventional source of funding – he applied for the prestigious Echoing Green fellowship. This fellowship is awarded to 15 social entrepreneurs from around the world every year...

"It's a very tough, very competitive process which takes six months. I literally put my heart and soul into it!."

And Dhruv's effort paid off. He was chosen as an Echoing Green fellow for the year 2009. The fellowship amount –

"I was always socially inclined but I had strong perceptions like the sector does not pay you, it's not professional, it's for people who don't want to make it big..."

approximately $60,000 – would be released in installments, over the next 24 months.

Just the miracle that Mirakle needed to not just survive, but thrive.

The focus now shifted on operations – building systems and infrastructure. As of March 2010, Mirakle couriers is handling 60,000 deliveries a month.

"My target is 200,000 deliveries a month – by next year. To do that we need tracking systems, but we can't simply go out and buy what's already in use..."

That's because commonly used technology gives a 'beep' everytime a barcode is scanned. What Mirakle needs is a visual signal – that had to be developed and is slowly getting implemented.

Meanwhile, the courier business operates in classic 'factory' fashion – extreme sub-division of tasks.

"The girls are in charge of the sorting. When volume is high, boys also chip in."

Sorting is done pincode wise and every boy has been allocated one specific area. So Churchgate (Mumbai 400020) will be handled by the same boy, every day.

"Each boy knows his area and develops his own route. We try not to change it unless there is an emergency."

Sometimes the address is incomplete so the girls use Google Maps and write down a landmark like a church or temple, which helps the boy find the place easily.

"There is absolutely no problem in terms of deaf people making deliveries. And if they need to, they find a way to communicate."

In fact, with every letter or parcel delivered, Mirakle attaches a basic 'Indian sign language sheet'. But most receivers simply sign on the POD without exchanging a word.

"I am really high on experiencing things in my life."

"The beauty of this model is you don't need to know the boy who delivered your courier is deaf."

But there is a feel-good factor to receiving a letter stamped: 'Delivered, sorted and accounted by deaf adults'.

"One of our clients is a magazine. The editor called me to say his subscribers are saying, 'I am really happy you are using Mirakle.' But will they pay me one rupee more per delivery?"

The answer, sadly, is no. And it's not just the little people but the Who's Who of the corporate world who will demand the 'same rate as Vichare'. Or less.

"Out of 45 clients only one pays Mirakle a better price and she is a foreigner."

And Dhruv says it's not about charity, the cost of operating a business with differently-abled people is a little higher. In addition, Mirakle gives all employees minimum wages as well as benefits like Provident Fund.

Purchase managers shrug, "*Guru*, that's not my problem."

Because Corporate Social Responsibility (CSR) is something CEOs talks about. But that's on television. In the mundanity of managerial life, it means nothing.

"In the US, diversity is a huge issue. Some states even have laws which favour suppliers who employ minorities or disabled people."

But no, Dhruv isn't complaining. He's taken the situation in his stride – like any young entrepreneur.

"We use the disability card to get a foot into the door. After that it's an equal sum game, you simply have to deliver."

In fact, in the first few months, Mirakle was making deliveries for as little as ₹ 5.

"The boys were new, I wanted them to get trained. So I said let me absorb the loss while they learn their areas".

It was a smart decision.

"I don't do deliveries at those prices anymore," he adds. "Even if it means letting go of some business."

Mirakle's client list included giants like Mahindra & Mahindra, A V Birla group, Godrej & Boyce group – to name a few. But Dhruv is now pitching to banks, which have large volumes. And to handle that kind of scale he realised Mirakle needed something he did not have.

The wisdom of experience.

"I decided to hire an operations manager, someone who knew the courier business inside out."

Eight candidates came for the interview; seven of them said, "You can't run an operation without any verbal communication!"

The eighth person was Sameer Bhosle, a man with 16 years of solid experience with AFL, Elbee and Velocity couriers.

"He jumped at the offer and honestly, it was the best thing that could have happened to Mirakle!"

Bhosle understands the nitty gritty of the courier business – and the tooth and nail of execution.

"I wanted to hire someone who is exact opposite of me. I am really good at strategy and getting business but Sameer is a master when it comes to day-to-day operations."

Mirakle is now building a classic hub-and-spoke model. The town office is now housed in space provided by the Aditya Birla group, at Industry House in Churchgate. A second office – managed by Bhosle – has been set up in Andheri. To take care of suburban deliveries.

In March 2010, business was a steady ₹ 1.5 lakhs a month. Breakeven is only six months away, maybe even sooner. So where does Mirakle see the business heading?

"Our strategy is to get an entry as a pro-disability organisation. After that, it is an equal sum game. We have to deliver!"

"I would love to hire a deaf or blind cost accountant – but I simply can't find one!"

"I want to be the DHL or Fedex of the courier business, but employing only people with disabilities!" declares Dhruv.

Because every disabled person with a job is empowered. In many ways.

"One of our stars is a boy called Bhupesh. He comes to office everyday from Bhiwpuri – it takes two hours one way," says Dhruv.

Bhupesh's father is an alcoholic, without a job. His brother is also deaf. For Bhupesh – who is barely 10th standard pass – working at Mirakle is about respect.

"It's the first time anyone has trusted Bhupesh, given him responsibility."

Then there are the girls – Vanita and Reshma – who work as supervisors. They track the deliveries – how many shipments picked up, how many have reached. What's more, the boys come back in the evening and report to them.

"Imagine the sense of confidence the job gives them!"

In fact, Reshma is being groomed for next level – she is learning Tally.

All employees at Mirakle have PAN numbers, group insurance and salary accounts, with ATM cards. Which is a big deal because most banks do not issue cards to the deaf.

"The issue is verification – which is conducted on phone."

Of course, having a card doesn't mean you use one.

"Mostly they keep it home," sighs Dhruv. "Twenty rupees is all a girl will carry, while travelling from so far!"

Then there's the issue of late hours. The Mirakle office shuts at six in the evening – whereas most courier companies work into the wee hours.

"Parents don't want girls to travel in the night.

So they come in early, and leave early."

Currently Mirakle employs 58 people, out of which 55 are deaf adults. As it grows, Dhruv plans to employ the blind and the deaf-blind. How?

Break the chain in such minute detail that even people with disability can master a particular job or function.

"So you see, delivery will remain with the deaf, but the back office can employ the blind. We'll find a way to integrate them into our system."

The dream however, goes beyond employment for a few hundred, or a few thousand disabled people.

"We want to change the way the disabled are viewed, to prove to corporates they have what it takes. The hope is that this will have a snowball effect – that more organisations will become inclusive and open their doors to the disabled."

Working with the deaf, Dhruv is keenly aware that employment is not a complete solution. There are any number of issues from sexual ignorance to 'where will I live once my parents are gone'.

But, Dhruv has taken a call.

"This is a cut-throat business – we have to focus, we have to go to scale. But five years from now, I will definitely set up a foundation or a trust which works on disability-related issues.."

Even as Mirakle struggles with the challenges of growth, there are some challenges on the personal front.

"I hardly pay myself anything," he admits. "My girlfriend is not happy about that!"

As for parents, well, they are proud and supportive. But Dhruv has a philosophical take on 'what people think'.

"You know, it's funny. When I joined Merrill Lynch, everyone was happy. Then, I left to work for an NGO and people said,'*Ek number ka gadha hai*'."

Then, Dhruv got a full scholarship to Oxford and suddenly it was like, "We always knew this boy was special."

"When I came back and started Mirakle, again I had to face flak. But after I got the Helen Keller award and the Echoing Green fellowship, I became a 'star'."

Ultimately, whatever you do, there will be people who will encourage you, and people who discourage you.

"Just don't listen to those who say,'*Nahin ho sakta hai*'."

Sometimes you just have to play deaf, and pray for a miracle.

<u>ADVICE TO YOUNG ENTREPRENEURS</u>

Just do it – that's my advice.

I used to be insecure, I used to wonder, "Do I have enough money?" Now I look back and think I should have started right after college.

As far as experience goes, yes I had work ex. But I had no background in logistics. Also I believe if you don't know something, you can think more creatively.

The conditioning in college is that everybody has to do CAT and join the corporate sector.

Nothing wrong if that suits you but don't do it if it doesn't feel right.

Take some time off, do some introspection. Find out what your true calling is, then go follow that path.

CHANGEMAKERS

A single person is all it takes to start a movement. While the world laments 'what is', the changemaker takes a small step towards making it as it should be..

THE SCIENTIFIC
SOCIALIST

Madhav Chavan,
Pratham

Born into a political family, Madhav Chavan almost became a Communist leader. But the winds of change led him in a diferent direction. Madhav returned to India after his PhD and made 'education' his life's mission. Today, Pratham is the largest NGO in this sector, working with the government to impact millions of children.

The son of a businessman, joins business.

The son of a filmstar, joins films.

The son of a politician, joins politics.

Not Madhav Chavan.

Born to freedom fighter parents, brought up amidst trade union leaders, activism and *naarebaazi* came to him naturally. But education in the US and exposure to the world made him rethink old ideologies.

And redirect the course of his life.

Since 1989, Madhav has devoted his time, his energy, his heart and his mind, to making education a reality for the other India. The India that attends municipal schools, government schools or no school at all.

He brings to this exercise the empathy of a politician, the rigour of a scientist, the enthusiasm of a child.

As he shares his story – and a late lunch of *idli-sambhar* – I think to myself, "Here is someone who could have spent his life playing with chemical equations inside an air conditioned lab."

Instead, Madhav immersed himself in the world, creating new equations. Using the oxygen of education to ignite minds.

THE SCIENTIFIC
SOCIALIST

Madhav Chavan,
Pratham

Madhav Chavan was born and brought up in Bombay.

"My grandfather was a judge in the princely state of Kolhapur. My father had the advantages of education, environment... but at 17 he became a communist and threw himself into the freedom struggle."

Madhav's parents met in 1942, when his father was an underground political worker, hiding in her house. Later, he became a trade unionist.

"I am the only child but I grew up among many adults. Our house was popularly called a commune, which means his colleagues – sometimes their families – all lived in one place.

By night it was a residence, by day it was an office where hundreds of people came in and out..."

Madhav's father belonged to the Lal Nishan Party – well known in political and trade union circles.

"I was introduced to social, political thought very early. After high school, I started participating in leftist political work, student activities. This was in the early 70s."

Madhav joined Jai Hind College, for FY and Inter Sc. While most of his friends went into engineering and medical, he went to the Institute of Science on Madam Cama Road.

"But that too was not very serious. It was just something that you... finish your graduation. My main preoccupation used to be student union work or other political work."

After completing his BSc, Madhav worked for a year with the Lal Nishan party. But then, Emergency was declared and for a variety of reasons, he decided to go back to college for further studies.

"By this time I had decided I did not want to work full time in politics."

Madhav enrolled for an MSc in Inorganic Chemistry. Not very serious in the first year, he applied himself in the second and got a distinction.

Then the question was 'what next?' Madhav applied to IIT for a PhD but was rejected. Meanwhile the US seemed to be inviting anybody and everybody who wanted to do a PhD, even offering scholarships.

So it was that the student union leader who was demonstrating outside the US consulate in 1973 lined up for a student visa outside the same consulate in 1978.

"I completed my PhD from Ohio State University which was considered 'top 10' for Chemistry. I can't say I could have won a Nobel prize but I understood chemistry much better in those years than I did before."

More importantly, Madhav's entire world-view changed. He became aware of issues in Latin America, Vietnam, China. And found himself challenging long-held beliefs.

"Imperialism, capitalism – these are words to describe the system. But when you meet people on a daily basis, you realise they have no real meaning."

What impressed Madhav the most about America was the sense of 'equality' in everyday life and interactions. And yet, after completing the PhD, securing a faculty position and even a 'green card', Madhav felt the urge to return to India.

"I faced a simple choice. Live in the US and face the challenges of US society or come back to India and face the challenges of Indian society. I chose to come back."

The year was 1986. Prime Minister Rajiv Gandhi had initiated the 'scientific pool officer' scheme, inviting scientists from abroad, to come back to India. Madhav joined the National Chemical Laboratory (NCL) in Pune as part of this scheme.

"My father never got a salary; it was my mother's job as a schoolteacher which sustained us. But we had everything we needed!"

Soon after, he got an offer to join the UDCT (University Department of Chemical Technology) and shifted to Mumbai. While Madhav enjoyed teaching, his research proposal got stuck in red tape for over two years.

In the meantime, he once again got sucked into politics.

"Lal Nishan was like family – I was thrown right into it. I attended meetings and even helped out in the publication of the newspaper they were bringing out."

By this time a section of this small party was rethinking along the lines of Gorbachev. Change was in the air.

Internationally, Communism was reinventing itself. In fact, in 1986 Madhav had a chance to visit China on the invitation of the Chinese Academy of Sciences.

"I had grown up reading and admiring Maoist literature. In China, I heard from the younger generation how *they* saw the Cultural Revolution and why it was wrong. That came as a shock!"

India too was changing. Slogans like *garibi hatao* were replaced with new ideas, new initiatives. One such initiative was the National Literacy Mission, the brainchild of Sam Pitroda*.

The idea was to make a very strong intervention to bring down adult illiteracy. Which, in turn, would impact other development parameters.

"This is very home-grown thinking. It was not UNICEF, World Bank, or anybody telling you. Just like you need pulses, just like you need water, just like you need technology, you need education."

The National Literacy Mission was looking for unusual people to take the movement forward. Madhav Chavan was certainly one

* Pitroda led numerous technology initiatives during Rajiv Gandhi's years as PM

such person. But *how* he came to the notice of the education ministry is a story in itself!

In 1988, university teachers went on strike, asking the government to implement the 4th Pay Commission's recommendations. Madhav led the brigade in UDCT. And at this time, he also wrote a letter to the Prime Minister.

The letter essentially said: "Colleges are closed, kids are wandering around and you are not even starting a debate on what's wrong with our education. Instead, the negotiations are stuck on issues like whether professors should sign a muster, whether the increase should be 5% or 7%. That's ridiculous!"

Apparently Rajiv Gandhi read the letter and marked it to Anil Bordia, then Secretary of Education.

The strike was ultimately settled but Anil Bordia asked to meet Madhav, to see *yeh kaun aadmi hai.* And he was in for a shock.

"I think he expected an elderly person, not a 34-year-old!" laughs Madhav. However, the initial interaction was not a happy one. Promises were made, which were not kept. But on another trip to Delhi – on behalf of the Lal Nishan party – Madhav met Bordia again.

The two had a long conversation and somewhere close to midnight Bordia remarked, "You talk about social revolution and social justice; print posters and pamphlets. But you're not bothered that the people you write them for...can't read!"

"And suddenly... everything seemed to come together at that point. My background in the US, what I had seen about equality, democracy. My rethinking on Marxism, what I had seen in China".

That midnight conversation was a Eureka Moment. A 'turning point' in Madhav Chavan's life. From 1989, he devoted most of his energy to the field of adult literacy. While he continued with his day job at UDCT, the real kick came from working in the slums of Chembur and Dharavi.

"It was amazing how hungry young people in the slums were to show what they could do. The question was, how exactly can I help them?"

At that time, the National Literacy Mission was running a program called Mass Program for Functional Literacy (MPFL). Madhav decided to rally around all the people he knew working for various causes – around this program.

"I had friends working for women's liberation. I had friends working for popularisation of science. I said to them – none of the things you want to do are possible if people cannot read and write!"

And they agreed to join the movement.

"Basically the appeal of the National Literacy Mission was that it was not just another government program. It was a *people's* movement".

Madhav registered an outfit called CORO, Committee of Resource Organisation. The idea was to put together a list of people in Mumbai who could be resource persons for the literacy program.

The Government of India gave CORO a grant of ₹ 1 lakh. But there was a great deal of confusion on how MPFL would be implemented. Could students of various elite colleges under Bombay University actually teach illiterates? Madhav didn't think so.

"When I actually started going on the field, I felt that there is no connect. How can you get Xavier's and Ruia students into a Dalit slum in Chembur? And on the other hand, there were a lot of young people in the slums itself who were 8th pass or 10th pass and had the desire to do something."

CORO tapped into these young slumdwellers and started a programme to teach adults and adult women in the slums of Chembur and Dharavi. Despite this innovative approach, one year later Madhav discovered that his program had only a 10% "success" rate.

Teaching an illiterate person to read and write was far more difficult than anticipated!

The truth is, CORO could have submitted a report claiming 50% success, or even 90% success and it would have been blindly accepted. But Madhav did not belong to the *chalta hai* school of thought.

"The point is, if it's not working, we have to change it!"

Even though it meant that the Government of India stopped giving its grants. After much soul searching, thought and discussion Madhav reorganised the literacy program.

"I have not rejected the idea of Marxism or anything. But I had questions in my mind."

"We started having classes at night, taught groups of people together and changed our methodology as well".

All these changes led to new energy, new interest in the program. And its influence soon went well beyond literacy.

One idea was to bring women from different slums together in one big hall and expose them to inputs from various women's organisations.

"So one organisation talked about income generation, another about domestic violence. One group from Pune spoke about how they had stopped the illicit liquor dens functioning in their area."

They said, "It's very simple, we simply get up and destroy them. End of story."

That same evening, as the women headed home in buses, one of them said, *"Hamein bhi aise hi karna chahiye"*.

And they literally went home, got together and demolished the liquor dens in their community. This idea spread like wildfire.

Meanwhile, in 1991, the Government of India relieved Madhav of his teaching duties at UDCT and sent him on deputation to the National Literacy Mission. At this point, Madhav became involved with the 'Total Literacy Mission'.

"After Ernakulam became totally literate, the Government of India asked every district to set up a total literacy mission. I was trying to develop that plan for Bombay."

Awareness and community mobilisation were the basic principles, but Madhav went the extra distance.

"I went to the Railway Board to get permission to put up signs inside stations. Then we went to the postal unions and they agreed that postmen would participate. None of this was happening anywhere else."

"Everything that came afterwards – Information Technology, telecom – equal to that or more important was the Literacy Mission."

The National Literacy Mission was a grand plan on paper. But there was a huge gap between the intention and the implementation.

For example, O & M had created a beautiful television campaign around the theme of *"Padhna likha seekho"*. At the end of the ad there was a small box which said: 'If you want to teach someone, write to us and we'll send you a literacy kit'.

Lakhs of people wrote in, but the National Literacy Mission did not have kits to send out. So they simply asked the agency to remove the line exhorting people to write in.

"It was a hugely disappointing marketing plan. If you're going to advertise a product, that product should be available. It's a very simple principle!"

Another simple principle Madhav discovered was that a 'system' may be slothful, but if you can fire up individuals within that system, you can work wonders.

Madhav recalls how he was able to get Sujata Khandekar, then an employee of MSEB (Maharashtra State Electricity Board) to become a resource for CORO.

"I went to Mr Sharad Pawar – then Chief Minister of Maharashtra – and told him CORO needs Sujata, but we cannot afford to pay her salary. He picked up the phone and called the Chairman of MSEB..."

Soon after, Sujata Khandekar joined CORO while MSEB continued to pay her salary!

Then there was a lady called Medha Kulkarni who worked with All India Radio.

"Medha called me once, to give a talk and we struck up a rapport. The result of that was a whole series of radio programs around the theme of literacy. Not only me but even our youth from the slums got trained as program editors."

What the Ministry of Human Resource Development could not get All India Radio to do at an all-India level, Medha Kulkarni did for adult literacy at the regional level. Simply because she became passionate about the cause.

The show was a 10 part series called *'Shaalebaherchi shaala'*, and it was very different from AIR's regular programming.

"I put together 10 groups of people at different stages of literacy. On day one I sat with some shepherds, completely illiterate."

Madhav chatted with them in the studio for 25 minutes and in the end they said, "Yes we want to learn!" The show was aired with minor editing.

Episode 2 featured some women who had just learned to sign their name. Week by week, the show took listeners through the whole process, the benefits of literacy. But in an interesting manner, with great music and top quality production – all done at All India Radio.

Around the same time, Madhav also hosted a prime time television serial on Doordarshan called Akshardhara. The show ran for one and a half years and it was the only social sector programming aired at prime time.

Again, it was born out of the passion of one individual to promote literacy. It started with the idea of producing a 30 second clip with small vignettes – like a vegetable vendor's son teaching his illiterate mother.

When Madhav first proposed the concept to Vijaya Dhumale – the Assistant Station Director of Doordarshan in Mumbai – she said, "I want to first *see* what you do, before we think about it."

After visiting the slums and speaking to the boys and girls helping out, she did not want to do a 30 second clip – she proposed a 30 minute program!

"Madhav," she said, "Have you ever written a script for television?"

Madhav had not, but gave it a shot.

"It's perfect," she said. "Why don't you also become the presenter?"

The program turned out beautifully and Vijaya managed to air it on prime time when one of the regular producers failed to deliver his weekly episode..

For the next airing, Vijaya roped in her former assistant Nitish Bharadwaj – much loved for his role as 'Krishna' in B R Chopra's 'Mahabharat'. With a two minute introduction by Nitish *Akshardhara* topped the ratings that week and the show became a regular fixture at prime time.

Madhav got the platform he needed – to send out his message. And creatively speaking, he had an absolute ball. At its peak, Akshardhara got a TRP of 25, as opposed to Ramayan's 44. The program was a huge success; the only trouble was there was no commercial angle.

"I did all the work free of cost – and that was absolutely fine with me. The problem was that the government had stopped supporting CORO. So I needed to raise some funds to keep that work going."

CORO was running on a shoestring budget, but that money had to come from *somewhere*. As luck would have it, the Department of Science & Technology (DST) had initiated a program on sanitation and waste management. The idea was to convert waste to energy and also to spread the concept of 'pay and use toilets' in slums.

The secretary at DST and advisor to then Prime Minister P V Narasimha Rao was Dr Vasant Gowariker. Madhav knew Dr Gowariker through family connections. But more importantly, Dr Gowariker had seen Akshardhara and hence asked Madhav to make a film for him on pay and use toilets.

"I went there and found the toilets were good, but the management system created was leaking. Contractors were literally fleecing the government."

Madhav suggested that the toilets should be managed under a co-operative system, by the locals.

"Let the people working there earn from the revenues. There will be no need for contractors or government funding."

Dr Gowariker agreed to try this scheme out in newly constructed toilet blocks and it was a huge success. Many of the CORO volunteers got employed thus. Other youngsters had learnt production techniques at All India Radio and those skills were in demand.

All these earnings subsidised the literacy work and allowed CORO to stay afloat!

There were hardships, but there was also a sense of movement. It looked like much would be achieved quickly. But in December 1992, there was a huge setback. The Babri masjid was demolished in Ayodhya. Riots followed in Bombay and the city became extremely tense.

"Even though the slums we worked in were not directly affected, the mood changed. Literacy became low priority and we lost the momentum we had created."

Around the time Madhav was unceremoniously evicted from 'Sahas' – the Saksharta Haq Samiti under Bombay Municipal corporation. There was no notice, no reason given. It was another turning point in his life.

"That day I decided if I ever do anything after this, I will build it independently. Not that I won't work with the government but I will make sure I have ownership of what I do."

Around this time – 1993-94 – the idea of Pratham started taking shape.

"People think I came up with Pratham but the first thought along these lines actually came from UNICEF".

In 1991, the thought of Public-Private Partnership (PPP) in education was voiced for the first time at the Jomtien conference. The UNICEF office in Bombay started holding meetings on the concept of PPP. This initiative was led by two remarkable UNICEF officials – Richard Bridle and Amy Watanabe.

Richard Bridle said, "We have to build the idea of a 'societal mission'."

"I wrote to Rajiv Gandhi, if you want to really have a battle then battle on the content of education and how it is to be delivered!"

UNICEF was obliged to support the government and the municipal corporation, but by themselves, these institutions could not deliver results.

"You need business, NGOs and citizens to take ownership and work with the municipal corporation. Make it a societal *mission*, to improve the status and quality of primary education".

At the time Madhav was not a 'recognised' social worker, running a registered NGO. So he was not invited to these meetings. But his colleague Farida Lambay, a lecturer at Nirmala Niketan College of Social Work, was present. And she introduced him to the group.

Eighteen months and several meetings later, there was no progress. In fact, there was a stand-off.

The NGOs said, "Show us the money, then we will show you a plan!"

UNICEF said, "The community must take this forward."

Business said, "Show us a plan and we'll see what we can do!"

The municipal corporation said, "When you figure out what you can do, come to us!"

There was no energy, no agreement. Since Madhav was one of the few who said it *can* be done, UNICEF asked him to take over the project.

The agency gave a grant of ₹ 2.5 lakhs for an office and basic staff, and employed Madhav as a 'consultant'. But to make it a *societal* mission, more stakeholders were needed.

The formal decision to set up Pratham Public Charitable Trust was taken in December 1994, at a meeting called by Sharad

"Because I came from a science background, I insisted that we test and measure the success of our literacy program; otherwise we could have just written a report saying, '*Haan haan, ho gaya, ho gaya*'."

"My entry into the sphere of education, was not because of an educationist belief. It is more from a social-political belief that this will give people more rights, make us a stronger democracy."

Kale, the Municipal Commissioner of Bombay. Several eminent citizens, among them SP Godrej, J B D'Souza and Armaity Desai were present.

It was decided that the body would have ex-officio members from the state government, the municipal corporations as well as socially minded citizens. Madhav Chavan was appointed as 'executive secretary' and asked to build the organisation from scratch.

"We had a trust, we had trustees. But we had no money and no program. The question was, where to begin?"

Well, a good place to start is *understanding* the problem.

As per secondary data, it appeared that close to 2.5 lakh children were out of school. If these children were to be educated, many more classrooms would be required. But what about existing municipal schools. How good *were* they?

This information was not available; someone would have to go and find out. But how do you conduct such an exercise across the city without any money?

You scratch your head and come up with a creative solution.

"I went to the Indian Medical Association and told them I need doctors who will volunteer to inspect municipal schools. See if they are well ventilated... do they have drinking water... are the bathrooms clean?"

The secretary of the association was taken aback.

"That is the job of sanitary inspectors!" he exclaimed.

Madhav explained the importance of the exercise. The word of a doctor counted far more than that of a sanitary inspector. Besides, doctors had no vested interest.

"Women started telling their husbands, '*Sharaab peekar, ghar ke andar nahi aana*'. If you want to drink, go lie down in the gutter outside."

It took some convincing but the IMA agreed to Madhav's proposals. Close to 400 doctors volunteered and surveyed 900 municipal schools across the city. The feedback was tabulated on a creaky 386 computer in the Pratham office.

The results were shocking. The doctors found that 75% of municipal schools were 'okay'.

"How is that possible?" wondered Madhav. "I have been to municipal schools myself and seen the dirty toilets!"

"India mein kaun sa public toilet clean hai," replied the doctors. They were practical people, who dealt with everyday realities of health and hygiene.

Madhav was pleasantly surprised at the positivity generated by this experiment. An added bonus was that the cost of conducting this giant exercise was a mere ₹ 25,000!

So school buildings were all right, but what about the staff? Pratham decided to focus attention on training and upgrading teachers.

The trouble was, teachers were not very interested in being trained. And they did not feel the training was *relevant*. During a feedback session, one teacher remarked, "All this is very good, but is it useful for our kind of classrooms?"

Madhav took this feedback seriously.

"In my experience the most important things is to keep your eyes and ears open. Listen to dissonance and see what people are really saying."

One issue which kept coming up was that children enrolled in municipal schools had no pre-school exposure. Which meant they did not come to class one knowing that school means sitting in one place, listening to instructions, being able to concentrate.

"Can you do something about this?" the teachers asked Pratham.

It was a *kuch kar ke dikhao* kind of challenge, Pratham saw it as an opportunity and came up with a very simple idea, improving upon an existing model in the municipal system.

"Community Development Officers had started *baalwadis* in some schools. They made space available and authorised a person to run the show."

The person running the *baalwadi* was authorised to collect a small fee – say five to ten rupees per child per month. A sound entrepreneurial model – no 'salary' burden.

Could the *baalwadi* program be scaled to municipal schools across the city? The corporation officers were reluctant.

"I was not about to take 'no' for an answer," grins Madhav. "We had run adult literacy classes in the slums, in the bylanes. Why can't we do the same with the *baalwadis*?"

Thus was launched the 'community *baalwadi* model'. The idea was to identify a good person, preferably an enthusiastic young lady who wants to 'do something'. Her job would be to play and sing with the children, make sure that they come for two hours; get used to a class environment and listening to instructions.

Pratham paid this young lady ₹100 per month. Any fees she collected over and above that were hers to keep. The space was provided by the community or the instructor herself.

Mandir, masjid, church, Shiv Sena office, Congress office, gully, verandah, somebody's house – any place was acceptable. As long as there was no interference in what was being taught, and no political or religious message.

The benefit of this very flexible, open-source model was that in the short span of three and a half years, there were 3000 *baalwadis* across the city.

"We had a team of 11 people, each in charge of one ward. In each ward we found locals and told them to recruit a person from the community, to run the *baalwadi*".

Once the model went to scale, of course, the issue of monitoring came in.

"Very often we found that we were falling short. But by and large the model was serving its purpose. When *baalwadi* children entered schools, they performed far better."

Pratham also found that the young women who ran the *baalwadis* became more confident, more aware of their own capabilities.

"The *baalwadi* became a sort of 'internship' for these girls. Many went on to college, got another job. And even as young mothers, they were better equipped to raise their own children."

As the *baalwadi* program grew, so did Pratham's credibility.

"Government officials don't take what NGOs say too seriously because they say you know how to teach 100 children, maybe even a thousand. But we are dealing with lakhs of children!"

Demonstrating a solution which worked on scale opened many doors and many minds to the idea of Pratham. The idea of thinking out of the box.

Another initiative pioneered by Pratham was 'joyful education.' At the time British Airways had just started the 'Change For Good' program, where passengers were urged to donate their spare change for a good cause. Pratham was one of the first beneficiaries of that program.

What Pratham did was again, very simple.

"Teacher training programs were not working, so we stopped them. Instead, we said, let us simply encourage them to do good things!"

Pratham provided material worth ₹100 to each classroom. Spread over 5000 classrooms, this was an investment of ₹ 5 lakhs. Returns came in the form of teaching aids, toys and games made by the teachers.

"Not all teachers made the most beautiful or the most useful things. But what we got was enthusiasm because nobody had said, 'I am telling you what to do.' We were saying, 'Tell us what can *you* do'?"

On its part, Pratham mass produced some of the most interesting toys and teaching aids. The teacher's name was printed on the

"When you are trying to create a movement, the '*zindabad murdabad*' type of social activists are not useful. You need creative people, people who can do things differently".

item and it was distributed to all schools. The idea was to make the teachers feel enthusiastic about their jobs – and it worked.

"Teachers started coming out and saying that they would like to do more."

At this point, Dr Rukmini Banerji, a PhD in Education from Chicago joined Pratham. She assessed the performance of the children, from the learning side. While a few children scored well, the majority fared miserably.

In fact, a large number of children enrolled in 3rd, 4th and 5th standards could not read, or do basic maths.

Pratham asked the teachers to identify these children and devised a program to teach them separately – for two hours, everyday.

"Sometimes all a child really needs is a pat on the back, somebody to sit next to them and say, "I am there for you". It was not just about reading techniques but giving individual attention."

Initially, full time staff was recruited to take care of the additional workload. But then Pratham came up with a bold suggestion.

"Why don't we offer you a volunteer from the slum community who's probably been your own student? She will come and teach the children for two hours inside your classroom and we will call her a *Baalsakhi*".

People said *yeh kaise ho sakta hai?* But Pratham had a simple argument: Either teachers agree to do it, or let us do it our way. And that clinched the decision.

Baalsakhis were paid ₹ 200 a month – not a large sum – but a fellowship of sorts for girls from slums who were going to higher secondary or college.

"I believe money alone does not motivate people. They want some recognition, they want to learn something and it feels good to be part of a larger movement. To be making a small difference".

And all these 'small differences' added up, to create a big impact.

Economists from MIT evaluated the Baalsakhi program through extensive randomised trials in Baroda and Mumbai. They found that it led to massive improvements.

"In 1998, for the first time, the Government of India acknowledged the need for remedial education. I think this is one of the big success stories of Pratham, so much so that it influenced thinking at a policy level*."

This was also the time that the government started talking about out-of-school children and what Pratham could do about it. The problem with reintegrating children who had dropped out of school was that they usually disappeared again.

Either they could not follow what was going on in the class, or they found it too boring.

Once again, Pratham turned to its *baalsakhis* to hook these kids onto the idea of sitting in a classroom. And give them the confidence they needed in themselves, and the system.

The astounding thing is that all this activity was undertaken – and achieved a fair degree of success– with a laughably small amount of funds.

In year one, Pratham had a budget of ₹ 2.5 lakhs. This went up to ₹ 18 lakhs in year 2 and by the third year it swelled to ₹ 40 lakhs. Thanks to a grant, from ICICI.

In fact, it was the personal conviction of Mr N Vaghul – then Chairman of the financial giant – which made it happen.

Mr Vaghul said, "I like your work, we will support you. But I want to see exactly what you do, before giving you more money!"

And true to his word, he went to the slums where Pratham was operating.

"He observed the young girls teaching and responded in his broken Hindi and great sense of humour," recalls Madhav.

---

*The current Sarvashiksha Abhiyaan gives money to state governments to run remedial education programs.

"If you want to activate an institution, you need to activate a person inside that institution. Create a champion."

Mr Vaghul went on to become a champion of Pratham and its work philosophy. And this had a ripple effect.

"Mr Vaghul's support gave confidence to business leaders such as Ajay Piramal, Azim Premji, and Mukesh Ambani. They too started supporting us."

Thus, Pratham became the first NGO in the field of education with a strong corporate support base.

But despite increase in funding, Madhav kept one simple rule of thumb: 'Whatever program we create, it should not cost more than 1% of the municipal education budget* '.

The idea was to remain tight and efficient, and reach out to ever larger numbers.

Until 1998, Pratham was focused wholly and solely on Mumbai. But as its work got noticed, demand to replicate its model started coming in. The Secretary of Education, Mr M K Kaw, invited many government officers to Bombay to see what Pratham was doing.

Both the UP and Rajasthan governments invited Pratham to help in 'mainstreaming' their children. But who would actually go to Jaipur and Lucknow to do that job? The same young men and women who had worked with Pratham in the slums.

"They had never seen the outside world but they were brimming with confidence. We sent them out to spread our programs."

In Jaipur, the administration was shocked when a young girl – Rekha Jadhav – and her colleague Sachin set up 30 bridge classes within a matter of 3 weeks. Such a pace was simply unheard of...

Rekha's story is the story of Pratham. She started as a *Baalwadi* teacher, displayed leadership ability and grew within the

* *The municipal education budget was approximately ₹ 400 crores at the time.*

organisation. When the Jaipur project came up, she raised her hand and said, "I will go."

Jaipur *ho ya* Mumbai, the formula was simple.

You walk into a community and say, *"Tumhare bachhe school nahi jaate, tumhe sharam nahi aati?"*

No survey, no bureaucracy. You go and connect at a person to person level and simply set up a class. Once a couple of children join, the rest follow in Pied Piper fashion.

"And the best part of it all was we didn't need government money to start. We quickly demonstrated the job can be done, the model works. Later, the government took over and it went to scale."

The conversion rate of the program was also encouraging. 55-60% of dropouts actually went back to school and most of them stayed there.

Meanwhile, requests were coming in from individuals to replicate the Pratham program in their states. Madhav recalls attending a conference in Delhi where the gentleman sitting next to him said, 'I like this idea of Pratham, how can it be started in Delhi?'

Madhav replied, "You say, 'I will do it in Delhi'."

The gentleman waited for a couple of seconds and said, "Okay. I will start Pratham in Delhi. Now what?"

The gentleman was Mr Vinod Khanna, a well-respected former ambassador and IFS man. He took it upon himself and he set up Pratham, Delhi. In a similar fashion, Pratham initiatives started in Ahmedabad, Baroda, Lucknow, Allahabad, Bangalore, Mysore, Pune and Rajasthan.

"There was a spontaneous replication of Pratham – with some ownership. Either the government had to take ownership or a group of socially minded people or business people had to take ownership".

The essential thing was that a group of people from different segments of society get together and set up an autonomous trust. Madhav even suggested that each trust should have its own name.

While Bangalore took the name Akshara Foundation, the others all came back and said they wanted to call themselves 'Pratham'.

"I was a little defensive because there was talk in NGO circles, *'Yeh Madhav apne aap ko kya samajhta hai, pataa nahi'*. He's trying to create an empire!"

But ultimately he agreed.

Thus came into being Pratham Delhi, Pratham Allahabad, Pratham Baroda – however, it was never a 'franchise' arrangement. Each Pratham is an independent entity, held together by the central gravitational force of common purpose.

"Of course, we constantly interact with each other, learn from each other. We have agreed on common accounting and financial principles but the rest is open".

The way you teach in Hyderabad can be different from the way you teach in Jaipur. But certain fundamentals like the scale at which Pratham operates, the cost per child and other such parameters remain constant.

Madhav likens the Pratham model to the ubiquitous Udipi restaurant.

"All Udipi restaurants are broadly similar – menu looks similar, décor is similar, the food basically tastes similar. But, they are not identical. It's not like a McDonald's where everything is supplied from a central location."

Of course this model implies a great deal of trust. And faith in the basic 'goodness' of people. But it worked for Pratham, allowing the movement to spread quickly, all over the country. Although with scale came the issue of raising more funds.

"In 1999, ICICI became ICICI Bank, and reduced its contribution to Pratham."

At this point Pratham started raising money in the US and UK.

"We also consolidated our operations, tightened our belt".

By this time, both the government and other NGOs were starting their own *aanganwadis* and *baalwadis*. This suited Pratham fine – the point was not *who* did it but that the work was being done.

The year 2000 was a turning point in other ways. Political equations changed and some union leaders and elected representatives alleged that Pratham was being 'favoured'.

"I always wanted to work in partnership," says Madhav. "But if the other side doesn't want you, there's no point!"

Pratham decided to move out of municipal schools and convert its entire program into a community based effort.

The cornerstone of this initiative is the '200 household pocket' or *basti*. In each such pocket, Pratham would first do a complete survey to find out the number of children in school, number of dropouts, numbers struggling with reading – and design a program to fit the requirement of that *basti *.

At the same time, Pratham decided it was time to focus not just on numbers but on the qualitative aspect of remedial education. It all boiled down to a simple question; how much *can* a child learn in two-three months?

From his experience in adult literacy, Madhav knew that if you isolate something learning can be faster. You just teach some parts. But what is the *critical* part? Pratham decided to focus only on reading – with remarkable results.

"We found that in a very short period of time, 7-10 year olds were able to significantly improve their reading skills. In fact, children could become fluent readers in 30-45 days*!"

Of course, Pratham worked out a technique to make this possible. Firstly, it adopted the *barahkhadi* chart from the work of Prof Jalaluddin, an expert in literacy. Then, came a simple assessment tool.

"Any person could actually go into a village or into a slum community, test children, and say, "Ok, this child is at zero level, this child is at alphabet level, this child is at word level, this child can read sentences."

Whatever the level, there was a *specific* way to take that child forward.

The secret of the 'accelerated reading' program is: Make it like a game. Mix up saying, doing, reading, and writing – do it all at once.

Simple teaching aids like alphabet cards, paragraph cards, small

* *In 2008, Pratham worked with 180,000 householholds in 900 bastis of Mumbai.*

stories and the *barahkhadi* chart were all that was needed. Apart from an enthusiastic teacher, of course!

"We discovered that innovation is not about doing something completely new but bringing pieces together which fits this particular group!"

The success with the reading program energised Pratham. If it could be done with alphabets, surely the same could be done with numbers as well? The trick was to identify the most crucial missing component.

"We found that children did not know how to deal with the 'place value' – units, tens and hundreds. That is because they are not doing things with their own hands and this is the basic principle of any kind of learning. You have to *do* things to learn."

The maths initiative did not do as well as reading, but these experiments changed the way Pratham functioned. From longer duration *baalwadi* and *baalsakhi* programs, the focus shifted to learning cycles of 2-3 months.

Teach a batch of students, integrate them into the school system; move onto the next batch.

But Pratham is not content with just putting kids in school, making sure they can read. Like any forward thinking enterprise they're always thinking 'what next'. And thus was born the 'library program'.

"We started introducing libraries in the community and we found that children liked the idea. The problem was we could not find enough books!"

Soon, Pratham started publishing its own. This enterprise – known as Pratham Books – was led by Rohini Nilekani and her colleagues in Bangalore.

"But then we learnt from our colleagues at AID India in Tamil Nadu that you can create a reading card. And a card costs merely one rupee. So now we have started bringing out reading cards in 100s."

If you create 350 reading cards, 350 kids can take them away. And the cost will be 350 rupees. In the same amount of money, you can give away only 30 books.

Going one step further, Pratham actually created a children's newspaper in Bihar. Printing four pages – in tabloid size, black and white – costs as little as 50 paisa. The idea was to send 20-25 copies per school, per fortnight.

The initial experiment was well received; the Bihar government has taken it to state-wide scale on its own.

"Pratham is not required... that is success!" exults Madhav. As he and his team push ahead, in new directions.

There is always a sense of movement, of 'what more can we do' at Pratham. Some efforts work spectacularly, some fail. But the point is to keep trying.

From 2004 onwards the 'learning to read' program – 'Read India' – spread to 40 urban centres as well as 120 rural districts. Pratham also worked in Amethi, the constituency of Sonia Gandhi.

When the new government came to power, Madhav was put in the National Advisory Council. He suggested that the government should come up with an Annual 'Status of Education' report. When that did not happen, Pratham took the task upon itself.

Madhav realised that because of 'Read India', the organisation's ability to reach the entire nation – to the last village – was within striking distance.

He asked a colleague, "Can we do a survey across India?"

"And this is the other characteristic of Pratham. Maybe it's a weakness also... Nobody says 'no'. Everybody said, 'Yes, we can do it'!"

It took three months from start to finish; from the point when Madhav sent his first email to the release of the report in January 2006. The sample was three times the size of NSS and yet the cost was a mere ₹ 2 crore.

As always, the effort was led by volunteers.

"Pratham was able to mobilise 20-25,000 people to do this survey, because our message was right. We said, "If you're going to pay an education cess, you should know if children are learning or not!"

Just like its original exercise in the municipal schools of Bombay, Pratham now has a national, state wise number and to some extent, district-wise number of school enrolments, dropouts, and other vital parameters.

More than anything else it's done, Pratham is now known for its Annual Status of Education report.

"All our expertise of mobilisation, teaching, analysis and testing came together and ASER became our flagship product," says Madhav.

With this data in hand, Pratham can tell the government, "50% of schoolchildren can't read – let your policies address this!"

And it is happening. As we speak Pratham has launched the second phase of its Read India program...

Which brings us to the question, what has been the impact of Pratham on the lives of those it touched? It's significant and yet, hard to measure.

Take the *baalwadi* program.

Pratham did conduct one simple study in a few communities, where it surveyed children 16 years and under. They found that once a *baalwadi* started the percentage of children who had left education, started falling. But the scientist in Madhav remains unconvinced.

"The economy is changing, aspirations are rising, people want education.. so you cannot pinpoint the cause and effect; you can make a lot of claims."

But the thing you cannot dispute is that Pratham is a unique model, a scalable model – a 'success story' in the social sector. So what's the secret?

"The first thing is that we have kept things very simple and transparent. Typically, NGOs don't tell you who's funding them because they worry somebody will snatch their donors*."

Secondly, Pratham allows people freedom, within certain boundaries.

"As long as you are not asking me for extra money, and you are achieving the overall objective, you are free to operate as you see fit. Because I don't own your soul; you are a thinking, feeling human being."

* Corporates still contribute, but 80% of funds now come from US & UK donors.

In fact, Pratham implicitly encourages its staff to grow and to even leave the 'nest'. Right from '98-99 Madhav encouraged local groups and leaders to create their own *mandals.*

"In Maharashtra today there are 20-25 organisations led by people like Usha Rane, who started with Pratham. They are not only creative workers, but also leaders. In Mumbai, there are four such organisations and all Pratham programs are actually executed by them."

What's the difference? Nothing and yet everything. These organisations are free to work with the municipal corporation and get grants from district governments; Pratham does not want 'ownership' or credit.

"What we do want is to be better than we were last year, and the year before that."

And to do that, sometimes you have to actually pause and take a step back.

"The Read India program that had spread to over 370 districts has been scaled down to 250 districts. The focus is now on higher quality of learning, all round development."

To make all this happen, there are new incentives.

"Our rural program was based completely on unpaid volunteers. Now, they get 'in kind' compensation or 'shiksha ke badle shiksha'."

Which means volunteers can access the computer center in a nearby village, and become digitally literate.

As if all this wasn't enough, Pratham is also deeply committed to the eradication of child labour – and 'vocational skilling' of the youth.

While the Pratham family takes most of Madhav's time and attention, his own kids – Nimisha and Joi – have been a source of joy, and inspiration.

"The way little Nimisha suddenly learned to read gave me the idea of introducing the 'Learning to Read' technique of Pratham."

Of course Nimisha is now a twenty-something, just like Pratham is a feisty sixteen year old – with a mind of its own.

But a mission that is still as relevant, still as unique.

For there are miles to go and promises to keep....

Miles to go, before we can all read.

ADVICE TO YOUNG ENTREPRENEURS

First, it is important to decide what you want to do and why. This seems relatively simple at the first level of iteration.

I like to revisit my 'what' and 'why' every now and then. It is the HOW of things that tests whether you have been honest to yourself in deciding the what and the why. I like questioning my 'what', 'why' and 'howz constantly. It causes chaos every now and then, but helps me to stay on track and to improve.

Finally, I ignore superficial praise and superficial criticism. Both are harmful, if taken seriously. I feel good within when I have done something good and right. If I do not feel good, I must do better.

THE NAKED
TRUTH

Anshu Gupta,
Goonj

Trained as a mass communication professional, Anshu
Gupta decided to communicate an entirely unusual
message to the masses. Through systematic collection,
sorting and delivery Goonj reaches every scrap of waste
clothing from urban India to *someone* out there. To use
with dignity, wear with pride.

I ring the bell at J93, almost expecting a dumpy Punjabi matron to open.

Sarita Vihar is a typical middle class address. But Anshu Gupta of J93 is anything but typical. And neither is his mission in life.

"We talk about *roti, kapda aur makaan* but how many people realise clothing is an issue?" asks the handsome man with intense eyes.

He takes me to his 'processing centre', five minutes away. This is Madanpur Khadir, the village where Anshu and his team give old clothes new life. And make the distribution of clothing a matter of dignity; an art and a science.

Goonj does not measure its success in numbers.

This is a movement, an idea, a bridge between two Indias.

The India of J93, and the India of Madanpur.

The next time you give away old clothes for 'earthquake relief' pause a moment and realise that you feel relieved as well.

Your burden is being carried by Goonj on the wings of angels.

In a village somewhere, your old sweater may be saving a life.

THE NAKED
TRUTH

Anshu Gupta,
Goonj

Anshu Gupta was born into a middle class family.

"An honest middle class family. My father was in MES so after every three years, we had to move somewhere – mostly in UP and Uttaranchal."

Coming from a family of engineers, getting an engineering degree would have been the done thing. But when he was in class 12, Anshu met with a major accident and was completely bedridden.

"During that time I realised engineering was not my cup of tea. I got a lot of time to read and realised I was very keen on journalism."

Anshu started writing for various newspapers, especially a children's magazine called *Suman Saurabh*. He also started writing serious editorial pieces for a local newspaper called *Doon Darpan*.

"They actually measured the size of the article and paid me ₹ 5 per centimeter or something," he recalls.

Anshu enrolled for a BA in Economics in Dehradun and then did a PG course from the Indian Institute of Mass Communication

(IIMC). Strangely enough he completed not one but two diplomas from IIMC – the first in Journalism, and a second in Advertising and PR.

"I did the second one so that I could enjoy the hostel, but they did not give me the hostel. So I started doing freelance writing to support myself."

Not quite sure what he really wanted to do, Anshu joined an advertising agency – Chaitra – where he took a shot at copywriting. The year was 1992 and his take home pay was ₹ 2000.

In a few months Anshu realised that he was passionate about taking pictures. He quit the ad agency, intending to make a full time career out of photography. But then, a strange thing happened.

"I was about 22 years old, and I got cataract in my right eye. That was a major shock – I realised my photography career was over."

Anshu got operated and meanwhile, there was an interview call from PowerGate, a public sector company. Although he was not keen on the job it seemed to be the sensible thing to do, so he joined. He spent two years with the company before moving on to Escorts, also in corporate communications.

"Back then it was a very mundane kind of job – you came out with a newsletter or annual report. And if one of the directors did not like the photo, or the font you redo it again and again, so you are busy".

You are busy for 8-10 hours, but at the end of the day you don't have satisfaction of 'doing something'.

"Also I cannot remember any boss of mine with whom I got along."

Given the lack of excitement in his career, Anshu was getting his 'kick' from other sources. And that story started in 1992, when he wrote a moving piece for Hindi newspaper 'Saptahik Hindustan'.

"I was a new journalist so I went to old Delhi to look for a story. There I see a rickshaw, and on that were the words 'Delhi police corpse carrier'. So I wrote about this man whose job was to pick up unclaimed dead bodies from the roadside."

The man received ₹ 20 for every body he brought in, and a piece of white cloth. Two things he said really shook Anshu; in fact they haunted him for a long time.

The corpse carrier remarked, "In the winter business is good, sometimes there is so much work that I can't handle it."

And his five-year-old daughter added, "When I feel cold, I cuddle a dead body and go to sleep".

Something stirred in Anshu's subconscious mind. The year before, he had been to Uttarkashi to help after an earthquake hit the region.

"I bunked my classes for 15 days and that was my first exposure to 'village India'. I roamed here and there and I saw how people are not worried about houses, or food. They were only talking about warm clothes and blankets."

Anshu was struck by how relief agencies were coming in and giving irrelevant materials. And actually taking away the dignity of the affected people.

"It started bothering me – how kids could remain without clothes in winter. But fortunately or unfortunately I did not know anyone in an NGO, I had no idea what I could do about it."

Lekin kabhi na kabhi kuch karna hai – that he knew.

In 1995 Anshu got married. Wife Mini joined the BBC, and they were 'okay' financially. Horribly bored at work and also charged up about doing 'something' to make a difference, Anshu quit Escorts.

On 22nd July 1998, he wrote a a small note about what he wanted to do under the umbrella of 'Goonj'.

"We did not form an NGO – the note just said that some of us have come together to address the issue of clothing for the poor, especially children".

The movement started with 67 clothes – donated by Anshu and Mini.

"We decided to get rid of all the stuff we had not used in three years, since we got married. Leaving aside a few zari sarees, we took out everything".

Anshu also undertook a collection drive from people's homes. In the evenings, he would pick up Mini from work and they would collect material door-to-door. Around nine pm they would head back home and dump the clothes into their own washing machine. Ready to go out for distribution.

"I am a hands-on type of a person and I know how to stitch a sack and how to fill it – I have learnt it."

The first such exercise, in the slums of Delhi, did not go smoothly.

"Firstly, people expect too much from you, they doubt your integrity. Another thing is that if you get something for free then you don't value it!"

Goonj then decided to target the people camped outside hospitals like AIIMS. Coming from out of state many are ill-equipped for Delhi winters and don't have money to buy woollens either.

On a cold January night Anshu was outside AIIMS, and noticed an elderly woman rummaging through the clothes Goonj had to offer. She had put aside many pieces in good condition.

Anshu asked, "*Mataji* what exactly are you looking for?"

She said, "I am looking for a black shawl".

It is midnight, freezing, why black?

She said, "*Beta*, I have a red saree and black colour will match well with that".

That day Anshu realised that even the poorest of the poor have dreams. They have preferences. And they have needs. Matching the right clothes with the right person became a priority for Goonj.

"Plenty of old clothes are given away by rich people. But there is a gap because you always give what you have and don't want anymore – not what people need".

This was especially true when it came to disaster relief.

In 1999, there was an earthquake in Chamoli. Anshu collected five sacks of clothes and one sack of shoes and despatched them through the Red Cross.

"The Red Cross is like an icon for you whenever you talk about relief. So their vehicle coming to your doorstep and you donate six gunny bags of material, that was a kick, I remember we were so happy!"

"When we made a letterhead for Goonj, we started putting two dots above the Os. My thought was that single dot is a full stop whereas two dots is continuity."

It was moments like this which kept Anshu going. Day to day, life was difficult.

"I had used up all my PF money. We did not have money to rent a godown so we sold the furniture in one bedroom and used it to keep the collected materials."

A few volunteers came forward to help but money was very tight. In 1999, when there was a cyclone in Orissa, Goonj collected many truckloads of material. But once again it was sent across through Red Cross.

"I remember Goonj did not have even ₹ 1000 so I could not travel to Orissa myself. And I was sad because when I visited the godown of Red Cross I realised they did not value the things and know how to distribute as efficiently as we did."

That same year, Goonj became a registered NGO. Anshu's closest friend remarked that more than half of the registered organisations commit fraud. "So you have also started it..." he said.

Duniya aisi hi hai – cynics abound.

Even funding agencies showed no interest because the issue of clothing was never on their agenda.

"I remember, when I wrote to funding agencies they would give a very pat reply: 'Your initiative is very good but it does not fall under our parameters'. Had we been working on AIDS awareness it would have been easy to get ₹ 3 lakhs just to make jackets and caps with some kind of message!"

The believer is determined, but not stubborn. You adapt, you change, you find new solutions.

In a few short months, Goonj decided to stop distributing material in slums and focus on the villages where the need was more acute.

"The handicap was that we did not have funds to visit villages. So we started having partnerships with the villages."

Goonj started channelising the materials it collected through local village groups. But even that required money.

"Every unit we distributed had a logistics cost. Logistics is nothing but resources – whether it is space, manpower, money, transportation, whatever."

It wasn't much – maybe ₹ 15-20,000 per month was all it needed to run a 'flourishing operation'. But raising it was a challenge. People were happy to donate in kind but when it came to money, they would generally favour a more established organisation.

"We didn't have rich friends and the ones who lived corporate lives couldn't understand why we were doing this. They lived a parallel life. So we got small sums like ₹ 10/-, 50/-, 100/-..."

Goonj also raised money by collecting raddi paper, beer bottles, iron cans – and selling them. Another source of revenue was handmade bamboo clocks.

"We brought bamboos and tools, and I literally learnt how to use the saw and how to nail things."

A big break came in the form of an order worth ₹ 22,500 from 'The Home Store'.

"We worked hard on the order, and made the clocks, and just before delivering them we polished them. My friend Ajay and I put everything in the Maruti 800, and went to deliver the clocks".

On reaching the store they discovered that the newspaper they had used to wrap the clocks had left an imprint on the fresh polish! The order was cancelled.

But life goes on. Goonj took up a stall at Delhi Haat in February 1999.

"People saw us, understood what we did, and they were interested because our volunteers were very decently dressed and talking differently. We were not asking for money but only for your old things".

Calls started coming in – as did more people, carrying materials.

Goonj 'expanded' by taking up a balcony and then an entire room on rent for ₹ 600. It also hired its very first employee for a sum of ₹ 700 + lodging & board.

"Subhash was our maid's husband – he used to roam around doing nothing, just drinking. But we took him on and he actually made himself quite useful!"

The Gujarat earthquake in January 2001 was a turning point of sorts.

"We found people coming all the way from Rohini to Sarita Vihar, to give things to Goonj. Even though there were dozens of camps to collect materials put up in every locality. It gave us a lot of confidence – that we were doing something right – and that the word was spreading."

But again, Goonj did not have the money to physically go to Gujarat and distribute the goods. What Goonj did was perfect a system of sorting. This ensured that clothes were not haphazardly sent here and there – and every bit of cloth was used to make some difference.

The tsunami in December 2004 was where Goonj was able to really make its mark – on a massive scale.

"During the Gujarat earthquake, the media beamed pictures of clothes lying unused on the roadside. Why? Because these clothes were oversized, or culturally incompatible."

Agencies collect and despatch jeans, ladies suits, t-shirts from urban India, but village women want a saree, blouse and petticoat. Some of the clothing received is dirty, or torn – you will even find used undergarments!

"Disaster-hit people, they are not traditionally beggars. Shahrukh Khan stays near the sea, we say he stays in a seaside bungalow. But what about the people living in the tsunami hit places – they used to live in seaside bungalows too. Who gives you the right to send your old undergarments to them?"

One hundred truckloads – or two million units of clothing – lay unused in government godowns post-tsunami. No one had a clue what to do with it.

The Tamil Nadu administration said, "These are old clothes – nobody wants them."

Anshu said, "Half the country survives on old clothes, how can you say no one wants them?"

Goonj signed an MOU with the Tamil Nadu government.

"We give away old clothes and act very pricey, ask if it will go to the right person or not, but who in the world gives away a useful thing?"

"There was a major North Indian versus South Indian issue but ultimately with the help of one very nice officer – Mr C V Shankar -we signed an agreement."

Among the first 1 lakh units Goonj sorted, there were 1300 monkey caps. Monkey caps to Chennai? Yes, many such unmindful though well-intentioned 'relief consignments'. It's the same story during any disaster – riot, earthquake or flood.

The market is vast, limited only by how much you can take on.

The organisation Anshu started with 67 pieces of clothing from his own almirah now collects and distributes 50,000 kgs – or 50 tonnes – of material every month. Along with clothes, Goonj redistributes used footwear, toys, stationery, small furniture, books and even computers.

"During any disaster, the quantities go up dramatically," adds Anshu.

Apart from a core staff of 100, Goonj operates with the help of hundreds of volunteers as well as 150 partner groups – from the Indian Army to village panchayats.

Volunteering could be as simple as someone coming forward and offering their home as a 'collection centre' in a particular city. Some get so involved that they make a full time commitment to Goonj. 24 year old Rohit Singh, is one such example. After volunteering for a year, he quit his job with Hewitt and now handles the activities of Goonj in Mumbai.

"My team is full of young people. The number two at Goonj is Ruchika. She joined when she was just 19, not even a graduate!"

Dealing with massive amounts of material also requires a well planned, well-oiled system – in Delhi, where Goonj is based.

Madanpur Khadar village behind Sarita Vihar is where the materials are cleaned, then sorted into wearable and unwearable. Wearable clothes are ultimately despatched to partner groups for distribution. In some districts like Khandwa, in MP and Chapra in Bihar, the model has further evolved.

"We have started a 'cloth for work' program. The villagers might dig a well, repair roads, clean the locality – depending on the need of that community".

Aptly, the program is now called *Vastra Samman*. And that respect is seen even in the careful manner in which Goonj handles collected material.

"We take out undergarments, dirty, torn, oversized and Western outfits. Also wash, repair and make complete sets."

For example, 50% of ladies salwars are donated without a *naada*. Volunteers take care of such details, and even match pairs of socks!

The clothes are also classified – 'women', 'kids', and so on. Before despatch clothes are coded by type and quantity so that Goonj can keep track of exactly what was sent where. And there is a method to that too.

"We send warm clothes to cold places; salwar suits to Muslim areas and gowns to West Bengal where women wear them all day. It's all about optimum utilisation of material".

A similar process is followed with school uniforms, export surplus and in fact any and every kind of material collected. From *bartans* and shoes to old furniture.

Meanwhile, the unwearable clothes are also converted into items of use – school bags, *dhurries*, yoga mats, baby bedding and most importantly, sanitary napkins.

"We started working on the idea in 2004-05; it was almost like a laboratory conducting experiments with all that waste cloth. 45

"I remember in the first year, this young couple came and gave us ₹ 5000. We couldn't believe that someone could trust in Goonj so much!"

ladies working with us were involved and it was right down to basic questions like should there be a loop or not..."

But how did the idea of converting waste cloth into napkins come about?

"I remember observing lot of clothes hanging on the ropes of middle class, government colonies. Somewhere you would notice strips of checkered bedsheets and wondered what it was."

Years later, when he started Goonj, Anshu realised that there were women in poor regions like Orissa who wore sarees without blouse or petticoat, because that was all they could afford. They probably did not even have undergarments, so how did they manage those five days?

"It's a taboo subject – no one wants to talk about it. Then we found out that they use sand, they use ash, they use pieces of jute, even newspaper and polythene."

One lady apparently used her blouse – she got infected from the rusted hook and died of sepsis.

Today Goonj produces over two lakh sanitary napkins a month, a simple solution to enhance the health and hygiene of thousands of women, across India.

It is women who also form the backbone of Goonj operations – it's not a 'job' for them but a way of life.

"It is not a top-down system but a guided democracy. Ownership lies with each worker," says Anshu.

"I will give you a very simple example; in sorting we have calculated a minute-by-minute average. But instead of setting a 'target' we say you have the potential to sort 3 gunny bags.".

When people work for themselves, they work from the heart.

Yet, the nuts and bolts of an operation do require cold, hard cash. Goonj now has an annual budget of ₹ 3 crores per annum. Close to half of that comes from individual donors; 15-20% through sale of products, newspapers. A small but significant chunk is the money received by Anshu as 'awards' *.

And finally, corporates are also coming forward. But money is really a means to an end, and this is a social venture; Anshu is determined to keep it that way.

* *From Ashoka Fellow to the World Bank Global 'Development Marketplace' award, Anshu has received close to ₹ 50 lakhs as prize money.*

"Our Board could easily decide to sell 10% of the material – the good quality material – and subsidise the remaining 90%. The entire world will say, 'What a business model!' We have the option but we will never go for that."

The moment you add Excel and make a PPT you have a business model.

"But my issue is that if I want to do a business then I will do business. But I would not like to treat social issues like business."

If Goonj visits a disaster-hit area it will not be content with serving the people in one district.

"A person may die in Madhepura but you will not send him the relief because you do not want to move out of your targeted approach. We can't operate like that."

Systems are important; there is a blueprint for everything that Goonj does so that anyone, anywhere can replicate it.

"But it cannot become a system oriented organisation; it has to be a *people* oriented one. That is the difference."

Goonj sees itself as a movement, and hence numbers are irrelevant.

"If you get into these number games, then you will give one cloth to one person and say I have one beneficiary. Like many NGOs and corporates will come and say, 'We have adopted 100 villages'. What have you done there? Put up a hand pump, or painted a school – it is all so vague!"

The way Anshu sees the impact of Goonj is in the fact that cloth is an issue today.

"Many people have copied what we do. Previously we were the only ones who spoke about warm clothes in Delhi winters. Now events are being inaugurated by film stars so somewhere the awareness is coming up!"

Another interesting thing is that after AIDS, the major funding goes to Reproductive Child Health or RCH. However none of these projects had a budget for sanitary napkins. Now, self-help groups (SHGs) are taking this up as an income generation activity.

Speaking of income, with Goonj becoming 'stable', Mini too decided to quit her job and join the organisation 3 years ago.

"I call her the 'backbone' of Goonj," says Anshu.

Goonj is an echo; an echo in the hearts of the 'haves' for the 'have-nots'. It is work; it is family; it is all and everything Anshu knows and does.

ADVICE TO YOUNG ENTREPRENEURS

Think out of the box and think practically. I address a lot of youth and meet many who are idealistic, who feel that something has to be done.

But if you sit here and say that everyone should get food, people won't get it. Someone has to make effort. And this is the golden time, because there are a lot of transparency issues, the right to information, the country growing – a very positive atmosphere.

And if you want to make a difference, it does not have to be 'full time' for everybody. Do it alongside a job. You have time for movies, parties, music, going on long drives, weekends with your family, chatting on the net. Why can't you have one hour to volunteer for some cause? Even one hour makes a difference.

There are people who are spending their lives on these issues, you just need to flow with them.

THE ART OF
WAR

Trilochan Sastry
Association for Democratic Reforms (ADR)

An IIT-IIM graduate, Trilochan Sastry could have been one of the many armchair critics who despair about the state of the nation. But his simple, courageous act of filing a PIL raised the standards of Public Life. And is slowly but surely changing the way we elect our leaders.

The year was 1992 – my first as a student.

And his – as a professor.

A newly returned PhD from MIT, we knew him as one of the most brilliant – and most laid back – faculty members on campus. Clearly he did not care for the things many professors did, but what did he care about?

I discovered that a decade later, when I picked up the newspaper and read about a landmark judgement from the Supreme Court asking politicians to declare their assets and criminal records.

Who would be crazy enough to file a petition like this? The very same professor. Clearly he cared about some things passionately enough to move mountains. And his passion moves others – to support, to contribute, to get involved.

Thanks to his efforts, we have the Association for Democratic Reform (ADR).

Because of ADR, anyone standing for election must declare their assets.

Because of this decree, politicians are slowly but surely becoming more accountable to the country they are supposed to serve.

Because of one man's gumption, guts and downright *gustaakhi* towards the system, our world is a better place.

I sit on the yellow rexine sofa in his office and think, there is so much to learn from this professor – not just inside the classroom, but outside it.

THE ART OF
WAR

Trilochan Sastry
Association for Democratic Reforms (ADR)

Trilochan Sastry grew up in Delhi. "My parents, brother and I lived in the same place for 21 years."

It was a very 'stable' childhood. The two brothers walked across the road every morning, and took a bus to Mount St Mary school. Then, Trilochan went to IIT Delhi which was within walking distance from his house.

Trilochan had no 'ambition' in life, as such. *Kuch to padhna hai, to chalo, IIT hi sahi.*

"In those days it was a five-year program. Nothing very remarkable but you are 16 and first time out of home – so it strongly impacts your outlook on life."

A wonderful experience but at the end of five years Trilochan once again found himself asking, "What next?" There were the standard 3 options: Take up a job, go to IIM or America. For no logical reason – he chose to study management.

Trilochan joined IIM Ahmedabad in 1981. He was not a very driven student and mostly remembers having a 'good time'.

"I used to do a lot of jogging… in fact I ran two marathons. I spent time hanging around with friends, reading lots of books – never took the course very seriously."

Ah. But one thing which always concerned Trilochan – even when he was at IIT – was the whole issue about society and poverty.

At the orientation in IIT, Trilochan recalls the director saying, "You are the cream of the country, the government is spending 50,000 rupees on each student per year." A lot of money back in 1976!

And he thought, "What the hell have *I* done to deserve these 50,000 rupees. Just because we are a little intelligent does not mean so much money needs to be put on me!"

During his first year at IIMA a professor called Nirmala Murthy called Trilochan to her office. She knew about his interest in 'other' issues and had a summer project with an NGO called Seva Mandir.

"Do you want to go to Karnataka, Rajasthan or Bihar?" she asked.

"Bihar," replied Trilochan.

"Why?" she asked

"Because it is a very challenging place," he replied. Imagining a Disneyland of social problems waiting to be conquered.

The good professor sent him to Rajasthan, which was equally 'exciting'. An IIM senior called Biswajit Sen working with the organisation took Trilochan under his wing.

"I spent two months in Rajasthan which was a big eye opener for me. I had never lived in a village... here I went to the back of beyond and they had chosen Kherwada – which was the 'most backward block' in the country at that time. No roads, hardly any electricity, nothing decent to eat."

Trilochan had to survey government departments and that was another shocker. He realised that government departments did no work at all.

"Those two months really changed my perspective on many many things in life."

In hindsight.

But back then, after coming back to campus, Trilochan went back to 'having a good time'. When placement came he was not particularly keen on any job.

"The question of trying to make money, slogging to make money, pardon me... it seemed very stupid to me (laughs). It has never excited me."

"My parents never advised me and I never asked them for any advice. I have always been a free spirit."

But a man's gotta do something. So Trilochan explored the idea of joining an NGO. It didn't work out. The next best option, he thought, was to join the public sector and serve the nation.

One year with ONGC rapidly convinced him that public sector is a bad idea.

But working in the Chairman's office had its benefits. ONGC was India's biggest company and largest profit earner. Trilochan's boss – Col Wahi – was a very powerful man.

"Two things about Col Wahi – firstly, he worked extremely hard. Secondly, he was very savvy. Just by sitting around and observing him, I learnt quite a bit."

But meanwhile, there was a personal tragedy. Soon after he joined ONGC, Trilochan's father passed away.

It was a difficult period for the close-knit family. And added some sense of responsibility to Trilochan's carefree shoulders, at the young age of 23.

"My brother was already in the US doing his PhD. I too was thinking of pursuing academics but felt I should stay back in Delhi with my mother."

She said, "Don't worry about me. Go!"

Trilochan started applying to various programs and was accepted at MIT. Studying at one of the world's greatest universities was another 'life changing' experience.

"Why is MIT such a great institution – I used to wonder. Of course one reason is they have such great faculty and students but there must be more. I used to think about it and discuss, some ideas got into my head."

As usual Trilochan made lots of friends and travelled the length and breadth of America in his second hand car. On the academic front, also as usual, he did not take the PhD too seriously. But writing a thesis came easy – and he liked the subject – *so ho gaya.*

Once again came the question what next? The big decision before him: "Do I stay back in the US or return to India?"

Trilochan's heart said, "India."

"When I told my adviser he was silent for 10 seconds. But in America they believe in individual freedom so he didn't try to stop me."

Trilochan returned to India in January 1992 and joined IIM Ahmedabad as a professor in Operations Management. In his free time, he started networking with NGOs, trying to find out what is going on.

"I had this vague idea that somehow we must bring all the NGOs together and collectively do something good."

Good idea, good intentions – but not easy at all, to get it done. NGOs are run by people with strong convictions. Getting them to work *together* is tough.

Life went on.

Trilochan Sastry, the professor, was teaching, publishing papers, going on the occasional Himalayan trek.

Trilochan Sastry, the activist, was going nowhere. Yet ideas were constantly brewing in his head.

Slowly, he found himself drawn to a cause. A 'hopeless' cause.

Like all thinking middle class people, Trilochan was pained by the country being 'messed up' by politicians. Prime Ministers were being implicated in criminal cases. All kinds of people in very high positions were openly looting the country. But what can People Like Us *do* about it?

Trilochan decided to file a PIL. He believed that a Public Interest Litigation asking politicians to declare their criminal records just might open the door for change.

Friends and colleagues were lukewarm. His brother declared it was 'stupid'.

"But I still thought it was a very good idea," recalls Trilochan.

He met lawyers in Ahmedabad, all of whom advised filing the PIL in the Supreme Court.

Even if the lawyer agreed to work without a fee, who would bear his travel expenses? A professor's salary did not allow for such luxuries.

But Trilochan felt that somehow, a way would be found.

He had a chat with activist H D Shourie, father of Arun Shourie and founder of 'Common Cause'. Although Shourie had filed several PILs, he too felt this one was unlikely to work.

"I listened to him politely and... I still thought it was a good idea."

And he kept his hopes alive.

One government was elected in 1998. It fell in 1999 and another election was declared. The time was 'ripe', felt Trilochan.

This time, with the help of friend Ajit Ranade, he found a lawyer in Delhi. The lawyer advised that the PIL should be filed on behalf of an association and not on behalf of an individual.

"So what is an association anyway? I looked through the faculty list at IIMA, got a sense of who might be interested, picked out 10 names and called them. Eight of them agreed. Ajit Ranade and Sunil Handa* also joined."

Ten people somehow squeezed into Trilochan's office at IIMA and signed a one page note prepared by him which laid out what the association would be doing. The Association for Democratic Reform – or ADR – would fight for democratic reforms.

And its first plan of action was to file the PIL.

Filing a PIL meant numerous trips to Delhi. Soon enough Trilochan realized that his lawyer – although an eminent personality – was giving them the run around and not doing anything.

Trilochan got hold of another lawyer by the name of Prashant Bhushan.

"By this time I had developed a lot of expertise – which I still have – which is that you can contact anyone in the country, if not in the world (laughs). You call this guy, call that guy, get his number through this that and the other means."

Everybody knows everybody else through *somebody*. With a bit of practice – and luck – you can reach that person. But do you have something to say which will make him sit up and listen?

* *Ajit Ranade works as chief economist with Aditya Birla Group, Sunil Handa's story is chapter 9 of Stay Hungry Stay Foolish. Both are IIMA alumni.*

"I had nothing to lose... *Kya farak padta tha, kya hoga*?"

When Trilochan Sastry explained his mission to Prashant Bhushan, in five minutes flat the lawyer agreed: "Yes, this can be done."

He agreed to take the case.

But one day, as they were discussing what to do next, Prashant introduced Kamini Jaiswal and said, "Trilochan, she is going to be your lawyer."

Trilochan was a little taken aback but was assured that Kamini would do a good job (which was absolutely true, as time would tell!)

Even as Kamini prepared the PIL, Trilochan was busy doing his homework.

"I must have spent hundreds of hours on the net trying to find out what are the disclosure norms in America, UK, France, Japan. We put together a lot of material while she prepared the legal documents and filed the PIL".

Trilochan's mother passed away in November 1999.

The PIL was filed in December 1999.

Kamini filed the PIL in the Delhi high court so that in case ADR lost, it had the option of an appeal in the Supreme Court.

"As luck would have it, we won in the Delhi HC and the government appealed. And this drama continued for the next 18 months."

In May 2002 the Supreme Court gave a landmark judgement saying that candidates must disclose their income, education and criminal record, if any. The judgement made front page news in all papers, and it achieved the impossible.

Politicians of all parties got together and agreed on one thing: "This ruling had to be overturned."

A strategy was chalked out at an all-party meet on 8th of July, 2002. One week later, a draft bill to amend the Representation of People Act had been circulated. In sum and substance, it said "We don't have to disclose all this information. We are politicians after all!"

"They tried to fix Tarun Tejpal, gave him a pretty hard time. I think he is a very gutsy guy and deserves lot of respect."

By this time many people working in this field came forward, realizing that 'something was happening'. NGOs such as Loksatta and Transparency International, as well as influential individuals such as Maya Daruwala, Kuldip Nayar and L C Jain offered support.

"All of us would meet and discuss what we should do if the bill is overturned, what is our action plan after the judgement comes. A sort of network started developing."

Some people on the network knew a lot of scientists and arranged a meeting with Dr Abdul Kalam at Rashtrapati Bhavan. Dr Kalam listened to the delegation for one hour and agreed to one of the suggestions made by ADR. Which was, to return the bill.

It was a symbolic gesture, but an important one. Although, going by the Constitution, the President had no choice but to sign the bill when it was sent to him a second time.

In August 2002, ADR decided to go back to the Supreme Court and challenge the constitutional validity of the amendment proposed by the politicians. An amendment which was trying to deny the voters basic information about their candidates.

In a record time of just six months, the Supreme Court gave its verdict. In March 2003, the court upheld ADR's petition and threw out the amendment as 'unconstitutional'.

This was a huge victory but, the real work had just begun.

ADR decided to use the Gujarat elections of 2003 to 'launch' its movement. The movement to create awareness in the minds of voters, and fear in the hearts of candidates.

"We decided to collect the information being declared by candidates as per law and widely publicise it."

ADR's instinct was that the data which candidates had to file – as per law – would just lie with the returning officer. ADR decided to physically collect the info, and channelise it to the media.

But first, an important decision had to be made. You are about to release the murder and criminal records of powerful, well connected politicians.

"Do we really want to do this?" asked a Devil's Advocate.

Everybody was silent.

Trilochan said, "Yes! We must."

The Devil's Advocate said, "Not "we" – someone has to agree to put himself out there in public view, be the spokesperson for the movement."

Without hesitation, without fear or fumble, Trilochan said, "I'll do it."

"Everybody was unsure because nobody knew what was going to happen."

What could be the consequences of taking on goons and *goondas*?

"Well, I am running around, and no one has gunned me down so far," Trilochan laughs.

Matter resolved, an action plan was made. Step one was the formation of a high level committee.

"We invited retired Chief Justices, IAS officers, former IIM directors, DGPs – all people in eminent positions who were non-political – and formed a Gujarat Election Watch committee."

ADR then went and met 8-10 editors of leading newspapers in Gujarat.

"We were a little more focused on Gujarati because in our analysis those who read English papers do not matter – they never vote. So we focused more on Gujarati and local medium which is a strategy we have always followed."

The Election Watch found tremendous support from all the editors. Raising money from friends and wellwishers* the Gujarat Election Watch campaign did release some newspaper ads. But most of the publicity was 'free'.

Nearly all papers – English and Gujarati – had banner headlines such as 'Modi government has 34 criminals!' TV channels did their bit as well.

* *The first Gujarat Election Watch campaign cost approximately ₹ 15 lakhs.*

ADR also conducted sample surveys – along with other NGOs – to find errors in electoral rolls. The survey was conducted in Mumbai, Delhi, Hyderabad, Ahmedabad and Bangalore – and found there were 40% errors in the voter rolls. This data was also released to the press.

"In fact Election Commission officials came running to our office saying tell us – what can be done!"

And through it all there was no pressure, no harassment, no threats at all?

A couple of minor incidents – like an intelligence officer landed up at Trilochan's office in IIM Ahmedabad.

"I remember doing a double take but decided quickly that I am *not* going to take this lying down. It was all in a matter of seconds."

Trilochan asked the man, "*Aap kaun hain, kahaan se aaye hain* – show me your I-card."

He added, "As soon as you leave this office I will email 40 journalists and 300 NGOS all over Gujarat and say that you, sent by such and such officer from the IB department is harassing me."

The officer stammered, "No sir, I am only doing my job. "

I said, "*Tum logon ne naukri kar kar ke desh ka bhatta bitha diya hai..* you get out of here!"

He left and Trilochan never got any more such visitors. There was one phone call from a joint secretary in the external affairs ministry asking ADR to explain 'foreign funding'.

Trilochan replied, "We have taken money from overseas but from Indian citizens."

ADR had photocopies of the Indian passports of every donor. And that was that.

"A journalist told me that politicians are actually scared of ADR."

Why?

"Because they didn't know how to 'fix' us."

The powers that be decided to mind their own business.

And truth be told, despite threatening to usher in an era of cleaner politics, Gujarat Election Watch did not make a 'a jot of a difference'.

> ## "Our strategy is not just to influence citizens. Our strategy is to use media exposure to put pressure on political party bosses not to nominate such candidates or make them ministers."

"There was a lot of publicity, people got to know about the campaign, but in terms of actually bringing about change it did nothing."

So what next?

Trilochan wanted to spread the movement around the country. One of the ADR members did not agree. He said, "If it's a good idea, it will spread. It's not our job to take on that responsibility. *Desh bhar ka theka nahin le rakha hai humne."*

"My thinking has always been: "*Desh bhar ka theka le rakha hai. Maine to liya hua hai."*

And so, the movement went national.

ADR held a conference in Ahmedabad. The idea was to invite NGOs from across India to see the work of Gujarat Election Watch. And ask them to replicate the model in their own states.

With Rajasthan, Madhya Pradesh, Chhatisgarh, Mizoram and Delhi were going to the polls, ADR concentrated on pulling in NGOs from those states. The strategy worked.

In the year 2004, ADR decided to hold another national conference, this time on electoral reforms. It was important to simply meet once a year, keep the network oiled; thoughts, ideas and action plans whirring.

By this time Trilochan had joined IIM Bangalore.

One day, as he was mulling over where to hold the ADR conference, the dean suggested, "Why don't we do it on the campus?"

Um, because, this is a 'hot potato' kind of subject. Would the institute be comfortable?

The dean said, "No problem."

The director also extended his support. And so it came to be that a conference on criminalisation of politics was held in the IIM Bangalore auditorium. The Chief Election Commissioner came, NGOs came, citizens came, and so did a representative of the Ford foundation.

Which led to a first round of funding, in November 2005.

"We got $ 200,000, spread over 2 years. Actually it was just about comfortable.. not too much, not too little."

The 'business plan' envisaged an Election Watch in all states, as they went to the polls over the next couple of years.

With funding coming on, the structure of ADR was also formalised.

"The structure really is trustees – there are 7 or 8 of them. The active trustees are Sunil Handa, Jagdeep Chhokar, Ajit Ranade and I. I am the chairman and Jagdeep is the secretary. We all work in an honorary capacity – we don't get any money. Of course, we also have full time staff."

The ADR 'head office' is based in Delhi – where all the political action is. One of the early recruits was Bibhu Mahapatra, who had conducted Election Watch in Raipur while he was with the Commonwealth Human Rights Initiative (CHRI). Bibhu built up the organisation, and in fact took it to the next level.

"Bibhu loves traveling and interacting with grassroots NGOs – they call him Bibhuda. He smokes a lot of cigarettes and drinks rum at night..."

And over shared smokes and shared rum, Bibhu built up a network across MP, UP, Bihar, Orissa, West Bengal. The idea was to work with partners, and give them full freedom to do an election watch in their state. ADR insisted only on one thing: Be politically neutral.

You could call it a 'franchise' model of sorts except that each organisation worked under its own name.

"What we bring to the table is contacts with the media, with the Chief Election Commissioner and so on."

ADR also provided overall moral and motivational support. And not from an armchair, but by actually being there. Going state by state, spending time at the grassroots level.. days, weeks, months!

"Bibhu travelled more than me but I also visited Bihar several times during the 2005 elections. Because the instinct was – going back to Nirmala Murthy – if you can do something in Bihar then things will change."

Trilochan decided not to concentrate on Patna alone but go to the districts to hold workshops and meetings.

"In every district we would call the local NGOs, some local businessmen, local media people, some college lecturers, students and discuss various issues. We found tremendous enthusiasm."

When people feel they are being heard, they start using their voice. And when many voices come together, the cry for change becomes loud enough to be heard.

The process of mobilisation in Bihar went on for 3-4 months. And the impact was visible.

There was intense media coverage, particularly from the two local channels Sahara Samay and ETV Bihar.

"Both channels had tickers running throughout the day, saying that such and such RJD MLA was charged under *dafa* 302, and so on."

But did these criminals get re-elected? Some of them did, some of them didn't. But that is not the main point. The political leadership woke up and realised it could not treat the issue lightly.

"Pankaj Pachauri, who runs the Hindi version of NDTV's 'We the People', flew down to Patna. All political parties in Bihar came on the show and were grilled on the number of criminals they were fielding."

The media scrutiny was so high that Nitish Kumar was asked repeatedly, "What are you going to do about this?"

Finally, he declared, "We will not make such people ministers."

A promise that he stuck to.

So for the first time in living memory, Bihar got a cabinet which, at least on paper, was criminal-free. And this, the Election Watch in Bihar can legitimately claim is entirely due to their efforts.

ADR met with equally good success in UP in 2007.

"I remember Rahul Gandhi actually called our campaign office. First his secretary spoke, then he himself came on the line and he said Congress *ummeedvaaron ke jo aankade hain wo mujhe bhej do.*"

Trilochan also received an email from L K Advani saying 'thank you for your report'. Ironic, because when ADR was fighting its case, the same L K Advani – as Deputy Prime Minister – had dismissed them saying, "People who have never fought an election are trying to reform the election system."

Perhaps that's why they succeeded.

After polishing its act through various state election watches, ADR faced its moment of truth: the 2009 national elections.

ADR used all its ammunition – the NGO partners, media supporters and even a public service campaign featuring Aamir Khan – to send out the message loud and clear. "No criminals in politics".

Did it have the desired impact? Yes and no.

"Serious criminals like Mukhtar Ansari lost. I don't claim he lost because of ADR alone but the general trend is that the very big thugs either lost the election or were prevented by the Supreme Court from standing in the first place."

So people with 10 murder cases did not win, but those with 1-2 murders cases – some of them have won. But again, the Union cabinet – is clean.

"In 2004 people like Shibu Soren had become ministers and the party was even defending them. That has changed."

Of course, there are new issues ADR is taking up now. Like, declaring assets is well and good. But how do politicians account for this income zooming by 1000% between one election and the next? ADR may go back to court to fight out that one.

Meanwhile, it has also taken up the issue of inner party democracy* and transparency in funding.

"We filed an RTI saying that Income Tax returns of political parties should be out there in the public domain. After 4 months and 2 hearings in the Central Information Commission, they finally made it public."

Another idea is to keep monitoring politicians – and not just at election time. So ADR will track how many times your MP

---

* *Top BJP, Congress leaders have given oral support to pass a bill on political party reform; committee drafting bill includes Trilochan Sastry from ADR*

attended Parliament, did he participate in any debates and what, if anything, did he do with his discretionary fund?

"Basically, we will tighten the screws a little."

It started with one man holding that screwdriver. Now, it's a national movement.

You would think '*nahin, kabhi nahin ho sakta*'. But it did happen.

"If you ask me why, why did ADR work, I think three things. Firstly, luck..."

"Second is the initial team we had – Jagdeep, Sunil, Ajit and I – the four active trustees."

"Third, we had a very clear, practical vision and action plan. And we never aimed to do a perfect job from day one. We just start and then things keep improving as we go along."

And to think in addition to all this, Trilochan holds a full time job – as professor and Dean (Academics) at IIM Bangalore.

"I manage... Actually, I have 3 jobs. I teach, I run ADR and I spend my weekend in the villages – trying to run two NGOs. All totally unrelated! You should do what you find interesting!"

True. But can you do so many things and do them well? Trilochan certainly believes so. The academic load he's always worn lightly. Teaching, writing research papers – that stuff comes easy.

With ADR the initial years were the toughest.

"I spent more time then, when nothing was happening, than now."

Because now there is an organisation, and really smart people to take it forward. A cause like ADR is a magnet which attracts the brightest of minds.

"The guy who's heading our Delhi office now, he's started two companies and sold them. A very high caliber chap – I don't have to worry much. Only look at new things, what to do next. And of course, keep looking for funding."

It is the third aspect of his life which actually keeps Trilochan busy – and charged up – these days.

"I am and continue to be passionate about lifting large number of people from poverty. This has always been my dream."

While in Ahmedabad, Trilochan did try to get into developmental work. Language was a huge barrier.

"I wanted to work directly in the rural areas but my knowledge of Gujarati was limited. One option was to sit down and learn the language. But I never got around to doing it."

In 2001 Trilochan joined ISB in Hyderabad. And suddenly, doors opened.

"All because I speak Telugu."

Trilochan quickly became trustee to an NGO and got involved with a World Bank project. He did not quite fit into ISB and decided to quit within 2-3 months but stayed on in AP. He spent the next 7-8 months traveling around the state, with just one guiding principle.

"I was clear that I am not going to read books or papers – I'm going to directly go to the field and observe what's going on. Talk to the poor."

The World Bank project CEO, an IAS officer, invited Trilochan to 'name his terms and conditions' and come on board. He had just one request: a cell phone. And, he added, "I don't want any money."

The CEO asked, "Why don't you want any money?"

Trilochan replied, "I don't know anything about poverty and I don't want to make money in the name of the poor!"

The World Bank project had offices in 6 districts and using them as a base Trilochan visited villages across the state – by train, by car, by ST bus. The young chaps working for the project – mostly IRMA graduates – were happy to show him around.

"I came to 2-3 very simple conclusions. Firstly, there are many projects working towards health, education, empowerment and so on but no one talks about how to raise the income of the poor."

"Secondly, I decided to work with those whose distress, whose need is higher."

"Lastly, I was clear – and still am clear – no subsidy. We won't give anything for free."

Trilochan quickly realised that in rural areas farming was and still is the chief source of livelihood. And that the majority are small and marginal farmers who get 'screwed' for a variety of reasons. For example, only 30% of India is irrigated while most marginal farmers live in non-irrigated areas.

Many are forced to come to the city and work as daily wage labourers. We pass them, sleeping under the flyover, and turn our faces away in disgust.

"By the way there are some 600 million people in this mess – it's not a small number – it's just that we don't interact with them and it really bothers me a lot. And it will bother me till I die, I suppose."

Trilochan wondered where he could begin, where he could 'plug the leak'.

"Where I decided to intervene is, they don't have marketing facilities. They don't know how to market their produce."

Take the example of a small farmer in a remote village with 20 bags of groundnut. He needs to sell it right away, so he goes to a middleman. *And woh log uski bilkul topi utar dete hain...* they simply fleece him."

Not only are interest rates very high, farmers are cheated on the weights – 50 kgs is certified as 40 and the seller has no option. Take it or leave it!

Trilochan's NGO – the Centre for Collective Development, or the Sahakar Mitra Sanstha – organises farmers into producer groups or co-operatives. Now, instead of selling to middlemen, they sell to their own co-operative – at the right time and in the right market.

"In Adilabad, which is a tribal area bordering Maharashtra in northern AP, this year the co-operative earned a profit of ₹ 35 lakhs . Which means each and every member earned ₹ 5000 more. And we did not give them anything for free."

In fact, farmers benefitted from the rise in soyabean price from ₹ 1450 a quintal to ₹ 2100.

Sahakar Mitra Sanstha has also set up India's first co-operative *dal* mill in India in a tribal area. It was inaugurated on 15th March, 2009.

"This season net of all costs they've made ₹ 11-12 lakhs in profits. I think if things go on track, in 3 years time they would have repaid all the loans as well."

Sahakar Mitra Sanstha has a 'head office' in Hyderabad and currently works in two districts of AP covering 50 villages – impacting about 2000 people.

"We could have easily expanded it to 20-30,000 people if we did not stick to the 'no subsidy' model. But just like with ADR, we are clear that some things are non-negotiable".

Trilochan is the CEO, but he has an able team on the ground, making it happen. Idealistic young fellows who've taken up the challenge. And are doing a very fine job.

"I am lucky to have a project manager who is a tribal, and an MBA. And the guy managing the *dal* mill is actually a gold medallist from IRMA. He's from Rajasthan, a Marwari by the name Biyani. Very smart guy, very happy doing this work."

And the work is really to empower villagers. Make them own the idea that things can change for the better − if they all come together as one.

Initially, Trilochan would go to a new village, people would gather and he would start a discussion.

"I don't go and say, 'Here, I've got the solution − do you like it'?"

Instead, he draws them out, gets them to start thinking.

"We have a general discussion on life. We talk about how many people live there, *kitni zameen hai, log kya karte hain...*"

At some point Trilochan will ask, "Where do you sell?"

They will reply, "To the *dalal* − the middleman."

If there is a blackboard someone is asked to start calculating how much the *dalal* is cheating them. Simple calculations reveal that the farmer is losing at least ₹ 2000 a year.

"True, but what can be done about it?" they say.

There is silence.

Then invariably some bright spark will say, "We need to get together and do something."

That's when Sahakar Mitra Sangh actually steps in and offers to help.

"This is all social mobilisation, whatever I instinctively feel. I haven't learnt it formally."

The reason the solution has to come from 'within' is there are so many barriers. One of the biggest, is caste.

A typical village meeting is held in a school building. On a *chataai*, right up front will be sanstha workers and people from the forward caste. The backward castes will sit against the walls and the Dalits will be right at the back.

"As soon as someone comes in, he knows where to sit down. And elephants cannot pull him out from that place."

"Marriage was never a priority for me, and one never made any efforts in that direction. It was not that I decided to remain single to do social work."

After some time, Trilochan asks his staff to conduct the meeting and goes out. He stands with the Dalits.

"I'll say, "*Beedi veedi pilao*" and a conversation starts.

After 10 minutes they say, "We agree with you but..."

"The co-operative will give us a good price. However my daughter is getting married in March, and I need to borrow ten thousand rupees. Will your co-operative lend me the money?"

Trilochan was clean bowled, "middle stump down".

Eventually they found a way to deal with the issue but the learning was that even the most efficient, logical solution may not 'work'. You have to understand your customer, your end-user and make it work for him.

Trilochan believes this two-district experiment can be taken to a national scale. Recently, NABARD has sanctioned a loan of ₹ 70 lakhs to set up an oil mill in Anantapur.

"We have funding from Sir Dorabji Tata Trust, HIVOS (a Dutch donor agency) and from the Ford Foundation. But to take this to the next level, I am trying to raise some ₹ 50 crores."

If he gets that Trilochan says he will quit his job and spend all his time on the rural poverty project.

"I'll buy a Scorpio and travel around India – start from Chhatisgarh, go through MP, Jharkhand, Bihar, Orissa and Karnataka. My idea is to network all the NGOs working on a similar livelihood agenda".

Many of these NGOs are already conducting Election Watch for ADR.

"I will say, 'Let's do this the same way. We've tested the co operative model – it works. Now you implement it in your area."

Then there are other dreams. Like building a house in the hills – from where you can see the snow-capped Nandadevi peak – and writing a book or two on the subjects he knows and loves best. Politics and poverty.

"One has to think a little bit whom you are writing for and... what purpose. But my instinct is, write what you have to say – and to hell with it."

And that just about sums up his whole attitude to life!

———

ADVICE TO YOUNG ENTREPRENEURS

My advice is very simple – don't read books, don't take advice from anybody. Go into the field, spend some time and learn about the issues first hand.

If you talk about primary education, go to the villages or slums – talk to the children and their parents. If you're talking about rural poverty, go and talk to the poor. If you're talking about women's issues go to the women and talk to them.

Whatever it is you choose to do in life – even if it's not social entrepreneurship – just go and immerse yourself in that, learn from there and out of that a sensible action plan will come.

If you feel strongly about something – go for it.

I also believe that each person is unique (and perhaps brings with him/her a whole baggage from previous lives if one believes that... or genes if you want another explanation).

This is what we call 'sanskar' or *samskara* in Sanskrit. That plays a powerful role in our lives. Hence my life or anyone else's for that matter, goes largely along that path.

THE GIRL IN THE
MIRROR

Shaheen Mistri,
Akanksha

As a student, Shaheen Mistri got her friends to volunteer their time teaching kids from the slums. That small initiative with 15 children in a single borrowed classroom now covers 3500 children in 58 centres and 6 schools. And continues to inspire the youth to do their bit, for a better India.

In 1989, Shaheen Mistri was teaching kids in the Ambedkar Nagar slums.

In 1989, I passed by those very slums every single day, on my way to college.

Shaheen went inside the slum and connected with the human beings who lived there.

I observed the slum from the giant windows of the TIFR bus, and rued the day the encroachment began.

Shaheen had an open heart, while mine was closed.

Shaheen decided it was she who had to make a difference whereas I – and millions of middle class citizens like me – decided it was none of our business.

Shaheen's story speaks to my soul. It affirms that you are never too young.

Never too rich.

Never too privileged.

To dedicate your life to 'doing something'.

And you can do it in your own unique way. Shaheen is passionate and compassionate, yet practical and tactical. She may be into social work but she does not look like a typical social worker.

Shaheen has a sense of personal style and dignity – which is all her own.

At the Akanksha office in Voltas compound, we sit crosslegged on a carpeted floor.

"You don't mind, do you?" she asks. "This is so much more natural... comfortable."

I'm not sure it is, in Levi's jeans that are slightly too tight. But the real source of discomfort is her story itself.

It made me think, "How come I, born and brought up in India, never felt the way she did when I looked at a slum child?"

THE GIRL IN THE
MIRROR

Shaheen Mistri,
Akanksha

Shaheen Mistri is a child of 'no fixed address'.

A child, so to say, of the world.

"I was born in Bombay, both my parents grew up in Bombay, went to school in Bombay…"

However, when she was just a few months old her father – a Citibanker – moved cities and Shaheen celebrated her second birthday in a whole new country – Lebanon.

"We were in Beirut for three years – my brother was born there. When war broke out we shifted to Greece. Actually, we were on vacation in Greece and never went back."

Shaheen started her schooling in Greece and then moved to Indonesia – Jakarta – where she studied upto class 8. By which time Shaheen had attended 'many, many different schools'.

"I was in about 10 different schools; started out in a French school system, then the English, the American, then the international school system. Everything except the Indian school system."

The family then moved to the US where Shaheen joined Greenwich Academy – a small private girls school in Connecticut. After high school, she joined Tufts University.

"All through my childhood we would come back to Bombay because we had grandparents and family here. If not every year, at least every two years."

And these long summer breaks were not just about having fun. From the age of 12, Shaheen was doing volunteer work at the Happy Home School for the Blind.

"My mum actually, was one of the founders for the EAR School for hearing impaired people... so I sort of grew up on doing that."

When Shaheen was 18, in her second year at Tuft's, she was in India for her summer holiday and made a radical announcement.

"I decided that I should stay in India."

Why? Well, that's a story in itself.

"So, by that time I knew I *loved* working with children and animals – those were my two big passion areas. I actually went through the big dilemma of whether I should work with kids or whether I should work with pets."

Also, by this time Shaheen was feeling a little 'rootless', having moved so much. Although she didn't feel Indian, she was very curious about India. The stark contrast between elite suburban life in America and poverty-at-every-street-corner in India hit Shaheen hard.

Hard enough to want to stay on here, and make some kind of difference.

"At the high school I graduated from, the only conversation would be about the size of the car you got on your 16th birthday! So I think the contrast when I came back to India – when I was 18 – it really, really hit me."

Shaheen asked herself: "Why am I going back?"

Her heart replied, "Whatever you do here can be – perhaps – more useful then anything you do there."

It was not so much a 'head' decision, more just an instinct thing. Why not try it out?

There was a safety structure – the option of going back to Tuft's the next year. Which made it easier.

"Initially I told my parents, 'Let me take off for a year and see what it's like. I can always go back if I need to'."

Shaheen's parents agreed, although they had doubts about whether she would get admission into a good college in India. After all, it was already three months into the college year.

> **"I had come from a place where in my naivete I felt like everyone had so much... and coming into a situation where people have so little. Later I realized how stupid all that was."**

"The first college I went to was Xavier's, because both my parents were from Xavier's and I thought, "If I get in there, they'll will be happy."

They said, "You can't just get admission in Xavier's... the admissions are already over and you can't even meet the principal."

When the door is closed, find a window. Well, that is what Shaheen did – literally. She snuck in through a back entrance and walked into Father Emil D'Cruz's office.

She said, "Look I really want to do something and I want to be in India and want to do *something* good... and I don't know exactly what that means but I really need to be here. So you need to give me admission."

"Father was so taken aback by this stupid girl coming in who was so different that he said yes, he had some small management quota I think. And that's how I got admission."

Won't take no for an answer – it's the hallmark of any entrepreneur.

Shaheen thus joined Xavier's and the first thing she tried to do was discover this new world all around her.

"I really felt a need to understand this city in a different way than my cousins and my family around me did. So I actually went to *The Times of India* and met this reporter there and I said, 'Can I intern with you... just follow you around for a couple of months'?"

And that was how Shaheen's immersion into the 'other India' began. She visited courts, jails, police stations – and was completely fascinated. At the same time Shaheen discovered the Social Service League – or SSL – at St Xavier's. One day they were going on a trip to the slums (Ambedkar Nagar, in Cuffe Parade). Shaheen asked to tag along.

"I sort of entered with them but somehow I just made my own way... They were doing some work with women or some medical thing that day. But I actually went and met this girl who was exactly my age. Her name is Sandhya."

"She was one of those people... I had this immediate sense of connection with her. She had this really warm, welcoming smile."

Shaheen did not speak a word of Hindi.

Sandhya did not speak a word of English.

But the hearts speaks when the tongue is tied. *Dil ki ek apni hi zubaan hoti hai.*

Sandhya welcomed Shaheen into her house and that little hut became a 'base' for the idealistic young woman in search of she-knew-not-what. A home away from home.

"Everyday from college I would just go and hang out there at her house. A few days later some kids peeped their heads inside and said, 'Didi teach us English.' And some mother came with a sick child and said, 'Will you help me take the child to the hospital'?"

So Shaheen started doing a lot of 'individual one-off things' and started a little class in Sandhya's house, teaching a few of the children and found she really loved it.

"I would research and look up things, think back to my school days and figure out activities to do with the kids."

In fact, Shaheen really looked forward to college ending so that she could come and spend 3-4 hours in the slums with those kids. That was 1989.

In the summer vacation, Shaheen visited her family – they had moved to Saudi Arabia – and suddenly she had a very uncomfortable feeling.

"I thought to myself, 'What I'm actually doing is making a few people dependent on me. What if I go back to the US next year? Does this make any sense'?"

Shaheen realised that if she really wanted to do something it was time to commit to something long term. To be thoughtful and really make a difference.

"So I came back from that trip with this conviction that I want to be here, I want to do this but I don't know exactly what that means. I know it is with kids and I know it is with poverty and that changed a lot of things. Even though it was a mental decision it made me see things very differently."

Along with a friend, Shaheen went around the slum and conducted a survey of sorts.

"We visited 400-500 families, just asking if we were to do anything, what would you want us to do?"

Two things came up. One was various issues around housing (slum demolitions were common in those days and rather 'inhumane'). When the BMC squad was done, the area would almost look like a war zone, she recalls.

But the second big issue was the pressing need to get the kids out of the slums.

"I felt like if they are here it is really hard to teach them because two more kids come everyday, someone gets dragged out and someone gets called for work."

The kids Shaheen was working with at that time has never seen a school and she strongly felt, that unless they see a school they would not want to be in a school.

That's when she had an idea. Why not get a space where the kids could actually come to. Every evening.

So many schools had empty classrooms which could be utilised after hours. All that was needed was volunteers to teach. As they say charity begins at home, so the first people Shaheen decided to tap were her classmates at Xavier's.

"I actually went back to college and asked a whole bunch of people around me whether they would be interested in helping. The thing that was truly amazing is that nearly 98% of them wanted to do something."

And they weren't doing something just because they did not know what to do. Or they felt that as one person they couldn't really make a difference because the problems were so overwhelming.

So when Shaheen said that in addition to everything else that you have in your life – your movies, friends, your college work, all of that – wouldn't you be willing to take out 2-3 hours a week to do

"I remember so clearly the first time I saw my kids' homes demolished – they would literally get bulldozers and not care whether there is a puppy in the way or a child sitting there."

something that is going really make a difference? The answer was a resounding "yes".

Saathi haath badaana is the theme song of every enterprise and more so, in a socially driven one.

So the 'teachers' were mobilised. Finding the space, however, was a big issue. Shaheen visited 20 different schools and they all said no, for the most illogical reasons.

One principal, a nun, actually said, "Your kids are fishermen's kids, they wear glass bangles and the bangles will slash our desk".

Talk about a creative way to say 'no'!

Others said, "It's a lovely idea but so revolutionary. Our kids will get diseases from your kids by sitting on the same desk..."

All the rejection only made Shaheen all the more determined – to get her way.

"I think I was really, really angry. I was thinking, how can we in today's world be talking about the idea of basic education being revolutionary?"

Finally the 21st school – Holy Name High School – became the first Akanksha centre.

"Father Ivo D'Souza was just incredible. I have always felt through all these years of Akanksha, it is like suddenly someone comes to your rescue and you don't even need to explain your case to those people. They just get it."

Father Ivo looked at Shaheen and said, "What's wrong?"

She said, "I have been to all these schools and all I need is a classroom."

No bathroom, no storage space, just one empty classroom.

"I will bring the materials, clean the class, we will leave with the materials. We just need a physical space to teach the kids."

Father said, "Sure – when do you want to start?"

Shaheen said, "Tomorrow."

Because she did not want to give him time to go back to the Board and for them to 'rethink' it. And that's how the seed of Akanksha was planted. In a tiny flowerpot, watered with love and sincerity.

Shaheen gathered a group of kids, got together the volunteers from Xavier's and started classes. Of course, the volunteers were clueless about how to teach. Which was good because the group ended up improvising and creating their own methods. More suited for kids who'd never been through formal schooling.

"We would sit on Sundays at each others' homes and sort of brainstorm on what we want to do next. We had this idea of projects – we chose one every week and taught maths and language through it."

Twenty years down the line, Akanksha has evolved to a different level – "it's a much more thoughtful programme and curriculum". But many of those *basic* ideas which came out of instinct are still part of the culture, the very DNA of the organisation.

"Whether it was the idea that teaching really needed to be interactive, or that we really needed to be friends with the kids. That they need to have fun, they needed to enjoy learning – all of that was right from the beginning."

In fact the original goal of Akanksha had very little to do with learning. It was really defined as 'a good time'. The idea was that every kid deserved a childhood and can we give every

"Some of the children I started teaching when they were 3 and 4 are now in the same colleges that me and my friends went to."

child the space – even if it is for 2-3 hours a day – to actually be children.

To be in a space where they were safe, where they are cared for, where they have fun.

"Gradually, things evolved and we started thinking a lot more about education and what they need and jobs – all of that came along later."

Akanksha formally came in existence in 1991. In 1992, Shaheen graduated from St Xavier's and went abroad – to Manchester University – for further studies. The course? Master's in Education.

Wonderfully enough, Akanksha had a strong and dedicated team – and carried on.

"I had a pretty regular group of volunteers and also a friend of mine – Aarti – who's still very much in touch with us. She is in Bangalore now... she assumed leadership while I was away."

At that time Akanksha volunteers would literally have to go from house to house, sometimes bathe kids, dress them, pull them out of home and get them to school.

"So Aarti would write funny letters about all this. Like 'today those kids came to school who haven't been coming' and 'today we had to drag 10 kids'. These were all the big achievements."

In 1993, Shaheen returned to India. And the exposure abroad helped in more ways than one.

"My degree was in Education but it wasn't a teaching degree, it was a degree in Education Project Planning for developing countries. I actually wrote my thesis, interestingly, on the role of the Indian college student in India's educational development."

A large part of these initial ideas are very similar to the whole 'Teach for India'* idea now. The challenge being: How does one really mobilise young people in India to bring about change in education?

* Different from TOI's Teach India campaign. See www.teachforindia.org

But this was to come much later. Shaheen's immediate concerns on returning were how to become a more formal organization. Different from the entirely volunteer-driven and student-powered effort of the initial four years.

"I came back and took a few very different decisions. We recognised that volunteers were a huge asset but there were also drawbacks on relying entirely on volunteers as an organisation, so that is when we got in professional teachers."

The teacher-student ratio was made more manageable, kids were divided age-wise. To raise the bar, Shaheen would have to do something she had never done before. She would have to raise money.

So far the Akanksha model did not *need* funds.

Volunteers taught for free. The space was free. The only cost was one bus which would go from Cuffe Parade to the school in Colaba which was about ₹ 20,000 a year. A small amount which could be raised easily from family and friends.

"We also collected resources like stationery in kind."

But professionalising the teaching meant salaries. So Shaheen started a scheme called 'Sponsor a Centre". After Holy Name, Akanksha moved to other centres. And it started gradually but then took off quite rapidly.

From a single class with 15 children, Akanksha grew to 8 centres handling 480 kids by 1998. In 2002 Akanksha also started working in Pune.

"The 'Sponsor a Centre' Scheme was really nice because they didn't cost a lot of money – just about ₹ 2 lakhs per year – and donors felt a direct connection to one centre."

So it was a kind of 'personal' bonding. Building an emotional connection between the donor and beneficiaries.

The reason so many people connected with Akanksha was that it was so simple, so idealistic yet so practical.

"The whole idea was that these children were in dysunctional schools. *Despite* that, how do you turn around the kid's life?"

The program developed very organically, over the years. Like a soup made special by chefs tossing in what's needed, after each tasting. A blend all its own.

The stock ingredients were basic English and Maths. To that a dash of values, self esteem and confidence.

"Then we must continue to build on the original idea of 'a good time' into everything we do. That led to all the extra curricular programmes and activities. And as our kids were growing up we realised that it's not just about the academics and the character, it's also about preparing them for a job. So we added that as a fourth goal."

"More recently we said, you know, even if we are not a school the reality is that kids need to pass the 10th standard exams. So how do we actually set that as a goal? In the older years we now give them a lot of extra study classes, do a lot of study habits. So eventually it became these five really big goals we wanted to focus on, with every child."

But the belief was still that this is 'supplemental', it's easy to replicate because a very big piece of the model was the fact that it used available resources.

"Even today we pay a nominal rent of ₹ 1000-1500 per month in some of the schools, but in general all our spaces are free. And we still use a lot of volunteers."

The whole idea was 'let's not create anything new', let's just find resources and bring them together.

Then about five years ago Shaheen began to question whether even *that* was enough.

"Even though we were seeing kids sort of turn around their lives we were losing many kids too."

Kids would go back to their villages when the slum was demolished, for one. And it was never taken as seriously by parents as school because it was, ultimately, a supplemental program.

"So we said, if we are really trying to be a school then why not just work within the system and actually take over schools? So our more recent program – and something I think Akanksha is going to move a lot more towards in the next years – is the 'Adopt a School' project."

Of course it wasn't a 'Quick Gun Murugan' takeover. It happened in phases. Starting with just trying to understand the system, then training teachers, putting Akanksha teachers into the system. and then, actually taking over a school completely and running it.

"We've now come up with a really interesting model that is demonstrating quite a bit of success in Bombay and Pune. And our hope is to grow these schools and to show that kids can not just achieve, but achieve at the *same level* as any child anywhere if you are able to give them opportunities."

"And we are not trying to create these schools as 'islands of excellence' where you pour money in and look very different. We're saying, within the same money that the government is spending, can we just use it really, really very differently? Invest it in our people in the school instead of peripheral things and really bring about dramatic gains in student achievement."

So far, Akanksha has 'taken over' six schools.

It's all hugely inspiring, but 18 years down the road, how does Akanksha measure the impact of its program?

"Great question," says Shaheen. Impact on a human being's life is intangible and yet, measurability is important. If only to help you improve on what you do, year after year.

Akanksha uses several parameters. For example, student achievement.

"We have a mid-term individual child assessment and an end of the year child assessment. All that data is stored and analysed and we look at trends. It's an internal assessment but it's not conducted by the teacher so there is a level of objectivity to it."

Akanksha also does a 'Model Audit' of its 60-odd centres.

"We look at a bunch of different criteria every single month through what we call a 'Model Centre Meeting' . The idea is to ask, "What's your model centre, what's your dream? And how does a whole team set the goal of moving towards that?"

The criteria includes everything from how well is your class display organised, to how effectively you have used volunteers in your classroom; to are you checking the understanding of the kids. All the information comes into the Akanksha office and the findings are shared with the whole team.

Most interestingly, the Akanksha schools are now working E-I or Education Initiatives, a company which administers the 'ASSET' test to students.

"We are benchmarking our kids – what we are doing in our schools – with kids in schools like Cathedral."

So where do the Akanksha kids stand? Shaheen feels it's a little bit early to say because its new schools start at the kindergarten level, whereas ASSET is available only after class three.

"But we started a school four years ago in Pune* with class 3,4 and 5 children. When we measured the kids they were between 50-70% below the national average. Within one year of working with us, on many indicators they had achieved the national average. And in some, they were just a little below. So there's been dramatic progress!"

Personally, I feel the most dramatic indicator are the alumni of Akanksha.

"We actually have this researcher from Cambridge University who has done a full blown 'impact assessment study' looking at every one of our alumni, comparing them to other kids in the schools they attended, as well as kids in the community."

The numbers are small right now (around 150) but the results are astonishing.

87% of the Akanksha kids actually sat for and passed the SSC exam.

58% of them went on to college – some are now graduating.

"In addition to studying they all work because they need to. Many of them today are earning ₹ 15,000-20,000 a month at part time jobs. Largely because of fluency in English. And confidence."

A successful student is the best reward a teacher can get. And Shaheen did go down this road because of her love for children, and teaching. But does she get to really teach anymore?

"Horrible, I am telling you it's horrible, I hate it. I think about this all the time. In fact, I was telling someone about 2-3 days ago that I just feel like going back into the classroom and being a teacher."

Over the last two years it has become difficult – Shaheen now focuses more on the growth and expansion, management and mentorship of various programs.

* In collaboration with the Thermax Social Initiatives Foundation

"But any chance I get, I go into classrooms and I still do lessons… though I don't have my own group of kids anymore."

It's important to stay connected and Shaheen also closely interacts with the communities directly.

"I actually think it really keeps you rooted in terms of why you are here and what you are doing. So I spend some of my own personal time in the community, especially with the older kids who I worked directly with. And many of our Akanksha kids are working here in the office. So that's great as well."

At one level there is still that personal touch but the organisation is now definitely 'large'. Akanksha is now 700 people (including 350 volunteers who are 'regulars').

The 60-odd centres employ 120 teachers. Then there's the staff – people who supervise the centres, social workers in the community, big group of helpers (mothers of our kids who are actually Akanksha's link to the community).

"We also have a very small core team of managers. There is a head of Bombay and there is a head of Pune and then there is a CEO who's not me because I've moved out now."

Why?

"I stepped aside to set up 'Teach for India'."

'Teach for India' is inspired by 'Teach for America', a program which invites young graduates in the US to spend two years of their lives teaching in inner-city schools. The idea being to sensitise young people to important issues and gain leadership experience, whatever career they ultimately decide to take up.

But it wasn't a case of studying 'Teach for America' and deciding to replicate the model. It happened differently.

"A group of us began to be lot more concerned about what's really the solution to all this. It's fine that Akanksha is changing the lives of a few thousand kids but really what is that, if you look at the size of the problem?"

"And you draw so much inspiration from seeing the Akanksha kids when they are older that you feel, 'Oh my God, every child needs to reach that potential'."

That really got Shaheen thinking about how does one bring about systemic change.

"There are 2 kinds of youth in India – one who choose to go and yell on TV and the others, who want to *do* something. For them, there is 'Teach For India'."

"I deeply believe that education is really complex, that there are no magical, miracle solutions. Educating a child takes a lot of time, it takes a lot of effort, you can't replace a teacher. The teacher is pivotal in all of this."

"So knowing that this is really hard but also really important but also being compelled by the scale and the need to bring about substantial change – that is how a few of us got together and started talking."

At the same time, coincidentally, a few 'Teach for America' alumni had come to Akanksha.

Shaheen was struck by these young people, full of passion for education. Young people who could have done anything but had chosen to teach in the most challenging classrooms. And, spoke so highly about the experience and how it had changed them at a personal level.

That's when Shaheen went to the US, to understand the 'Teach for America' program better and meet founder Wendy Kopp. Shaheen invited Wendy to come and see the context, to understand if a similar model could be implemented.

The answer was yes, and no.

" 'Teach for India' will adhere to a few of the core principles of 'Teach for America'. Like the fact that this is a movement of the people, you need to do it through teaching. You need to invest a lot in these young people so that they are really well trained and supported so that they can achieve excellence in the classrooms."

"The most important part of the model is that it's not just about putting teachers in the classroom. The idea is that you are putting your next generation of leaders in the classroom."

The program recognises that these very bright young people will complete a teaching stint and take up careers in business, technology, entertainment or even government. And when they become leaders – at that next level – they will bring about transformational change and really address the issue.

But in the nitty gritties of how it works, 'Teach for India' is evolving its own unique model.

In January 2009, 'Teach for India' invited applications for the very first time. 2000 young people sent in their CVs from all over the country. Fresh graduates, software engineers, investment bankers – all united by the idea of teaching as a way to 'give back' to society. As well as gain a completely different kind of work experience.

"We chose 87 'Teach for India' fellows in the first cycle. In our second cycle, we received about 6000 applications, and will be choosing about 150."

The chosen ones will teach at low income private schools in Mumbai and municipal schools in Pune. "So these are the first two places, the idea is that within 5 years we should spread nationally."

Scaling up is the biggest concern for any entrepreneur. At some point, it's not just about drive and determination but about funding as well.

"Well it is a huge concern. Akanksha is registered as a trust but you are absolutely right – the funding strategy needs to be really carefully thought through."

Most of the money for Akanksha came through word of mouth. Because people were able to see the kids, there were always a large number of volunteers involved and they spread a lot of goodwill.

Then, there was Shaheen's personal goodwill. Her family background and connections helped to open many heavy wooden doors, and wallets.

"Initially a lot of supporters were from the Citibank family – the people who worked with my dad who saw me growing up and thought, 'Well at least one of us is attempting to do something good while everyone else is going into banking'."

When you speak to Shaheen, you can't help being moved by her intensity. Like any great communicator, she knows exactly how to hold your attention. And that is a quality that has certainly come in handy.

"I think I also had the advantage of living in so many different countries and interacting with so many different kinds of people. So I have always found it very easy to tell my story. I mean I think that so many people have compelling work but the little additional advantage of being able to tell their story in a way that is compelling helps a lot in being able to raise money."

The strategy with 'Teach for India' is slightly different. The initial funding for the program has largely been from foundations while seed funding came from the Akanksha board. But now, money is being raised from more sources and more aggressively. And here too, it's about finding an angle that captures not just the mind but the heart.

"What we emphasise is that if you are donating to 'Teach for India' you are not just putting teachers in the classroom. You are really developing the next generation of empathetic and effective leaders."

"I think, people are increasingly seeing that there is such a crisis of leadership in the country so that is really an important investment for people to be making."

Like 'Sponsor a Centre', Shaheen now has a 'Sponsor a Fellow' scheme where each donor pays ₹ 6 lakhs for two years. This takes care of the fellow's stipend – ₹ 20,000 per month – as well as cost of training and support.

"If you think about that in terms of putting a teacher in a classroom it is a lot of money. But if you think about that in terms of investing in someone who in their life is going to be a leader and really help the country become better, and be part of a movement of people who are well-networked together… then you think about that investment differently."

The 'Teach for India' challenge is that costs are going to be higher – it's not the old *jugaadu* model Akanksha ran on.

"As you can imagine, if you are recruiting the best and the brightest and the most committed young people, then our level of execution to deliver everything has to be outstanding. So we need an increasingly high caliber staff … it is all quite frightening at this stage."

Funnily enough, Shaheen had no butterflies in her stomach when she set out on this path as an 18-year old. It's always tougher when you are 'successful' and need to live up to the reputation you've built.

And what a reputation it is. The Akanksha 'brand' has always been much bigger than its actual footprint.

"Akanksha only has 3,500 kids, so it is not a big organisation in terms of its impact yet. But it's been really significant I think in terms of its quality and how it works with kids."

Shaheen says she never consciously built the brand (though she is now trying to, for 'Teach for India'). It just happened, through goodwill generated from art auctions and the annual Akanksha musical. Both of which were started as initiatives for the kids.

"Our kids made stunning products and cards. The amount of brand it built for us without us knowing it really helped a lot."

The musicals also, were hugely successful.

"Again, the focus was on Akanksha and on our kids. We wanted to show the city that we can do the best musical in town. We wanted them to come in thinking, 'Oh it's going to be like any charity show' and leave feeling, 'Wow, you should get all these kids on a plane and take them to another country to perform'."

The intent and the honesty of purpose behind the events – and the fact that they were different and unique – generated a lot of interest from the media. Ergo, brand Akanksha did not have to spend a penny.

Intent and honesty of purpose are also most valuable when it comes to attracting team members. Retaining them, of course, takes even more.

"Giving people ownership over what they want to do – I think that helps a lot. We have an amazing group of people, they are so passionate. The second thing is choosing people that really fit in with the values of the organisation. Making people accountable and giving them really concrete goals."

And then it is about showing people the end result, the impact of their work.

"I work with kids so it is very flexible, it is not like I have a job where I am gone in the morning and come back at night and I feel scared to call my kids in between."

"Someone who is teaching five-year-olds may be going crazy in class each day... But if you show her a well put together alumni whose life has been transformed that is a really compelling reason to stay engaged with Akanksha."

Now you might be a socially motivated organisation but economic motivation drives the people working for you. And if you want to attract good people, certainly, you must be able to pay – if not a market rate – some minimum 'decent' sum of money.

Shaheen agrees.

"I really believe that this is one of the biggest problems in the sector and until we can really pay people competitively, we can never attract the best talent. You get that odd person that's willing to make the sacrifice."

"But having said that it is not so easy because we are dependent on donors and we are growing so quickly and we need so many people. It's not about raising the money for five great people, right? You are employing hundreds of people, so it is a complicated task."

Akanksha's approach has been "let's keep working on it".

"We were abysmally bad in the beginning, you know, we couldn't pay anyone anything. Then we paid a few people hardly anything for years. But now we are getting closer and closer to paying people well."

Shaheen too gets a salary. In the beginning it was 'very little'. Now it is 'more than enough'.

And what about the effect of being devoted to Akanksha... on her personal life? Has Shaheen managed to find that thing called 'balance'.

"I am not very balanced," she says candidly. "I have two daughters – a 5 year old (Sana) and a 10 year old (Samara)."

Where did she find the time for that, I ask and she laughs – "I know what you mean."

Yes, she was working till the very last day and no, she did not really take a breakthrough it all.

"I really literally was in a meeting when I went into labour and I went to the hospital. And I think a week after I was home I started working again."

Does Shaheen ever feel guilty?

"I really want my girls to feel like I tried to meet my potential in my own life. I don't want them to think I was a perfect mother, I know that they are going to get angry about the fact that I wasn't there for every birthday party. But to me that is significantly less important."

Shaheen hopes, when her girls grow up and talk about her they see a mom who really tried hard to do something with her life and really cared about people.

"That is the sort of legacy that I want to leave to them."

And luckily, she says, her girls are just incredible.

"They've never made me feel that I am not there enough. They are really well-adjusted, they are really independent, very creative, incredibly caring about different things."

"So I feel like somewhere – it's ok. But having said that it is difficult you don't have enough time for everything and it is exhausting."

There are some daily rituals.

"I am with them every morning, I get them ready. I am with them almost every evening and I don't go out a lot at night."

Because of the nature of her work Shaheen is able to take a couple of hours off in the middle of the day. Or put them to sleep and then go back to work late into the night.

"I've found my own strange balance," she says, "where I do what I feel like I want to do with them and what I need to do with them. But it is definitely not like a typical you know 'balance'."

Shaheen is lucky to have a wonderful support system – her parents, who now live in India.

"I actually use my parents' home as a base during the week, so from school they go there and then they go to their various classes. So by the time they come, it's usually 7-7.30 pm and I try to be home."

"Then I also have a lovely girl who's been with me for several years who is absolutely unbelievable; she is lovely, hardworking and adores the kids. And when I go out of town I think my kids are so blessed – they have 10 different people they can choose to spend the night with. From all their cousins, their friends..."

Shaheen feels it's really not been all that bad – it's been 'manageable'. But let's face it, a man would not even have to mention that point more than once. It would be understood, that he has 'different' priorities.

"I think at times it gets out of balance and I recognise that and I try to re-balance it a little. My mom always feels that I don't do it well enough but you do what you can do!"

Unconventional choices – that's Shaheen Mistri. And that extends to her personal life as well.

"I actually got divorced before my first daughter was born. So I was married for 4 years and then just when I was six months pregnant I got divorced. I basically brought them up on my own, obviously I am in contact with him because of Samara but other than that..."

She says it very evenly, matter-of-factly and I want to know more...

But it does not feel right to ask.

At the end of an hour with Shaheen I can only say, there is nothing typical about her. Including the way she dresses – which is rather too fashionable for an 'NGO' type.

"You don't look like a social worker", I say. You know, the *jhola-kurta-kajal* uniform...

"I tried for a while – when I started college here I only used to wear khadi saris. And it was terrible because my best friend in college – the first time she met me – came up to me and asked where the classroom was. She thought I was a professor!"

Shaheen has been through some 'crazy phases' but now, she is definitely comfortable in her own skin. Comfortable enough to wear jeans and a halter top to a panel discussion on 26/11 without worrying about how it will come across.

"I felt that when I came back, the most important thing, the thing that I value the most in other people is the ability to be yourself. I feel like you can't really pretend for too long to be somebody who you are not."

And yet, most of us go through life exactly like that. Like spectators, like passengers, like sleepwalkers. On the stage of life.

Shaheen wrote her own script, acted her own part, expressed who she was – with passion and intensity.

And that's why she is an inspiration – to each of us.

ADVICE TO YOUNG ENTREPRENEURS

I just think that you need to really believe, I mean that sounds so trite, but my biggest learnings have been that if you really want something to happen badly enough, you have enough belief in it you can make it happen.

I have seen that when we question things too much, we start to doubt our ability to get there. We don't try and so we don't reach.

There are some teachers who tell a child, "I believe in you. The world may have told you differently or treated you differently, but I know what you are capable of."

This belief makes that child start thinking about himself or herself differently.

Life is a lot about making a leap of faith, feeling passionately about something and then being able to *sustain* that passion and belief .

That is applicable to anything – whether it is the kind of career you want to make or what life you want to have.

I think people also feel like 'I don't want to do something small'. But to do something big, first you have to take small steps.

The days when nobody cares and nobody wants to sit and interview you and you have to carry trunkloads of books to the slums and walk – that's where the true learning comes from and I think being open to going through that really difficult phase is really important.

INTO THAT HEAVEN OF
FREEDOM

**Arvind Kejriwal,
Parivartan**

As an IRS officer, Arvind Kejriwal waged a secret war against his own department. This campaign – under the banner 'Parivartan' – later pioneered the use of RTI (Right to Information Act) to empower citizens. Arvind's dream is to see 'true democracy', where ordinary people regain the right to govern themselves.

Arvind Kejriwal has a smooth, unlined forehead. Which is a miracle, for a man who's been banging his head against the wall – for years.

Even a casual conversation about 'corruption', 'politicians' or the 'state of the nation' can depress the best among us. Things appear so hopeless, so grim.

But Arvind is made of sterner stuff. For the past ten years, he has waged a battle against various elements of the 'system'. His efforts have made a few dents, brought some small change – but there is a long long way to go.

Yet, he is cheerful. And certainly not cynical.

"The real issue is not corruption – that is only a symptom. What we need to work on is building democracy, in the real and honest sense of the term."

Which is what he is doing, through 'Parivartan'. Using the hammer of RTI and the nail of 'accountability', Arvind has created a movement.

But he needs more hands, to hit these nails into more walls. To put 'what must be' in place of what is.

So that into that heaven of freedom, may this country awake.

Amen.

INTO THAT HEAVEN OF
FREEDOM

Arvind Kejriwal,
Parivartan

Arvind Kejriwal was born in a village called Sivani in Hissar district of Haryana.

"My father was an electrical engineer. He kept changing jobs so I attended many different schools. But finally, he settled down with Jindal Strips Ltd, so from 8th class onwards I studied in Hissar."

A topper where academics was concerned, but zero in sports, Arvind's initial inclination was towards medicine.

"Till 10th class the desire to become a doctor was very strong. At the back of my mind I always had this element of wanting to 'serve the people'."

But a senior explained that 'whatever you do, you must do it in the best institutes'. But, seats at AIIMS are limited. Why not try for engineering instead?

That's how Arvind ended up joining IIT Kharagpur. And, after completing his Mechanical Engineering degree in 1989, he joined Tata Steel.

"I worked with Tata Steel for three years, and somewhere in this period I took the Civil Service exam."

In his first attempt, Arvind made it to the IRS (Indian Revenue Service). Keen to get into IAS, he took the exam again and got through the 'writtens'.

At this time, he went to the HR department at Tata Steel and asked for a transfer to the social welfare department.

They said, "That's not possible."

So Arvind quit and joined Mother Teresa's Missionaries of Charity.

Why the sudden desire to take up social service?

"I have no clue," he says.

The UPSC results were due in March. Arvind spent the next four months with Christian missionaries in the tribal areas in Bodoland. He then spent some time with the Ramakrishna Mission.

Then, the interview call came and Arvind went back home – to Haryana. But, he went and visited several villages and also did some work with the 'Nehru Yuva Kendra'.

"This period was more of learning. I would go to various organisations and see what kind of work they were doing. Several questions came up in my mind at that time, but then I got through the interview and once again got into the IRS." This time he joined, and the 'journey' came to an end. Working with the IRS – or Income Tax department as it is commonly known – was routine.

"I enjoyed working. People say that if you are honest, you are victimised. But I was never victimised. I got some of the best postings and I never faced any interference in my work. Neither was I ever asked to do 'wrong things'."

But at the back of his mind, the questions remained.

The Archbishop of Delhi had once said, "The biggest problem of our country is not Harshad Mehta stealing ₹ 3000 crores. It is when an ordinary person pays 200 rupees as bribe – and thinks it's okay." That impacts the psyche of the entire country. But *what* can be done about it? This is something Arvind often pondered on.

"A person wanting to lead an honest life does not have that option in this country. Can we provide him that option?"

After much thought and discussion, Arvind decided that telling people 'don't pay a bribe' was not enough. Someone had to provide an alternative.

"Let us start telling people that if a government official asks for a bribe, don't pay. We will pursue your case and get the work done for free of cost."

"While taking the IAS exams you feel
'I can make a difference'. Only when you
actually join this service do you realise
that's not going to happen."

It was essentially some like-minded people who came together under the banner 'Parivartan'.

"We started with the income tax department only and it worked very well."

At the time Arvind was still working with the Income Tax department – and yet, in a sense, working against it. Naturally, no one but his close family and friends knew about his involvement with the cause. The first thing Parivartan did was meet with the Commissioner in Delhi.

"We will bring to you cases where bribes are being asked for," they said.

The Commissioner said, "I will support you."

Parivartan then put up banners and hoardings in Delhi exhorting the *aam aadmi* to approach this forum, if anyone from the I-T department is asking you for a bribe.

"The moment these banners came up, the authorities decided we were painting them in a bad light. So they disowned us and, in public, the chief commissioner said that some disgruntled CAs and touts are behind this campaign – under the garb of 'Parivartan'."

Yet, a lot of cases did come. Parivartan would submit these cases, collectively, to the income tax authorities. As well as send the list of pending cases to members of Parliament, the Finance Minister, media and so on.

"For example, *Financial Express* did a half page story on all the cases that were with us, asking why the people were not getting their refunds."

This put tremendous pressure on the department and as a result, cases going through Parivartan were cleared in no time. "But overall, there was no change in the practice of the department."

The Parivartan campaign kicked off in January 2000. By August, Arvind felt that the scope of their efforts should be widened. He decided to take up an issue affecting all sections of the society. That issue was electricity.

"In August 2000, we started the same exercise with the Delhi Vidyut Board. We asked people not to pay bribes but come to us, instead. Parivartan will take up your case, free of cost."

The Chairman of DVB – Jagdish Sagar – was very co-operative. He appointed a special executive engineer in his office and said that whatever grievance cases come through Parivartan should be attended to immediately.

As part of the campaign, members of Parivartan – including Arvind – would sit outside the entrance of Delhi Vidyut board, distributing pamphlets. On one such occasion, an erstwhile colleague from Tata Steel came up to him and said, "What are you doing here?"

Thinking that Arvind had fallen on hard times, he added, "If you want, I can talk to Tata Steel and they will take you back!" Another time, a senior from the Income tax department caught him distributing pamphlets at Nehru Place.

But none of this deterred the double life of 'Officer Arvind, Citizen Kejriwal'.

"In end of 2000 I took study leave and till November 2001, we kept doing these activities."

But by the end of two years, Arvind started wondering, "How long are we going to do this?"

Tackling two departments in one city, Parivartan had its hands completely full. Yes, the effort was working, especially with the Vidyut Board.

"At one time there were more than 50 cases pending before the 'Bijli Adalat' every month. After we came in, the number came down to 3 or 4 cases a month."

But, how many people could Parivartan serve like this? How many departments could one organisation cover, how many officials could they meet?

"Parivartan is not a registered NGO.
You don't have to register, actually,
to do social work."

"I realised that we are not empowering people. We have also become middlemen, only unlike touts we don't take money."

The *system* was not shaken, in any way.

Even as Arvind wrestled with these issues, the government passed the RTI Act in Delhi, in December 2001.

"We got a copy of the Act and found it to be a very powerful instrument. But, no one knew about it!"

The Act states that every department will have an Officer declared as a 'Competent Authority'. Any citizen can submit an application seeking information related to that department. And the department would have to reply within a stipulated period of time.

Arvind decided to test if this worked, by sending applications to DSIDC (Delhi State Industrial Development Corporation), DVB (Delhi Vidyut Board) and MCD (Municipal Corporation of Delhi).

"In all these departments the Officers did not know who the 'Competent Authority' was. In fact, they were not even aware that such an Act had been passed in the Delhi legislature!"

Parivartan gave the officials copies of the Act. Nothing happened. So, they wrote to the Chief Minister and in January 2002, the CM held a meeting with officers of various government departments. Sheila Dikshit said, "RTI is law, and it must be implemented."

The following month one Ashok Gupta of Lakshmi Nagar, came to Parivartan with a grievance. He had applied for an electricity connection about 2 years ago. He was being asked to pay a bribe of ₹ 5000.

"Earlier we used to accept such cases. But this time, we drafted an RTI application and asked him to go and submit it."

10 days after he submitted his query, an officer from the Vidyut Board came to his house and said, "The connection is sanctioned."

This was surprising, to say the least. Because even cases routed through Parivartan usually took around 2 months to get resolved.

"From then on, we stopped accepting grievance cases. When anyone approached us we helped fill out the RTI application and submit it. And this way, their problems were quickly solved."

In the next 3 months, Parivartan helped to file over 200 applications. And all cases – many of them pending for years – were resolved in 15 to 20 days.

"We decided to use RTI in other government departments. 'If you have any legitimate work use RTI – it works better than bribery'. This was our message to people."

In March 2002, Arvind read about Aruna Roy and the *jansunwaai* 'social audit' she had undertaken in Beawar (Rajasthan). He went to meet her and understand the work of MKSS (Mazdoor Kisan Shakti Sanagthana).

MKSS was using RTI to battle corruption at the panchayat level. Much of the funds alloted under various government schemes were actually going to babus and middlemen. False entries in muster rolls were a common occurrence in employment guarantee schemes. Public works existed only on paper, but money was recorded as 'spent'.

"MKSS collected information from the panchayat and then, they would hold a public meeting. Villagers were present, the authorities were also present. People would then testify whether work had actually been done or not."

Arvind realised this was an extremely powerful exercise. He decided to implement the idea in Delhi.

"We have our office in Sundar Nagari, which is a slum area. We decided to file an RTI application to get records related to work carried out by various departments in Sunder Nagari, and neighbouring Seemapuri."

This exercise took much longer than usual.

"We can ask people to come to us and cases will be resolved. But as soon as we move out of the scene, the malpractices start again. This was a big worry!"

"It is a huge mafia, jobs were at stake. So they did not give it easily. But we kept pursuing the matter and finally, got information regarding 182 contracts."

Parivartan distributed this information block-wise and street-wise. Locality by locality, they beat drums, collected people, and held a public meeting.

They said, "MCD claims ₹ 2 crores was spent on the road in front of your house. ₹ 50 lakhs were spent on toilets."

The people came out and protested, "This is all a big fraud, no such work was done here!"

There was a lot of anger, lot of mobilisation. Parivartan then arranged for a *jansunwaai* where contracts were read out in the presence of authorities and the local MLA.

Ultimately it was found that of ₹ 1.3 crores allotted towards 64 contracts, items worth ₹ 70 lakhs were missing. 29 electric motors were shown as 'paid for', not a single one had been installed. 29 hand pumps were supposed to be paid for – of them, 15 were missing.

There were several roads which existed only on paper. "We verified each and every contract in this way. After this, we prepared a very detailed report which showed each and every item paid for, checking if they were all installed or not. We gave copies of the report to the Chief Minister and MCD Commissioner."

Wonderful, but no action was taken. No one was suspended. An order or two was half-heartedly passed. But 'systemic change' remained, only on paper.

"Our first suggestion was that anytime a new project is to be implemented, it should be put up on a public notice board. An order to that effect was passed but never actually implemented."

Parivartan decided to file a PIL in the Delhi High Court, asking for action to be taken. Under the court's directions, an FIR was registered. The case is being fought in the district court – for the past 8 years.

"Nothing has come out of it."

Frustrating, for sure. But Parivartan continued its efforts. A lot of energy had been generated in Sunder Nagari. People now came to Parivartan saying, "We are concerned about the overflowing *nallahs,* but first we need food to eat."

So it was that Parivartan decided to take up the issue of PDS. Commonly known as *ration ki dukaan.*

"We had a case where a very poor woman called Triveni – with monthly income of ₹ 400-500 per month – was unable to get ration. The shop would either be closed, or did not have stock."

This, despite Triveni having an *Antyodaya* – or 'poorest of poor' – ration card.

Parivartan helped her file an RTI application. The application asked for copies of the cash memos issued in Triveni's name over the last 3 months.

"After one month she got a reply saying that 25 kgs of wheat and 10 kgs of rice had been given per month. Of course all this was fake information!"

But before any action could be taken, the shopkeeper approached her. He apologised and promised to supply ration every month – so that was that.

Arvind decided that if one family could get its due, why not the entire locality? Parivartan requested all 17 ration shops in the Seemapuri area for their food distribution records over the past 6 months.

"That's when the authorities got together. They knew that if this information leaked out, there will be *hungama.*"

They said, "These records cannot be given to you as they are the property of the shop keepers.The government has no control over them."

Parivartan filed an appeal and won it. Then, the shopkeepers went to the High Court and got a stay order against them.

"At one point of time there were 132 stay orders against us in Delhi." Eventually, the court lifted the stay orders and records were verified. But, Parivartan workers were badly beaten up.

"A girl's throat was slit; our records were burnt. There was lots of *tamasha*. The Food Commissioner of Delhi was transferred out..." Subsequently, the people of Sunder Nagari boycotted the ration shops and finally, the Delhi Government made some changes in the system.

Now, for the ration department, there is no need to file an RTI. Any Saturday, you can walk in between 2 pm and 5 pm and the records will be shown to you.

If there is a discrepancy, then the shop will be cancelled on the spot. "When this order was first passed the Food Commissioners were very helpful and a lot of ration shops were closed down. But over time the department office itself became a battleground."

A mob of 300-400 shopkeeprs would gather outside and prevent people from going to verify their records. The few who managed to get in were beaten up when they came out.

"Again, I must admit, in some areas people are getting ration. But I don't think on a systemic level there has been a big change." But, every failure or 'half-success' only led Arvind to push harder. To find better, more workable solutions.

Next, Parivartan decided to take up the issue of 'water privatisation'. "In November 2004, I read a newspaper article about the Delhi Government's decision to privatise water. Several NGOs were opposing this move, so we decided to find out more."

Parivartan filed an RTI application asking for copies of all records related to this project. After 6 months, they got copies of about 10,000 documents.

"This was a World Bank funded project going on in complete secrecy, for the last 6 years. We studied this project and realised that if implemented, it would be a disaster. And this was not just our finding."

Parivartan sent these documents to IIM Ahmedabad and IIM Bangalore. 35 professors from IIMB and 15 professors from IIMA wrote to the Prime Minister, asking him to cancel the project.

"There was a lot of uproar. We distributed a large number of two page pamphlets all over Delhi saying that 'your water was at stake'. Finally, the Delhi Government withdrew its loan application from the World Bank.

"Now all these things – water privatisation, corruption, bribery, PDS – it got us thinking. There are so many sectors, so many problems, and in each case RTI is a powerful tool. But the battle cannot be fought by one Parivartan!"

Arvind decided to enlist foot soldiers to the cause. To make the mission a *movement*.

In 2006, Parivartan launched a campaign titled 'Drive against bribe'. This campaign aggressively promoted a single thought: "Don't pay bribe, use RTI to get what is due to you."

"We contacted NGOs from across the country and enlisted their support. 1500 volunteers were trained and there were also 8 media houses including NDTV, *Hindustan Times*, *The Hindu* and regional papers who came in as media partners."

From July 1-15, 2006, these volunteers set up help centres in 55 cities across India and helped people in filing RTI petitions.

"In 15 days, 22,000 RTI applications were filed. We had several success stories – typically work pending for months and even years was done in 3-4 days flat!"

The experience was an eye-opener, in more ways than one. Parivartan is not even a 'registered' NGO, so it is not funded by any corporate or developmental agency. People often expressed doubts whether such an organisation could 'scale up'.

"If you want to bring about a movement of the people, then money and time should come from the people. Only then they will feel this is our movement."

But lack of money – far from being a hindrance – actually helped mobilise support.

For instance, when Parivartan met with NGOs, the first question they would ask was, "Where will the money come from?"

Arvind's response was simple, "*Aapka sheher hai, aapka desh hai, aapki ladaai hai... aapko hi sab kuch karna hai.*"

And the NGOs raised their own funds.

Similarly, media houses gave free advertisements, in support of a good cause.

"One day we calculated – so many cities, so many people, so many volunteers – the 'budget' would have easily exceeded ₹ 15-20 crore rupees."

What Parivartan actually spent was ₹ 80,000.

"The other thing we ensured was that Parivartan remained completely in the background. It was *everyone's* campaign."

And even as an ongoing effort, that remains the philosophy. Parivartan operates with just 4 full-time staff and total monthly overheads of ₹ 40,000. That money comes from individual donors.

"*Logon ke chalne se chalta hai,*" is how Arvind likes to put it.

2006 was a watershed in more ways than one. It was the year that Arvind finally quit the IRS. After taking study leave, unpaid leave, and special leave, he formally resigned in February 2006.

It was also the year that Arvind received the Ramon Magsaysay Award for Emergent Leadership. A recognition of his commitment to the cause, and a chance to take the effort to the next level.

"With water privatisation, it was more of an ad hoc kind of reaction to a particular problem. I felt we need a system in place where we can study the various governance systems on an ongoing basis."

Thus Arvind set up an office called 'Public Cause Research Foundation' (PCRF), using the Magsaysay award money as seed capital. Apart from research the Foundation had instituted 'RTI Awards' to honour individuals, commissioners and officers who are doing extraordinary work in Right To Information.

"We studied 52,000 orders passed by 104 information commissioners in the country and ranked all of them." Naturally, this created a controversy of sorts.

"But the rating is only on the basis of their orders," he shrugs.

The RTI Awards themselves are funded by Narayana Murthy and the Tata Trust.

RTI was no doubt a stupendous tool, and it could be and should be put to excellent use. But the larger question remained.

"Wherever, you go, there are various problems. *Bijli, paani, sadak...* But the common thread in all these issues was lack of governance."

This 'democracy' – which we are so proud of – is actually a farce.

"The trouble is, you go out and vote once in 5 years. After that, as a citizen, you have absolutely no say in governance. *Koi aapko poochta nahin!*"

Over the last couple of years, PCRF has been researching this subject. What kind of governance system do other countries have? What kind of governance systems existed in ancient or medieval India? And what comes out is quite fantastic.

"We believe democracy is a modern concept, but democracy has existed in India since Buddha's time," exclaims Arvind. In fact, Vaishali was the first 'republic' in the world.

"If I tell you *desh mein do hazaar crore ka ghotala ho gaya*, it's just a story. But if I tell you the *kachcha* road outside your house has been 'made' last year, as per municipal records, then your blood boils."

> **"Some people work in education, others are opening hospitals; I ask that all people work toward making us a real democracy. Everything else will fall into place."**

"When I say republic, the first thing that comes to your mind is elections. But elections are not democracy. *We* have equated elections with democracy."

In Buddha's time, in Vaishali, there were no elections. The king's son became the next king but, these kings had little or no say in important matters. Almost all decisions were taken in *gram sabhas* or public meetings.

This system of governance continued to be in force till 1860, when it was dismantled by the British and replaced by the 'collector system'.

"All the powers that the people enjoyed earlier, were invested in the collector now. Each part of a person's life was departmentalised; education department, health department, irrigation department and so on."

Unfortunately, at the time of Independence, we did not change the system. We just replaced the British collector with an Indian collector!

"When you study other countries – the US, for instance – at the local or county level, all decisions are taken by the public. You have regular town hall meetings where you can decide on things which affect your life."

And hold your elected officials responsible.

"I don't think our government asks citizens these things *anywhere* in our country!"

When Parivartan met Sheila Dixit, she said, "The people want water privatisation."

Arvind countered, "People don't."

So who decides whether the people want it or not?

"If you have *mohalla sabhas* all over Delhi i.e. you divide the city into small-small parts and people meet on a monthly basis, they can decide whether they want water privatisation or not."

And the collective voice of these *mohalla sabhas* becomes the voice of the people.

"This is the kind of democracy we envision – we call it *Swaraj*. This is what Gandhiji talked about; that this country would be a federation of six lakh villages, every village a 'republic' unto itself."

So while RTI work continues, Swaraj is taking more and more of Parivartan's time and attention. In Delhi, the concept of Swaraj is actually being implemented, on an experimental basis.

"We spoke to some councillors, good people, who liked the idea and agreed to try it in their area. We have divided one ward of 40,000 people into ten parts. Each part is called a *mohalla,* and consists of approximately 4000 voters."

The first *mohalla* meets on the first Saturday; the second on the next Saturday and so on. This way you reach out to 40,000 people over ten weeks.

Before the meeting the councillor writes a personal letter to each family stating that there are things to be decided and we would like to know your opinion.

"Aap aaye aur mujhe bataiye kya karna hai."

At a typical meeting, around 150 people turn up. The councillor brings with him local officers such as the sanitary inspector, horticulture inspector, water inspector, electricity inspector. Each officer shares the budget allocated to him; people vote and prioritise on what things the money should be spent on.

"This has been started in two areas – in Trilokpuri and Sundar Nagari. Now we want to accelerate it and implement it elsewhere!

The results have been fantastic. People now have a voice. "If you come to the meetings, you would see that often a project gets sanctioned on the spot!"

It has also been an eye-opener for the councillors. In Sundar Nagari, the councillor said he had a budget of ₹ 70 lakhs.

"*Usme to kuch ho nahin sakta,*" he sighed.

Then people asked the junior engineer, "*Aapka kitna budget hai.*"

He said, "*Bahut hai. Aap batao kya karna hai...*"

The 'budget' is apparently, enough to get all roads in the entire mohalla made *pakka*. If the contractor lays it thick on the roads – not his own pocket.

"You see, people's demands are actually not even that many!" exults Arvind.

Someone wants the streetlight on his road fixed – the bulb costs ₹ 3000. Someone asks you to fill up a pothole – that costs ₹ 20,000. So a budget of ₹ 12-14 lakhs is usually sufficient to take care of *everything*. And yet!

"Now, the *mohalla sabhas* are monitoring everything. No payment is made to contractors unless the people vouch that the work is satisfactory."

And finally, at *mohalla sabhas,* the community decides who should benefit from the various government schemes for the poor. One such scheme provides ₹ 1000 per month per family – an attractive sum for any slumdweller.

But, in a gathering of 200 such, not one hand went up. Everyone pointed to one woman and said, "She is the poorest, give her the money."

"You have to be very needy to stand up and say, 'I need money' in front of your entire community. *Sab ko apni izzat pyaari hai – koi bheekh nahin maangna chahta*!"

People are basically decent – and this decency can be harnessed.

"Our ultimate dream is that the whole of Delhi would be run by *mohalla sabhas*. The people should decide what laws get passed in the Assembly."

But first, we need a law which institutionalises *mohalla sabhas*. In the meanwhile, Parivartan is selling the concept to councillors, and to citizens.

Councillors are slowly coming on board – two in Tigri Khanpur, five in Jahangirpuri...

"*Unko vote nazar aa rahe hain.*"

But, it's a double-edged sword. Once you are a known face, and accountable to your people, you have to deliver. *Phir dhandha paani kahan se aayega?*

"Let's see, it is very interesting. The day 30 or 40 councillors are ready to implement this scheme I know *mohalla sabhas* will come under attack. How and when, only time will tell. But then it depends how stiffly people resist and stand up for their rights."

Put this way, the future looks a bit bleak. Struggle, strife, even danger to one's life...

"You know when that girl's throat was slit, it was a difficult moment for us. We thought about what we were doing and why, where are we going, will it even bring any result?"

It was the girl herself who provided the answer. She was under tremendous pressure from her family to leave Parivartan, get married and settle down. But *she* questioned them instead.

"*Agar main nahin karoongi to kaun karega. Koi Amrika se aakar to hamare desh ko sudhaarne wala nahin.*"

And that kept everyone else's resolve.

"You have to accept all this – it's part of the battle."

While there is the option of legal recourse, Arvind is well aware how futile that can be.

"Whenever there has been an attack on us, we file a case so it goes on record. But we leave it at that."

Because pursuing the matter would only mean spending your life running from one courtroom to the next.

"Also, if we are to go about seeking punishment for everyone, it would not serve our purpose. That's because the people who attack us are just pawns of the system. By giving them punishment, the *system* will not improve."

Bold words, inspiring words, but just for a moment I pause and think about how he is managing it all. Does revolution run only on love and fresh air?

"Like I said the movement is funded by people. I myself get a fellowship from AID (Association for India's Development)."

And then, there is the silent support of his family.

"My wife is with the IRS. And no, what I do has not affected her career..."

Yet, it could not have been easy.

"Initially, there was a lot of opposition, now they have accepted it. If you look at it from their perspective, I did give them a shock."

Just like he is doing, to the system. The voltage is not enough – yet. But *andhere se ujaale ki taraf ka safar shuru ho gaya hai*...

More power to the people.

———————————

ADVICE TO YOUNG ENTREPRENEURS

The first and foremost thing is that you need to think. Yes, corruption is a problem; but don't just jump on that one point. Many issues are inter-linked.

Secondly, most of us think, 'I am an individual and I have a family'. And we would do anything for that family. But we don't have that same feeling for the country.

Now take for instance, when we had that 'cash for votes' scandal. MPs were sold. I thought that was the most shocking thing in Indian democracy.

I told many of my friends, "Let's go to India Gate and protest." They replied, "*Jaane se kya hoga, kuch hota to hai nahin.*"

I felt that even if 'nothing happens' if we keep quiet, things will slide further. At least some people would join in the protest and our voice would be heard.

When we go to see a movie, then do we ask, would there be any benefit in watching this movie?

So as we take responsibility for our families' welfare, in the same way, we need to think about our country's welfare. We have to think and there is no other option as democracy cannot work without active participation of the people. Otherwise it will collapse and it is collapsing.

In order for a democracy to work, *kuch hota hai ki nahin hum logon ko participate to karna padega.*

I am not telling you to join Parivartan. I am not saying participate in anything and everything. Make your choices, but participate in something. Something which attracts you, motivates you, inspires you.

INNER
ENGINEERING

Bhushan Punani,
Blind Person's Association (BPA)

As a young MBA, Bhushan made the unconventional choice of joining Blind Person's Association. To see if management principles could be applied to the social sector. 31 years later, the scale at which BPA operates makes the answer to that question a resounding 'yes'.

When I see a blind person, my first reaction is to look away.

"How can this person go through every day, as if it were the darkest night?"

You have only to close your eyes for a second, to know.

And yet, as I walk through the BPA campus, in search of Bhushan Punani's office, I am probably the only one with this morose thought.

All around me are blind people – young and old – going through their day with a sense of purpose. A smile is visible on most lips.

Soon I will learn more about the work of the Blind Person's Association. And its transformation from a single, small school and vocational centre for the blind, to a multi-campus, multi-purpose movement.

A movement to bring dignity to the life of the disabled, not just in India, but across the world.

At the helm of this movement is the unassuming Bhushan Punani. A graduate of IIM Ahmedabad, Bhushan joined BPA not as a teacher or social worker, but to learn for himself whether 'management principles' can be applied to the development sector.

The answer is a definite yes but, there is so much more that can be done. That sense of mission is what keeps Bhushan – and the amazing team at BPA – on their toes.

At the end of our meeting I wonder, how many young MBAs today would be satisfied with a salary of ₹ 5.1 lakhs – at age 23 – let alone after 30 years on the job?

Love and gratitude, a sense of true accomplishment; and sound sleep at night. These are the additional 'perks' Bhushan enjoys.

Things which those with long cars and fat bonuses are still seeking...

And find that all their money simply cannot buy.

INNER
ENGINEERING

Bhushan Punani,
Blind Person's Association (BPA)

Bhushan Punani was born in Hansi, a small, sleepy town in Haryana.

"I studied in a typical government school, Hindi medium – like most schools in those days. The only concern was, students should keep 'passing'."

Yet, Bhushan always felt different. Academically brilliant, he procured a state scholarship from 4th standard. Which meant the government paid your fees and gave you ₹ 10 per month for your books.

"A large amount in the early '60s," he smiles.

Apart from studies, Bhushan was also a state level table tennis player.

Like many bright young men of his generation, Bhushan wanted to be a doctor. But, he missed a seat in medical college by 3 marks.

"Actually, we did not have a chemistry teacher the whole year and so we did not know how to go about the practicals," he recalls wistfully.

So what were the other options? As a student with 'bio' background Bhushan was eligible for the prestigious dairy husbandry course in Karnal. He applied and got in.

"It was the institute where they take only two students from the state and groom them to be managers in dairy development and dairy technology."

While at Karnal, Bhushan once again topped the university. He graduated with two gold medals – one for getting the highest marks in his batch, the second for getting the highest marks ever secured in that course.

Bhushan was picked up by Milkfood to head the milk procurement division. A great honour for a graduate without any industry experience. While he did extremely well on the job, Bhushan quickly realised it was not his cup of tea.

"I decided to go for post graduation. Again, I got very good marks and was one of only five people selected for an ICAR fellowship to do PhD in animal breeding and genetics – my favourite subject."

In the meantime, Bhushan had also applied to IIMs for admission and got selected. He decided to take up the offer. But, from day one, he was very clear about his special area of interest – rural development.

"I had one year experience working in the interiors of Punjab. We think Punjab is a very rich state, it has so much agriculture. But still I saw people who were living in substandard conditions."

Not surprisingly, Bhushan spent his summer studying tribal unrest in Simdega, in the interiors of Bihar. He also worked closely with professors like Ranjit Gupta, who, along with Ravi Mathai, pioneered IIMA's rural development project in Jawaja.

By the time placement came around, it was clear Bhushan would not go for a usual, commercial job.

"So that year the placement brochure had an additional column titled – 'unconventional job'."

Such a job was offered on the second day of placement, by the Mafatlal group. The company needed someone to head its rural development division and Bhushan was an ideal candidate.

"I told them I will join on 15th of June and went home. But unfortunately there was a split in the Mafatlal group that year – in 1979 – and they abandoned this project."

"If a rich state like Punjab can have so many poor people, subject to exploitation, you can imagine what happens elsewhere."

The company sent a letter to Bhushan, withdrawing its offer. So, he returned to Ahmedabad, to explore other options – one from the government and the other from an NGO.

That is when Bhushan was approached by Manubhai Shah, a visiting faculty at IIM Ahmedabad.

Manubhai called and said. "I have a most unconventional job for you – would you like to look at it?"

Bhushan said, "Yes, of course."

Manubhai replied,"There is an organisation – 'Blind School' – looking for a manager. If you are willing, I can arrange for an interview."

The Blind People's Association (then known as Blind Men's Association or simply "Blind School") had received a grant from very large German organisation called CBM. Their condition was: appoint a professional manager.

The manager's salary for the first five years, as well as infrastructure support, would be provided by CBM. An interesting proposition, indeed.

Bhushan met Dr Jagdish K Patel, General Secretary of BPA and agreed to join.

But, only after three months.

"I had promised to help Prof Ranjit Gupta on a project in Kota. I had to keep that commitment."

In this interim period, Bhushan received a summons from the director of IIM Ahmedabad, Dr Vyas.

Dr Vyas said, "I am shocked to learn you are joining a blind school – a leap in the dark? Are you sure you are making the right decision?"

The director was especially worried because there had been some adverse reports about the school, a few years earlier.

Bhushan replied, "Sir, I have two very outstanding degrees with me. If I have to worry about my future there is something wrong either with the degrees, or with me."

But, practically speaking, Bhushan had decided to keep a two year perspective.

"If I find this job interesting I will continue. Otherwise, I will look for other opportunities."

'Losing' two years – in a long career – did not seem like a big deal.

Dr Vyas was convinced about the young man's commitment to his cause.

"Do keep me informed about your progress," he said while parting. "I would like to know how you are performing."

And so, on the 14th of September 1979, Bhushan Punani joined BPA as manager. His salary at the time? He did not know, because, he had not even asked.

"My boss called me after a week and said, 'What a stupid fool you are. You have joined us but you don't even know what salary we are going to pay you'."

Bhushan replied, "I leave it to you. I am sure you will give me a salary with which I can survive in the city of Ahmedabad."

The boss was a kindly man and benchmarked Bhushan's salary with that of a director in the government of Gujarat. Around ₹ 7000 (basic), adding up to ₹ 1 lakh a year.

"This was much lower than the salary I was getting before joining IIM Ahmedabad, but salary was not my concern."

The important thing was, the job was exciting. In fact, it was a challenge.

In 1979, BPA was a very small institute with 80-90 staff, headed by Harish Panchal. An engineer and former works manager.

"We had a blind school from class one to twelve, a workshop and a vocational training centre. There were around 250-300 beneficiaries and we used to get a grant from the government in addition to donations from the public."

BPA's 'bank deposits' were around ₹ 10 lakhs, against which the organisation availed of overdrafts of about ₹ 7 lakhs. The organisation had been in existence for over 25 years, although the Vastrapur campus was set up only in 1964.

The question now was, could the activity be scaled up by a young management graduate?

"The positive thing which really made a difference – where other IIMites run into problems – was that my boss Jagdish Patel was an outstanding person."

A man with foresight, understanding and a charismatic personality.

"He supported me through thick and thin," acknowledges Bhushan. "And luckily, there was no 'old-timers conflict'. They were only concerned with how I perform."

Having Arvind Lalbhai as President of BPA also brought that professional touch.

Secondly, Gujarat is a very philanthropic state. Charity is a 'way of life', especially among communities like the Jains.

"There is a sense of 'giving' to others and that has made a big difference to our organisation from day one."

Thirdly, although small, BPA was a very honest and transparent organisation. A rarity in the NGO world back then.

"Trustees were not here to make money. They get no monetary benefit from the institute."

And to top it all, it was a 'virgin' field.

"Disability was a new development area, not much was happening at the time. So we had the capacity to expand very fast."

Within a year, Bhushan realised there were two ways to grow. The obvious route – increase the scope of activities at the institute. But, to reach out to larger numbers, the organisation would have to think beyond.

Thus was born the idea of 'projects'. Instead of people coming to BPA, the institute would have to go out, to *them*.

And this is the two-pronged approach BPA has followed ever since.

> ## "People were not very happy about me joining BPA, they thought it might bring a bad name to the institute to take up such a job."

But the first thing you need – when you set out on any kind of mission – is people with both competence, and commitment. The first such person to join the new team was a young graduate of the BK School of Management – Nandini Rawal.

"Nandini could have gotten a job with much better salary, but chose BPA," recalls Bhushan.

One fine morning she rang up Bhushan and said, "Can I come and meet you? If you have an opening, I would like to join your institute."

Bhushan replied, "God has sent you to us. We are looking for somebody to head our projects and take them forward."

Nandini accepted the offer and thus began projects covering not only the blind, but the deaf and those with multiple disabilities. The unique thing about this program was the emphasis on CBR, or Community Based Rehabilitation.

"Our first project began on 19th February 1982 in Dholka in Gujarat and in Chikmanglur district of Karnataka. It is all about building local partnerships."

What BPA does is identify a local partner – a rural development organisation in the area. This organisation is appointed as the local implementing agency.

"We assure them the first 3 years of funding for the project. They have to identify a team of 10-15 people – field workers, supervisors and teachers."

BPA trains this team by sending its own people on location. Over the years, they have developed 'master trainers' in different states.

The job of field staff is to identify people with disabilities, complete formalities for them, give them access to numerous services.

"There are schemes for the disabled, but people don't know about them. Our project is aimed at empowerment. With some support in the form of training and micro-credit, they are able to perform like anybody else."

And in the process move from being a burden to an asset, to their community.

But is this decentralised model easy to manage? Yes, and no. If the local agency – or agent – is dedicated, then yes.

"Let me give you a classic. Viramgam is about 80 km from Ahmedabad, a lady doctor by the name of Ramila Jain lives there. Through the Lions Club of Viramgam we identified this lady, and gave her the responsibility."

Ramilaben formed a local trust, but yet is part of the BPA system.

"We monitor the program, send our people for the monthly meeting and give her constant feedback. We also keep giving the field workers refresher courses."

Ramilaben has been 'with' BPA since 1985. She now runs an eye hospital, works for a orthopaedic hospital, supports programs in education, assisted devices and vitamin delivery.

"Any activity we take up in Viramgam – Ramilaben is the moving force behind it."

Of course, for every ten Ramilas, there will be one 'Jitendra'.

"There was this very smart fellow, he was a teacher of yoga and even wore sadhu-like clothes. We were quite impressed by him and asked him to set up the local co-ordinating agency at Ghodadongli – a place near Itarsi in Madhya Pradesh."

One fine morning, he eloped with a young lady field worker.

In another such instance, the project head started siphoning off money. And a common problem is that full salaries are not paid.

"I joined because I wanted to see whether the tricks you learnt in management have any relevance to the developmental field. It was putting my knowledge to the acid test."

"For example, we are giving ₹ 1500 per field worker but they will pay ₹ 1000 and get a signature on ₹ 1500. Sometimes, they will have their own family members on the rolls, or simply make fake vouchers."

And such problems can crop up anywhere – from Gujarat where BPA has a very strong local presence, to physically distant states like Meghalaya and Orissa. Constant vigilance and 'ear to the ground' is the only solution.

"What we do is maintain very good relations with the field staff. If anything is going wrong they are the ones who let us know."

The moment any *gadbad* is brought to BPA's notice, the agency is terminated.

"Yes, we have lost money in closing a project abruptly but we can't afford to have rotten eggs..."

As long as there are many more people in this world with good hearts and honourable intentions, BPA believes it is worth the effort.

Of course, to manage this multi-location, multi-pronged campaign, you also need a strong team at the centre. To co-ordinate, raise funding and provide continuous nurturing and leadership.

"When we started the fund-raising division, a Master's in Social Work – Nautama Shukla – joined us. Another very smart young lady by the name Vimal Thawani – a teacher in MS University's Faculty of Social Work – came on board as 'vocational counsellor'."

For every new division BPA set up, it started attracting qualified professionals. Just like a company would appoint people to head each of its 'profit centres'. And as each division grew, the managers were continuously trained – to do their jobs better.

Take for example, Akhil Paul. An MSW from the School of Social Work, Indore, he also had a journalism background. When he shifted to Ahmedabad, he joined BPA as a coordinator for the CBR program.

"Within a year we sent him to America for a one year course in one of the world's best institutes. He became a great resource and now heads 'Sense International' – a UK based NGO."

Few companies would refer to ex-employees with such obvious pride – that's where BPA is different.

"Akhil was an all-rounder; he could do photography, he could drive a car, he could receive guests, he could work around the clock. Placing him elsewhere meant losing a very good person."

But Bhushan believes that if people get a chance, you must push them so they go up the ladder.

"In fact, I was in the committee that placed him," he grins.

And he is also firm in the belief that what is taken away, will be replenished. Soon after Akhil left, a lady with MA Political Science background applied to BPA.

"Since she had no social work background, we organised her training for three months."

Within six months, Brahada Shankar has almost replaced Akhil Paul in every respect. In fact, she was better than him in one aspect – her rapport with the children.

"Brada became our 'low vision' specialist. Now she is in Trivandrum, working for a national organisation from there."

Over the years, BPA has become an institution with its own 'alumni'. People who may physically leave, but not in spirit.

Take the instance of Hasmukhbhai Thakkar – the full-time legal officer of the BPA for many years. A day came when there were few legal issues left to solve.

Thakkarbhai said, "Sir I don't have much work here now. If you don't mind I want to start my legal practice."

Bhushan said, "Sure."

But, Hasmukhbhai added, "I cannot leave BPA, I will still come in on Saturdays and make sure everything is in order."

Thakkarbhai receives a token ₹ 2980 per month – one-sixth his original salary.

"It is just a token payment, he says this cheque is a sign of my attachment to BPA. In fact, his wife works as a volunteer and raises ₹ 10-20,000 per month for the organisation."

BPA alumni continue to contribute to BPA as visiting faculty and advisors to various programs. Others help with fundraising.

> **"In any part of the developing world social conditions are very similar, so our concept of community rehabilitation works – with some regional modification – in countries from China to Zambia."**

"Jasmine Anirudhan raises money for us in Dubai, Deepika Josh in US. Ashok Kumar now heads Indian Red Cross, Gujarat. He has given BPA more than ₹ 20 lakhs as grants for the eye hospital we set up."

It is almost like you can join BPA – but you can never 'leave'.

"Staff turnover is minimal," nods Bhushan.

There are three reasons for this. Firstly, salaries are as per Fifth Pay Commission guidelines – much better than most other NGOs.

"Secondly, there is lot of freedom to do your work the way you want to. This creates a sense of ownership."

Thirdly, staff members get a chance to grow professionally through courses and seminars in India and abroad.

"As we speak, four of the BPA staff members are studying abroad. They are pursuing courses in human rights, in leadership and in multiple disabilities in the US, Europe and Japan."

BPA works with agencies like the Ford Foundation, to make this possible.

In a lighter vein Bhushan adds, "The interesting part is that I have never been to America but I have sent at least ten people from BPA to study there. When these people return they are very motivated."

And raring to put into practice all that they have learnt.

All well and good, but what about results? What have been the achievements of BPA; the impact of its work?

Bhushan elaborates, "When I joined, we had just one campus.

> **"Most of my friends, my classfellows, they are in the ₹ 1 crore salary bracket. And I tell you, none of them gets sound sleep in the night..."**

Now we have eight campuses in Gujarat state. From a ₹ 10 lakh organisation, we now have a budget of over ₹ 20 crores."

But even that figure does not tell the full story.

"CBR projects are only co-ordinated by BPA, money flows directly from the funding partner to the local agency. So it does not get reflected in our books*."

Such an arrangement is preferable for a simple reason.

"We avoid handling too much of money, that gives you a temptation of ownership – that *you* are managing it."

What BPA gets for such projects is cost of training, co-ordination, some staff and hardware. Moreover, outside Gujarat BPA's involvement lasts for the initial couple of years only*.

"Of course, we keep calling for training programs, and they get back whenever they have problems."

But the mantra is local empowerment.

"In fact, BPA has evolved from a 'doer' organisation to a 'network' organisation. Our core strength now lies in training and co-ordination."

As the organisation evolved, so did its structure. In its original form BPA consisted of one general secretary, one works manager and one trust.

"Now we have five independent trusts – one main trust and four associate trusts. Each trust has a Board of Directors, but all are part of the BPA family."

---

* *BPA has co-ordinated CBR projects in125 locations across India, in addition to 225 talukas in Gujarat. It has also trained field staff in China, SE Asia and Africa.*

The five trusts are involved in different kinds of activities. For example, the National Institute for Blind – Gujarat branch – is a network organisation with branches in all the districts. Sadbhavna Trust is for non-disability projects while the Center for the Blind is for business activities.

"We produce and sell more than ₹ 8 crores of furniture every year!"

The profits from these sales constitute close to 10% of BPA's annual budget. And what about the balance?

"If I put all four trusts together, our government exposure is 20%-25%, while foreign funding makes up 20 to 30%. Another 10-12% comes from investments and the rest is public donations.

Slowly, BPA is also trying to tap corporates. And tweaking its service model to move from pure charity, to 'self payment', as per financial ability.

"At our eye hospitals, you will be surprised to know, the poor actually insist on paying. If they cannot pay, they will send produce from their fields."

It is an expression of human dignity. Which is exactly the spirit in which BPA runs most of its programs.

"We want the disabled to be employable, to be able to lead normal lives."

That is why BPA students are trained in IT, while physically challenged girls can take up beautician courses. The visually challenged can opt for physiotherapy and get jobs in BPA's own state-of-the-art physiotherapy centre. Frequented by the elite population of the state!

"At our eye hospitals, you will be surprised to know, the poor actually insist on paying. If they cannot pay, they will send produce from their fields."

"We also run a very large ITI, we have just been funded by the government to construct a new, modern building for it".

At the end of the day, BPA remains a proactive but pro-government NGO.

"If you go to any NGO, they always crib, '*Yeh grant nahin mila, woh nahin mila*'. But we have never had such problems."

Whatever money it is eligible for, BPA ensures it gets. The important thing is to get your paperwork right.

"As many of our trustees sit with ministers and with secretaries on a number of committees, once in a way we may use that influence to get the grant on time," he adds.

The work is not easy, but neither is it *difficult*.

"God is with me – I am never alone – He is always helping me."

And there is another pillar of strength in his life – Hansa.

"My wife Hansa is Gujarati and she is a lawyer by profession. We were friends before we got married, so we share a very good understanding.

Bhushan's working hours are long and demanding.

"I am generally in office from 9.30 am upto 8.30 pm. Even Sundays, I work at least till 2.30 pm."

But Hansa understands that this is not a 'job', it is a mission. And she has made adjustments.

"As she is earning more than what I do, money has never been a issue."

The couple has a daughter – Shachi – who has just completed her law degree.

"We believe in local empowerment. If BPA gets the money and pays for the project, it becomes ours. But if Ramilaben gets the money and pays the money it is *her* project. That sense of ownership is crucial."

> ## "I don't feel ashamed telling that my salary is less than the fresher of IIM every year – it has no meaning to me. I need just two rotis in the evening, the third roti is like poison to me. "

"She has never been a demanding or difficult child. In fact, she is very simple and down to earth."

So much so that when Bhushan wanted to take her out for dinner in Bangalore, where she was doing her internship, she said, "Papa, this restaurant looks very expensive. Why don't you wait outside – I will go and check the menu."

Ultimately, father and daughter went to a food court instead. Not that they cannot *afford* a fancy meal, but it just does not seem right...

"Honestly, my salary is not all that bad. It is printed in our annual report – ₹ 5.1 lakhs per annum."

And it is enough for a decent home, car, a house, simple food, simple needs. *Isse zyada aur aadmi ko kya chahiye*?

Bhushan knows that his father – the late Bhagat Chela Ram, who worked tirelessly for social reforms – would have been proud. But would *aajkal ke* overachiever parents – and children – feel the same?

At the annual IIM Ahmedabad festival 'Confluence', Bhushan shared the dais with CEOs and corporate head honchos. And he spoke passionately about how money has little meaning – what really matters is fulfillment, commitment and working for others to make a difference.

"They were saying we have created jobs for 1 million people. Or wealth of thousands of crores. Good – for them."

What Bhushan has done is created a wealth of knowledge, of network, and of empowerment.

"We have established that management principles have a role to play in development. We have touched the lives and hearts of thousands and made 'normal' life possible for them."

A life well lived – for others, with others.

Inner engineering makes everything else irrelevant.

You have only to look within, and learn that truth, for yourself.

———————————————

ADVICE TO YOUNG ENTREPRENEURS

You don't have to go and do research, you don't have to do a lot of thinking. Just go outside your house and look around.

Open your eyes and ears – who has a child who is illiterate, or not going to school? There may be an old lady suffering from cataract. There may be a *laariwala* whose son has cancer.

Just identify one person and ask that person what is his/her need. Then, within your capacity, help that person. Often what that person needs is only the right direction.

I will give a classic example. There are 10 hospitals in Ahmedabad which provide free cataract surgery but people are not aware of this. If you know a lady suffering from cataract, you only have to tell her, "Come and sit on the back of my scooter, I will take you to the Nagari hospital and get you operated."

See, how much money you have to spend! Going to Nagari hospital and coming back – just ₹ 80 – and the old lady can have her sight again.

Don't be a hypocrite and merely talk about development. If you pay for fees, books and uniform of a child in the nearby municipal school it will not cost more than ₹ 1000 a year.

The important thing is to make a difference – to some one.

THE SPIRITUAL
Capitalist

The ideal of service may be old-fashioned. But there are individuals who still choose to live by it. Because they believe purity of purpose and selflessness of spirit can transcend every limitation.

SOUL FOOD

Madhu Pandit Dasa,
Akshaya Patra

As a student at IIT, Madhu Pandit once came close to committing suicide. Then, he discovered Krishna and embraced the spiritual path. As head of ISKCON Bangalore, Madhu is now leading Akshaya Patra. A movement which combines missionary zeal and modern management, to feed 1 million hungry children everyday.

ISKCON Bangalore is the most opulent ISKCON temple I have ever seen.

It is also the most peaceful.

I sit in the office of Shridhar Venkat, Executive Director (Marketing) of Akshayaa Patra. He offers me 'Vedic' tea.

Regular tea and coffee is not served here, you see.

We are waiting to meet Madhu Pandit Dasa, President of ISKCON Bangalore, and a trustee of the Akshaya Patra foundation. The world's largest mid-day meal program, feeding more than a million school children. Everyday!

I am in two minds about this interview. Is there any big deal about temples taking up service of humanity? Isn't that part of their core 'business'?

Apparently not. Of the millions of *mandirs* spread across this land, collecting millions in daan and donation, how many actually take up charitable activities? Only a miniscule fraction.

And when they do, it's a case of 'doing the best we can'. They are limited by lack of resources, lack of systems. Unlike Akshaya Patra.

Akshaya Patra is a marriage of science and spirituality. The scientific method governs the design of the kitchen, of accounting, of marketing. But the missionary zeal of the operation comes from its spiritual base. The dedication and commitment of the *Hare Krishnas*, at all levels.

As I listen to Madhu Pandit, I think here is a monk who never aspired for a Ferrari. A man who found the answer to his existential questions but continues to search.

For answers to more ordinary questions.

"How many children go hungry in this country?"

"Can we feed one more such child, tomorrow?"

That is the magic of Akshaya Patra, the inexhaustible vessel.

Everyone's portion is decided up there, by the Supreme. But the cooking is done here, on earth.

SOUL FOOD

Madhu Pandit Dasa,
Akshaya Patra

Madhu Pandit Dasa was born in Nagercoil, but grew up in Bangalore.

"My father was a scientist in Indian Institute of Science. I finished 4th standard in Bangalore and then my dad shifted to ISRO in Trivandrum."

Madhu shifted from St Joseph's School in Bangalore, to St Joseph's School in Trivandrum. At school, he had a special interest in science and even did a lot of extra reading – beyond the curriculum – at the British Library.

"Another thing I was fascinated by was chess. My father was a good chess player so I learnt from him, when I was in class 4."

In his senior years in school, Madhu won the Trivandrum Junior District Championship three times. And one year – he cannot recall which, exactly – Madhu was the State Junior Champion in Chess.

"So during all this time, my focus was more on pursuing science and chess. I was not really serious about studies."

When he entered class 9, Madhu's father forbade him from playing chess anymore. It made a big difference to his academic performance.

"Even I couldn't believe that in one year, I could improve so much."

In the class 10 board exam Madhu was one of the handful of students in the state who secured 100% in mathematics. During the pre-degree course Madhu joined the Trivandrum

Science Club. He quickly developed a fascination for theoretical physics.

"I realised that if I wanted to understand more of physics, I had to study more of mathematics. You know, the language of modern physics. So, I started self-study outside my curriculum."

Around this time, Madhu also won the National Science Talent Search Scholarship. An award so prestigious that all IITs and BITS Pilani used to send an offer of admission without the entrance exam to the selected scholars.

Madhu chose IIT Bombay and enrolled for a 5 year integrated M.Sc. Physics course. The year was 1976.

"I was very excited as I felt it was the best institute and I thought I can really learn and pursue my subject."

But then came the big disappointment.

"The IIT atmosphere, oh my God! I didn't like it because it was too competitive and there was relative grading. Maybe for engineering it was good you know, to tease your brains, make you think faster. But it was not for me."

Madhu went through a depressing two years.

"I was studying physics and at that the same time, not studying any physics. I was just attending classes and tutorials, mugging and writing for exams."

At the end of two years, Madhu decided to switch to civil engineering. A less popular branch, hence less competitive. He wanted to join an easy branch, so that he could continue studying physics on his own.

"I would attend classes, bunk tutorials and then sit in the IIT library till 10 o'clock," he says, with a twinkle in his eye.

But even behind this love for physics, lay something else, something deeper. Since childhood Madhu had one question at the back of his mind, "What is the original cause of everything?"

"I was excited by science because it explored the 'cause behind the cause'. So I relished that process of discovery."

And after entering IIT, Madhu had actually started looking into life itself.The pursuit of physics acquired a philosophical dimension.

"Einstein shook the foundations of science with his Theory of Relativity. But, even on his death-bed, he was grappling with the truth."

"See, when a scientist tries to understand the atom, he finds it is made of electrons, protons and neutrons. Then he realises that there are further elementary particles within the nucleus. And it is all bound together by order and symmetry."

So much beauty, so much harmony in nature – perhaps there is a 'creator'? That thought, however, never crossed young Madhu's mind. As a soldier of science, he was looking for an impersonal cause.

An irreducible, fundamental particle, a single, unifying theory from which *everything* can be explained. Something that eludes physicists, even today.

Immersed in this Quest for the 'Cause of all Causes' – but naturally – Madhu's grades suffered.

"You see, everywhere I came out with flying colours, but here in IIT, I am average."

In other words, a 'six point someone'.

Madhu took to smoking, and then, during the last paper in his fourth year, something snapped.

"By then I had been reading a lot of philosophical books. Mostly, Western philosophy, because you see, I did not know Sanskrit."

One such book, by Bertrand Russell, proved to be the 'trigger'.

Said Russell, "If I get another chance to live, I will never touch philosophy. For the simple reason that for all these years of searching I do not know if what I am seeing is true or not. Does what I see with my eyes exist or not exist, is it true or not?"

If a man like Bertrand Russell 'gave up' after racking his brains for years, what hope did Madhu have?

At this point Madhu – and a fellow student from Trivandrum – decided to 'end it all'.

"What difference does it make whether we live or die? These IIT fellows have messed up our lives. We will jump off the main building and give them a bad name."

It was not about grades, or career, or unrequited love. It was about questions to which there were no answers – life, the universe and the meaning of everything.

Existential frustration.

"You see, when man gets very worked up in his mind, he can do anything. So we really got worked up about the question of 'what was the truth'? And why can't we find it?"

But once he had decided to commit suicide, there was a complete ease of tension. The night before, Madhu went into the library one last time and for reasons unknown, picked up a different kind of book. A book by ISKCON founder Srila Prabhupada, with a colourful cover illustration.

"I'd seen it before and thought there's nothing more than stories in this book – so I put it back. I didn't want stories, I wanted the truth!"

But that day Madhu decided to do some 'light reading'. And so he took the book with the glossy picture of Krishna on the cover to his room. Turning to the chapter 'Prayers by personified Vedas'.

Within five minutes, Madhu burst into tears. Tears of joy.

He cried, "My God! I can't believe it, how did this simple thing not strike me?"

The 'truth' was so simple. God – or Krishna – was the 'cause of all causes'. A Person, limitless in name, form, activities, energy.

"I continued reading and that's when I realised that I couldn't die. I had a purpose to live."

The revelation came to Madhu, at the age of 22.

"After that, he started reading Prabhupada's books voraciously. My view of the world changed completely."

Madhu realised the limitations of science. Limited, by definition, to the five senses.

"But there are many, many things beyond. For instance, the mind. We all know that we are using our minds and that the mind exists, but nobody can see it. Therefore the science of the mind – or psychology – is not considered a pure science!"

That is not the Vedic perspective.

"Our Bhagwad Gita and Bhagvatam understands the self as the 'body', the 'mind', the 'intellect' and then, the 'ego'. So there is a *hierarchy* of selves."

Without going into further details, let us just say, Madhu's universe expanded.

Of course, he admits, science cannot go beyond the five senses. Because then it will lose objectivity. But that does not mean there is nothing beyond science.

"Vedanta is the science of the self. The laboratory is our body. Your experimentation is with your own life. So I am still a scientist – only the domain is different."

The domain now includes the spirit, awareness and consciousness.

"In a nutshell, we are not this *body*, and we are eternal. And it does not end there, we are part and parcel of a Supreme Eternal."

Even as he digested this new found treasure chest of knowledge, Madhu completed his BTech and then joined MTech. Mainly because he could not bear to be parted from the IIT library. However he did not actually complete his Master's.

"Somewhere along the way I decided to dedicate my life to Prabupada's mission. I decided to join ISKCON."

Madhu's father – himself a religious person – was puzzled.

"Why are you doing this at your age? Renunciation is for old people."

Madhu replied, "This is different. I am pursuing spirituality as a science, as a seeker of knowledge. I am not becoming an ascetic or joining religion."

Of course, he could sit and be a philosopher but Madhu wanted to live this knowledge. To do that, he had to first submit to the process.

"Hydrogen and oxygen combine to form water under certain conditions of pressure and temperature. In the same way, you need to condition your mind, and your body, to become a *sadhak.*"

In short, you need discipline. Discipline to wake up at 3.30 am, bathe and then spend five hours in spiritual practices.

"When we cross a certain level, the organisation is only an instrument. We think that the Lord takes care *through* the organisation."

"The discipline is designed to facilitate the purification of our mind*. This is the science of *bhakti yoga*."

While ISKCON promotes *bhakti* to Krishna, it is not to be taken literally.

"Krishna is spoken of as a historical person in the Bhagwad Gita, but the shastric understanding is that Krishna means 'all-attractive'. And God's nature is that he should be all-attractive."

The ISKCON idea of 'Krishna' is therefore a Universal God, and not a 'Hindu God'. And the purpose of people working with ISKCON is to serve humanity.

"Part of the self-realisation process is to act selflessly. That is what is facilitated here. Someone may be a priest, another may sell books, a third may be in the 'management'. But it is all application of spiritual knowledge through devoted action, or devoted service."

In the process, the Seeker opens us up internally to higher levels of experience.

"As long as we are self-centred in our thinking, we do not open up to this higher dimension of spirituality. So this discipline, both the morning *sadhana* and the the devotional work work we do, give us an opportunity to dissolve that sense of false 'I' ness – for me and myself."

Your horizons expand into God, into humanity and ultimately you realise all is One.

Of course, self-realisation is a Journey. For Madhu, this journey formally began in 1981. After six months, he was 'initiated'. With shaven head and saffron robes, Madhu Pandit 'Dasa' became a *Hare Krishna*.

* In addition, Hare Krishnas are forbidden from intoxication, meat-eating, illicit sex, gambling and stimulants like caffeine.

> **"Srila Prabhupada instructed that in a 15 to 20 km radius of any ISKCON temple, no one should go hungry. So this was an inspiration for us to start Akshaya Patra."**

"For two years I travelled to remote villages in south India, giving lectures on Bhagwad-Gita and distributing ISKCON literature. I also worked with ISKCON in Trivandrum. Then in 1983, I came to Bangalore, and took up the opening of a centre here."

Around this time, Madhu also got married to Bhaktilatha, headmistress of Chinmaya School in Chennai and also a missionary. She resigned from her job and joined the ISKCON movement.

The ISKCON centre in Bangalore started from a two bedroom house. But, Madhu had big plans.

"When I joined ISKCON, my idea was to do big things. I never gave up whether it was in chess or physics or anything else!" he exclaims.

It sounds a little odd, coming from a 'spiritual' person. But, he puts it into context.

"Whatever Prabhupada has given to this world in terms of spiritual knowledge and in terms of service, should be spread. It is a big gift to humanity."

But this 'gift' will not just fall into your lap; you have to earn it. And the life of Srila Prabhupada has been Madhu's greatest inspiration.

"This is a man who went to America at the age of 70 with just ₹ 40 in his pocket. He adapted to living in a strange new culture and transformed people around him."

In fact, the entire institution of ISKCON was built in a scant eleven years – between 1966 and 1977. Exactly 'how' did he do it?

The explanation is simple – or complex – depends how you see it.

"When you work for a selfless cause, the sky is the limit. You are not bound by your *karma*. If you give full efforts, results will keep coming."

Cause, effort, result – you need all these things. But, you work without attachment to the *fruits* of your labour. And that work must start, somewhere.

At ISKCON Bangalore it all began with an abandoned quarry. A 'worthless' piece of land offered by the government to the trust.

While inspecting the site a devotee remarked, "We cannot have a temple here – there is so much pollution from factories all around, and no *pakka* road!"

Madhu kept quiet. He was observing a mud patch in the centre of all the rocks. A patch where *tulsi* plants were growing.

He told the devotee, "Don't see the smoke, don't see the road, just look at these tulsi plants. This place is where the Lord's feet have to come, it is destined for that."

And that is exactly how it happened. The wasteland was transformed into a majestic temple complex. From 'nothing' came something – the magic of Creation.

"In the mind of any kind of entrepreneur, there is a current reality and there is a vision. The brain works in such a way that it moves closer and closer until that vision *is* reality."

The vision for ISKCON Bangalore was to create a beautiful, modern temple. The funds for it were raised, from the common people.

"Mostly this temple is built out of individual donations. We had an innovative scheme called 'Sudama Seva' where we collected one rupee per day, so that anyone – no matter how poor – could contribute."

Drop by drop, ₹ 30 crores was thus collected.

"We got hundreds of construction workers, put up sheds for them to stay on the site and worked with petty contractors. Whatever we collected, we spent week by week, on construction."

The temple complex – as it stands today – was inaugurated in 1996. Initially – like all ISKCON temples – the focus was solely on propagation of the Bhagwad Gita and Krishna Consciousness.

And of course, as devotees flocked for *darshan* they were taken care of. You would not leave the temple without partaking of the delicious *prasadam*.

One fine day, in March 2000, two gentlemen walked into Madhu Pandit's office. One of them was Mohandas Pai, then CFO of Infosys.

Mohandas said, "It is nice that you are feeding so many people here, Swamiji. Why don't you feed the children in nearby schools?"

This, he explained, was a popular program in Tamil Nadu, a scheme initiated by the late MGR.

Madhu Pandit said, "Sure, why not? I have a kitchen facility but, I need a vehicle."

On the spot, Mohandas offered not one, but two vehicles. The meeting ended, the gentlemen left.

Madhu then sat back, took a pen and paper and started calculating how much food needed to be cooked.

"In my enthusiasm I had told him we will make as much food as the vehicles can carry. Now, I realised he is giving us two lorries!"

Calculations showed that could carry ten tonnes of food. Even for a kitchen as large as ISKCON, the volume was mind-boggling.

"Then I realised that in 15 to 20 days, the cost of the food would exceed the cost of the two trucks."

Madhu simply never factored in the recurring cost! Which is kind of strange...

"You know, that's where the Lord's hand is there, especially in these kinds of things. Normally people say that if you shoot for the stars, you will at least touch the moon. But in my experience, in the Lord's service, it has been the other way round!"

In short, aim for the sky and find you have been taken far beyond.

"For that to happen sometimes ignorance is good. Because if you are ignorant, you don't have fear. If I had done a proper calculation when Mohandas Pai was with me – a financial calculation – I would have hesitated."

Now, he had given his word, and he kept it.

"First of all, I set up a separate kitchen. In June 2000, we started a pilot project, feeding 1500 schoolchildren everyday."

This program covered five schools. Word spread quickly, many more schools wanted meals for their children.

"In the space of two months, we had enough applications requesting us to feed around 100,000 children. And this was just in and around Bangalore city!"

In just a few kilometres radius, so many children were going hungry to school. It was a shocking revelation.

Without conscious decision, or 'strategy', the program began 'scaling up'. In just four months, 10,000 children a day were getting a nutritious mid-day meal from the ISKCON kitchen.

And these meals were being financed purely by individual donations. Which are not easy to get.

"We had no government subsidy, or corpus. But we had faith that somehow money for the next meal would come."

Invariably, it did. But what if – one day – that did not happen?

In one such moment of doubt, Madhu stood before the temple deities, and prayed for guidance. Suddenly, all fear vanished.

He said to Radha, the Universal Mother, "Any number of children can be fed by you, why should I bother? I will just put in my best efforts."

And that effort meant many practical and worldly wise decisions. Such as creating a separate foundation, to manage the program.

"With the creation of a separate identity, there is no confusion about the management and most importantly, we can ensure that there is no discrimination among the beneficiaries."

"There is a lot of pep talk given in books that if you desire, if you think high, you think big, you will get whatever you want. It is not true. There is also the law of Karma."

The second reason was that such an organisation would find it easier to attract funds from corporates. And clearly, to feed more and more children, donations from individuals would not be enough.

"We knew corporates would seek transparency and accountability with regard to their money. So we brought in KPMG to audit our accounts (pro bono)."

The stamp of Mohandas Pai is more than evident. He came in as a trustee, in his capacity as an indiviual. Infosys – as a company – would get involved in Akshaya Patra much later.

Which brings me to an important question, "Who thought of the name?"

"You know it's very interesting," says Madhu.

It happened – just like that – during a meeting with Dr Murli Manohar Joshi. The HRD minister at that time."

Madhu said, "We are running a mid-day meal program, feeding 5000 children a day."

He responded, "So this has become an *akshaya patra*?"

In the Mahabharata, 'akshaya patra' is the vessel which would give unlimited food everyday.

"So when he uttered that word, I thought that it was the Lord telling me this should be the name of our mission."

So beautiful, so apt, so evocative. And true to its name, the vessel has been inexhaustible.

"Actually it is a divine programme. It will startle anybody with some finance knowledge to know that we have no corpus. We have huge recurring costs every month."

"Sometimes the cause is selfless but somewhere I think that I need fame, or name. You need to forsake even that. Then the Lord will use you as an instrument for greater works."

"We followed all the practices of the business world to build credibility for Akshaya Patra. Our corpus is our intention, recommendation, commitment and daily efforts."

An Akshaya Patra meal costs ₹ 5.50 to prepare and deliver. Initially, the entire cost was borne by the foundation. But, that was to change.

On 28 November 2001, the Supreme Court of India passed an order mandating "Cooked mid-day meal is to be provided in all the government and government-aided primary schools in all the states."

Akshaya Patra thus became eligible for government subsidy. Yet, even today, that does not cover the entire cost.

"The government gives ₹ 3 per meal but we spend ₹ 5.50. So we spend roughly ₹ 2 on every meal, everyday."

In the initial days, with 30,000 children to feed, the daily deficit was ₹ 60,000. Today, with over 1 million children in the program, the deficit is an astounding ₹ 20 lakh per day.

Yet, till date there has never been a shortfall.Through the magic of effort, commitment and intention, somehow the funds come.

"Initially, we struggled a lot. That is the time we launched this scheme where you could sponsor a child for ₹ 1200 for a year."

A non-profit organisation was registered in the US with Chaitanya Chitranga Das collecting funds – practically door to door.

But many NGOs and charitable trusts make these efforts. What sets Akshaya Patra apart is its unique form. Part missionary, part corporate, the foundation harnesses the energy of both worlds.

Like a modern-day Narasimha *avatar* born to kill a modern-day *rakshasa*. The *rakshasa* of hunger.

"We have missionary trustees but the majority of the trustees are external. They bring greater transparency and accountability to the foundation."

> **"Three things are required for creating anything – Gyana (knowledge or intelligence), Bala (strength) and Kriya (skill). You can acquire these qualities, you don't have to be born with it."**

And no, they do not necessarily believe in ISKCON. They simply believe in doing good, in lending their professional expertise to a worthy cause.

Similarly, while kitchens are a labour of love – and daily commitment – managed by the missionaries. People who can be counted to wake up every morning at three am and get the work started.

But technology and professional practices enable these kitchens to operate at the next level. From one unit with gas stoves and brass pots catering to 10,000 children, Akshaya Patra now operates 18 centralised modern kitchens.

"Our facility in Hubli district* alone cooks more than 180,000 meals on a daily basis," exults Madhu. This includes 15 tonnes of rice and 26,800 litres of sambar – all ready in less than six hours.

But, there is no fixed 'formula'. As the program expanded to the village level, kitchens actually had to be decentralised.

"We ran a pilot to feed 600 tribal children in five villages of Baran district in April 2005. A self-help group of women was formed in each village and these women were trained in various aspects of cooking, hygiene and nutrition."

An operation of this size and scale needs not just dedication, but direction from trained professionals.

In 2006, Shridhar Venkat chucked his IT job and joined the Akshaya Patra foundation – as Executive Director. He heads the

---

* The Hubli kitchen was set up in 2004-5 with a ₹ 10 crore grant from Infosys Foundation and personal donations from Sudha Murthy and Gururaj Deshpande.

team of professionals who handle finance, marketing and the supply chain. Social service it is, but managed with the ruthless efficiency – and ambition – of a corporation.

On the missionary side, Akshaya Patra is headed by Chanchalapati Dasa, who has been a *Hare Krishna* since 1984. In all, the organisation has 2500 employees and 50 missionaries, overseeing an ever-expanding operation.

"We are happy to state that we have achieved our earlier mission of feeding 1 million children by 2010, in early 2009," says Madhu.

Akshaya Patra's next milestone is reaching out to 5 million children by 2020.

All very well, but is there real value to providing a meal to a child? A value beyond the humanitarian gesture of filling an empty stomach? The startling answer is 'yes'.

The Department of Education, Government of Karnataka, conducted an independent study on the impact of the Akshaya Patra program. The study noted that 99.61% of the students felt that they could pay better attention in class.

Another study – by AC Nielsen ORG MARG found that attendance in schools, as well as learning ability of students, had increased.

But, these are all happy side-effects – not a result of a well thought out 'strategy'.

Madhu chuckles, "I will frankly tell you, it was not like I sat down and had a vision that so many children will get so much of education; they will have food in their stomach so they will come to school. In fact, we had no idea of the magnitude of this problem...!"

A journey of a million miles starts with a single step. A casual conversation, a stray thought. You may start barefoot, without a map, but somewhere along the way you find your rhythm. And fellow travellers join in step.

Akshaya Patra has changed not just the lives of a milion children, but the character of the temple. It makes ISKCON Bangalore* special, gives it a heart.

* *There is an ongoing dispute between ISKCON Bangalore and ISKCON Mumbai. The matter is currently under litigation.*

"Imagine us, such a big temple... without a social initiative. How would it look?"

If more temples worried about that, God would rest in his Heaven.

And all would be right with this world.

———————————

ADVICE TO YOUNG ENTREPRENEURS

Help yourself and God will help you. As for we helping ourselves, we should leave no stone unturned towards our goal or mission.

I also think that becoming an entrepreneur or creating something can be learnt. It's a process and you can train people into that process. Use *gyana* (knowledge), *bala* (strength) and *kriya* (skills) to make your vision a reality.

What is the difference in a person who is trying to create an empire for himself, his family, or even for his nation and somone working for a selfless, larger cause? The processes are the same. But the law of *karma* operates differently due to different intentions.

A person working with purity of purpose is not bound by *karma*. In your daily life, if you work without attachment to rewards, you can start transcending *karma*.

The Vedas have revealed that everyone's milestones in life are set but you have the freedom to run between the milestones. So endeavour upto a reasonable limit.

The Bhagwad Gita says, "Do your duty, and leave the fruits in the hands of the Lord." Why? Because there are many 'other factors'.

You are not simply going to go forward on your effort alone. Your background, your 'past life' actions – or the law of *karma* – must make you eligible for the fruits of the efforts.

This knowledge is there in our Indian culture. Unfortunately, because of the Western education system we are deprived of it.

Once you discover your relationship with the Lord and surrender to Him you will say, "Lord, you fix my milestones. I will run towards them."

That is life and you will see that He will always be guiding you beyond your *karma*.

ALL IN
THE FAMILY

Vinayak Lohani,
Parivaar Ashram

An IIM Calcutta graduate, Vinayak turned his back on corporate India to do something of service to humanity. That something is Parivaar Ashram, a residential facility for orphans, tribals and daughters of prostitutes. Today, Vinayak leads a 'household' of over 500 children.

It is a humid August afternoon; we have just finished a three hour long interview. And an extensive Bengali lunch.

I am feeling a little sleepy; not Vinayak Lohani. In his spotless white kurta and dhoti, he is looking fresh as ever. Raring to show me around Parivaar ashram.

First, the school building. Then the various dorms. Girls and boys of all shapes and sizes are enjoying a Sunday siesta. Those who are awake jump up, flash a huge grin and say "hello".

We survey the infirmary; the games room and TV room. The extensive library and impressive cricket ground.

"Now we will go to Nivedita house," says Vinayak. A building nearby which houses some more children.

I'm not sure why we need to, won't it be more of the same?

As we bound up yet another flight of steps and Vinayak breathlessly introduces me, I suddenly realise. These are not just any children, these are *his* children.

Like any proud father he wants me to see them all.

Parivaar is not an institution, it is a family.

It is a mission to make the world better, through the power of love.

ALL IN
THE FAMILY

Vinayak Lohani,
Parivaar Ashram

Vinayak Lohani was born and brought up in Bhopal.

"My father was in the IAS in Madhya Pradesh cadre. So till Class XII, I was at Bhopal and from there I came to IIT Kharagpur."

Post-IIT Vinayak spent a year at Infosys in Bangalore. Like most software engineers, he appeared for the CAT.

"I didn't really want to do an MBA, but it was a sort of challenge to successfully crack an examination. And when I got admission at IIM Calcutta I thought okay, let's explore this too".

However, within the first two months, Vinayak realised IIM was not the place for him. "I realised that even the highest point where this career path could take me would not be fulfilling. I lost interest in the course."

Culturally also, Vinayak did not feel at home. The moral universe in which he had been brought up was completely different. Vinayak's father was among the first generation of civil servants, a generation with a different kind of idealism and sense of 'national mission'.

"I admired Gandhi, Jayaprakash Narayan and Vinoba Bhave – who worked in the villages, for the common people. IIMs on the other hand are narrowly focussed on the corporate sector, there is no exposure to wider issues."

Attendance was not compulsory at IIMC, so Vinayak spent most of his time exploring the cultural and intellectual life of Calcutta. He also met numerous people running NGOs.

"The inflection point came when I withdrew from the placement process in the beginning of the second year itself. This exempted me from attending pre-placement talks, which I had no interest in!"

And so began the great adventure. You eliminate what you do not want; and set out to in search of the unknown. That thing which you really *want* to do..

The year ended and Vinayak remained unsure. He hung around the IIMC campus with friends from the FPM – or PhD – program, and had intense discussions. Finally, he decided to do a bit of travelling; see what the world had to offer.

"In June 2003 I went to Varanasi, where Magsaysay award winner Sandeep Pandey* had started a *satyagraha* against the ruling BJP government".

Vinayak did not care about the cause in particular, the idea was to experience what it was like to work at the grassroots level. During this period, he spent time in a dalit village in UP, a rural organisation in Madhya Pradesh and also interacted with volunteers from Mother Teresa's Missionaries of Charity in Kolkata.

"I realised there were many people who focused on very very simple, down to earth service. One such person I met was Brother Xavier, a priest who used to run a small home for children of women forced into prostitution."

Seeing the work of Brother Xavier, a tiny seed sprouted in Vinayak's heart.

"Let me start something like this – a residential home for orphans, homeless children, children languishing on streets and railway stations."

And let it start from *somewhere*, even if small. The question was, where to begin?

---

* *Sandeep Pandey runs the NGO 'Asha for Education' and is part of NAPM (National Association for People's Movement) headed by Medha Patkar.*

"I found myself moving further and further from intellectual frameworks of humanitarian work and more towards direct service in the spirit of love and with complete dedication."

At the time, Vinayak was friendly with a person by the name of John, who ran the night canteen at IIMC. John had worked with Missionaries of Charity for about 3 years and Vinayak had always believed in his potential.

"I helped John become a principal of a small school in rural Madhya Pradesh. But since he had never worked in organisational set up it did not work out and he came back to Kolkata."

John became the first 'employee' of Vinayak's new organisation*. Not that there was any name, any office, any concrete plan of what this organisation would do. But Vinayak continued his field work – building his understanding, his contacts and also an action plan.

The IIM tag helped Vinayak in getting appointments with senior people at NGOs. Two such organisations were CINI (Child In Need Institute) and Sanlaap, which works with women in different red light areas of Kolkata.

The plight of prostitutes somehow deeply affected Vinayak.

"Tears used to come to my eyes to see women who have been exploited in this manner. I was also impacted by the character of Waheeda Rehman in Guru Dutt's *Pyaasa*."

Vinayak discussed the possibility of starting a residential institution for children of prostitutes.

"Would you be able to refer any such needy children to me?" he asked.

"Thousands of children," they replied. "How many can you take?"

* Parivaar Education Society was registered in July 2003 with Vinayak as founding secretary, Sunita Singh Sengupta, IIM Calcutta professor, as President.

There was definitely a need, but would Vinayak be able to deliver? It was one thing to be an activist organisation, and quite another to run a 24 hour institution!

To run a residential place, the first requirement is land. Although he had no money, Vinayak surveyed many properties. Nothing was available for under ₹ 15 lakhs.

"I decided to make a 'business plan' because that's what we had learned at IIM. Then I took appointments with many people in corporate sector trying to 'sell' the idea to them."

Vinayak was no good at all at this. He was uncomfortable making cold calls, asking strangers for support in the name of 'CSR'. "I spent three months doing this but nothing came out of it. In fact, things were going nowhere..."

Matters came to a head on 13th November 2003.

"I remember that day because it was an alumni-reunion day at IIMC. I was invited to speak to the alumni and seek their help for my project".

Vinayak reached at 8 am, and was waiting for over four hours.

Then, the professor handling alumni affairs came out and said, "Oh! I had forgotten about you...!"

"I felt slighted and humiliated at that time. He then took me inside and introduced me in a very uninspiring way as someone from the 'voluntary sector'."

Vinayak did not have the heart to make his pitch; he quietly headed home. That afternoon, as he lay in his tiny rented room, feeling despondent, he recalled a chance conversation.

The head of CSR at ICICI bank had mentioned the name of a person called Venkat Krishnan* whom the bank was working with closely.

"Venkat's phone number was lying with me for many weeks, but finally that afternoon I decided to give him a call."

Venkat had a simple suggestion: "Why don't you directly write to each and every one of your batchmates – ask them to contribute?"

---

*Venkat Krishnan founded Give India (chapter 22: Stay Hungry Stay Foolish')

"You worry about your 40 children – don't take on the burden of the rest of the world."

And that is exactly what Vinayak did. 15 odd responded and surprisingly, these were classmates with whom he'd had little or no interaction. This gave Vinayak the confidence to reach out to the wider alumni base, through the IIM Calcutta website.

A roommate from Vinayak's days in Infosys – now working in the US – offered $ 500.

But Vinayak did not want to actually take any money until the children came; until the project had started. And that was still not happening...

One winter afternoon, Vinayak was having his usual rice-and-daal meal in a shop in Shaukher Bazar. He struck up a conversation with a boy at the next table.

"That boy said he was in the merchant navy and also that he was closely associated with Mother Teresa's Missionaries of Charity."

More importantly, he told Vinayak about one Mr Das, a former missionary of charity who was now running a home for destitutes in Antala, 8 kms from IIM, on Diamond Harbour road. Das cared for 30-35 mentally ill patients found languishing on streets, bus stands or railway stations.

"I went to visit Das and discussed with him my idea – a home for children which would be more like a 'family' than an institution. He was very encouraging."

In fact, Das offered to refer needy children from the surrounding rural areas.

"I was amazed because at that time I had nothing to show for myself. And yet here was someone willing to believe me and even help."

Vinayak returned to Kolkata and decided to quickly find a place to operate from. Why not simply rent a building? A suitable place was found, at a rental of ₹ 11,000. Which was more than Vinayak earned in a month, from lectures at CAT coaching classes.

"I promptly went to Erudite and TIME and offered to take additional classes. But we still needed money for initial set-up, repairs and running costs. I realised it would take ₹ 30-35,000 per month to support just 10 children."

And time, to make arrangements. On 31st December 2003, Vinayak's friend Munish Thakur* suggested, "Let's not hurry – start after 2-3 months."

But Vinayak was worried he would lose credibility with Das. "We keep talking – we have to start *doing* now," he declared. On 7th Jan 2004, Vinayak took a lecture at Erudite Coaching Institute in the morning. At 10 am he boarded a bus to Antala, to pick up three needy children identified by Das.

As he was leaving with them, Das said, "Vinayak, this is a new life you are entering. You cannot go back."

This one line had a profound impact on Vinayak.

"I realised that I have taken up a responsibility – this is like having your own child. I was no longer on an 'adventure'."

Back in Kolkata, a very basic 'home' had been set up. Bedding, blankets, and a cook – a lady from the same neighbourhood whom Vinayak was acquainted with.

"We had very neat arrangements, very austere arrangements. I gave up my rented room and moved in."

On 17th January, 2004, an NGO called 'Tomorrow's Foundation' sent over 10 children. A couple of days later Das sent three more. Thus a critical mass of 16 was quickly reached.

Vinayak opened a bank account and requested all those who had committed to help, to send in money. Which they did! Close to ₹ 3 lakhs came in.

In February, a small article on Parivaar appeared in *the Hindustan Times*. A Kolkata based businessman by the name of Mr Ravindra Chamaria was moved by what he read and called up Vinayak. He wished to donate ₹ 25,000 a month, to keep the good work.

"At that time, the scale of my work was so small, things were so uncertain... I felt humbled to see a stranger step forward and put so much trust in me".

* Munish Thakur was an FPM student at IIMC; he is now a professor at XLRI.

"I raised funds through individuals rather than collectives. Collectives wait for something that is a proven success story while individuals may trust you or get inspired by you, or simply give you a chance."

With a steady 'income' coming in, Vinayak decided to quickly expand the operation. He decided to focus on children of sex workers, especially girls. On 12th March 2004, 26 such children were added to the Parivaar, taking the headcount from 16 to 42 in a single day!

Vinayak then sent out a newsletter, not only to his own alumni, but to the alumni of IIM Ahmedabad. More messages of support – and cheques – came in.

"Meanwhile, we were preparing our children for a class which is suitable for their age. I wanted them to get admission to a good school, just like any father would want for his children."

Thirty of the children were thus enrolled in classes I to IV.

In May 2004, Outlook magazine published an article on Parivaar. Many people got in touch, the most significant of them was a gentleman called Ramesh Kacholia from Mumbai.

"Ramesh is an extraordinary person. In a nutshell you can say he's been a mentor and guide to a large number of very successful people. He runs an informal organisation called 'Mumbai Group of Friends'."

The Mumbai Group of Friends includes many very high profile, high net worth individuals. This group extends support to many worthy, grassroots organisations.

Mr Kacholia invited Vinayak to Mumbai in August 2004, to talk about his work.

"Every 2-3 months the Mumbai Group of Friends* gets together. They call it 'get-together with a purpose' where people interested

* In 2008-09 Mumbai Group of Friends gave ₹ 20 crores to worthy causes.

in supporting good organisations – and leaders from these organisations – interact with each other".

All these efforts started bearing fruit.

By December 2004 new people were emailing Vinayak everyday, saying they had heard about his work and wanted to support it in some way. In its first three months of operation (Jan-Mar 2004) Parivaar had raised ₹ 7.5 lakhs. By March 2004, that figure had jumped to ₹ 83 lakhs."

Vinayak decided it was time to purchase some land, and build something more *permanent*.

"This land where Parivaar ashram stands, as you can see, it is slightly away from the main road. Initially we acquired two acres at a cost of ₹ 20 lakhs."

Construction began in January 2005, in a phased manner. Three buildings costing ₹ 12-15 lakhs came over the next six months. With every increase in infrastructure, came more students. By the end of that year, the number of children had more than doubled – from 67 to 144.

But it was not just about quantity. The point of Parivaar ashram was always, to live like a family. And Vinayak's top priority is equal opportunity.

"I grew up in a middle class home, we had a simple life but education wise I never missed an opportunity. The right guidance, right study material, right motivation was always available."

The aim of Parivaar is to take a child upto the last level and highest level of education he or she desires and is capable of. For the bright ones that could mean engineering or medicine; the average ones would opt for diploma courses or ITI.

"The theme of education is woven into the very fabric of Parivaar. Now from 7:00-9:30 am we have our first tutorship

"At the time I started *parivaar* I was clear that I will not get married. From now on this is my family..."

session. Then the children have breakfast and get ready for school."

The first lot of children who joined Parivaar were admitted to regular schools, and are continuing there. But in 2007, Parivaar opened its own school on campus known as Amar Bharat Vidyapeeth.

The reason was simple: as the number of children at Parivaar crossed 200, there weren't enough seats available in nearby schools!

By this time, Vinayak had also been able to compare the performance of Parivaar with respect to children from educated families.

"Our children were outperforming children from privileged backgrounds. So we could be sure that our bridge course*, our tutorship program after school, our overall methods were effective!"

This gave Vinayak the confidence to set up an independent school on the Parivaar campus. Today 256 children study in this school, currently functioning upto class IV. 57 continue in regular schools while the rest are completing the 6-12 month bridge course.

In all, Parivaar cares for 500 children. And the numbers continue to grow. But no, it was not exactly *planned* this way...

In the year 2007, Vinayak decided to give Parivaar a thrust into tribal areas.

"There are certain pockets completely cut off from the world, where development has not reached at all. I decided to do something for these people."

Parivaar chose to work with the Sabar tribe in the Belpahadi area of west Midnapur district. The idea was to start a Parivaar-like institution which would not only focus on children but have other dimensions. Such as basic health care and livelihood for the general population.

"For 8 months, Parivaar did intensive fieldwork in 35 villages in the area. This included awareness drives as well as distribution

---

* Bridge course brings a child upto the academic level of his age. Eg: a 9-year-old is groomed to enter class IV, even if he has not attended class I to III.

of rice, particularly during the rainy season when starvation deaths happen".

But Vinayak failed to take one crucial thing into account. Belpahadi – or Lalgarh – is a Naxalite stronghold. Even as Parivaar was identifying children and had readied a building to start operating from, the Naxals struck.

"Some of our people were taken hostage at gun point – we could easily have lost those 3-4 men!" recalls Vinayak.

Fortunately that did not happen but this incident brought Parivaar's plans in the area to a grinding halt. The 150 children who were to be admitted were instead brought to Kolkata in September 2008.

In hindsight, Vinayak admits he was naïve and idealistic.

"Naxalites as a group don't believe in democracy and the nation of India as it stands today. They want to wrest control of forested areas right across central India from west Madhya Pradesh, Gujarat till West Bengal."

More than 100 out of 600 districts in India have been declared as 'Naxalite infested', these are areas where even the police do not have control.

"Even we were seen as outsiders, people who might act as informers to the state. Apart from that I think Naxalites feared our activities might capture the imagination of the people and they would lose their grip..."

And capturing the imagination is something Parivaar manages to do almost effortlessly. Running a 24 hour institution requires a cadre of highly dedicated people. And Vinayak was able to attract these people – inspire them to take up a life of service.

"Generally middle class families pay a premium on education although they may cut down on other things. Parivaar is one such family."

"Most institutions take responsibility for a child only upto a certain age, but we are a family. And in India parents don't say once you cross 18, you are on your own!"

"People ask me, why did you start this? The only thing I can say is, I had a certain sense of destiny, a mission to fulfil. And this mission has inspired highly idealistic men and women to join me."

They came from cities; they came from villages. Graduates and school dropouts. Young and old. All bound by one common thread: the desire to give of themselves for a larger cause."

"I call my people *'seva vrathi'*, which means one who is inspired by and vowed to the ideal of service. They are all extraordinarily dedicated people but they were extraordinary even before meeting me... I merely identified and channelised them towards the work of Parivaar ashram!"

Neither Vinayak nor his team members had experience in running this kind of institution. Or any diploma in child counseling or child psychology. But purity of heart and purity of purpose – combined with common sense – made it all possible.

Today Parivaar has 35 full time *seva vrathis*, with a core leadership team of ten. The entire movement in Belpahadi, for example, was spearheaded by Pulakda (Pulak Banerjee). A *seva vrathi* known for his genius when it comes to people mobilisation.

"Nimai Saha and Sandhya Nag are two others who have contributed immensely – to making this organisation what it is today."

At the centre of it all is the idea of *parivaar* – or family. It is not just a nice sounding *name,* it is a state of being.

"We haven't achieved anything at all just by admitting a child into *Parivaar.* It is not about 'saving' the child but giving each one a new life, a future".

Vinayak is the 'head' of the household. Affectionately called as 'dada' by everyone.

"The children are the centre of my imagination, my universe. When I close my eyes I can recognise most of the children – by their voice alone. In fact, I can recall the exact dates on which each of my first 200 children joined Parivaar."

I can only imagine the bonding, the unconditional love which makes such a thing possible...

As if reading my thoughts Vinayak adds, "The extraordinary love I have received, there won't be too many people in the world who've been loved so intensely by such a large number of people..."

Everything Vinayak does it is with the *parivaar*, or for the *parivaar*. "I take my children on excursions. We go to College Street or Oxford for books. Also to parks, museum, zoo and so on."

The only other trips he makes to Kolkata – or occasionally to Mumbai – are to meet donors or groups like Ramesh Kacholia's. At such times he catches up with his two sisters who reside in Mumbai as well.

"Actually in the initial years, I had cut myself off from relatives and friends. My entire focus was on this new life that I had taken".

Vinayak's logic was simple. His energy was his 'working capital'; too many outside forces and unnecessary questions would dilute it!

"Of course," he smiles, "In the last two years I have become much more liberal, much more open to discussion, debates and learnings. I am comfortable with who I am and where I am."

The writings of Swami Vivekananda have influenced Vinayak greatly.

"Swami Vivekananda's message is that there is divinity in each human being, that each human being has got infinite potential and this has been Parivaar's theme."

"We have 4.5 hours of tutorship everyday which is over and above schooling hours. The reason is we need to erase the backlog in their education."

"People ask me how has your management education helped you? I say that it has basically given me this tag of IIT and IIM, which opens some doors."

It is with this belief in his heart that Vinayak deals with his children, his team members and even his donors and supporters. And the difference is visible.

While most NGOs have been affected by the slowdown, Parivaar donors did not waver. In fact, in 2008-09, Parivaar's income actually *grew* – from ₹ 3.61 crores to ₹ 4.5 crores.

"Our core supporters see *Parivaar* as an essential family spending. Will you cut down on the education of your child during a slowdown? You wouldn't! In the same way they are bonded with our children, our mission".

Emotion hangs in the air, and then Vinayak breaks into a child-like grin. Parivaar is a responsibilty, and that's a serious business. But Vinayak has a slightly crazy streak in him and like any father, he shares with his kids all the people and things he loves.

From Roger Federer, whose Grand Slam titles are celebrated by bursting of crackers to Michael Jackson, whose death was mourned and his music celebrated.

"He may be controversial but I love Michael for the tremendous pleasure he gave me when I was a school boy. When he died the children created a shrine – a salute to his many achievements!"

Then there is cricket and cricketing history.

"Two days ago we celebrated *Don Bradman*'s birthday; last year we celebrated his centenary. We have a very competitive cricket team and my kids are trained to play with regulation bats and proper gear."

In fact, the cricket pitch next to the ashram has been carefully developed by the same curators who have done the Eden Gardens pitch at one time!

Like in cricket, life too can bowl you a googly. There are tricky issues to deal with, which come up in any family.

"We had some cases of hooligans teasing our girls on their way to school – that was dealt with firmly."

In fact as the kids grow older, there are greater responsibiliies.

"In many different ways one has to be very vigilant. Because even a small incident can mar the entire reputation of an institution like this or demoralise other people".

One such tragic incident was the drowning of a young boy in March 2008. It was during 'Holi' celebrations, when a playful mood turned into fatal recklessness. The boy who drowned was one of the first few children who had joined Parivaar.

The entire ashram was deeply affected; Vinayak himself went into depression.

"For 2-3 weeks I could barely function. How could such a thing happen, I kept asking myself...!"

Compounding the situation were police and the administration hassles.

"If there is a bereavement in the family, people come and console you. In our case we were flooded with questions... Even accusations."

Vinayak realised he *had* to pull himself together. Because life must go on. And from every experience, every encounter, you learn something.

"In the most seemingly ordinary people you find extraordinary things," says Vinayak.

"Amongst my chief inspirations are the women who have been exploited, victimised and who are still fighting to live with dignity, every day of their lives. In comparison to that I feel I have done nothing."

"I am inspired by all kinds of human endeavours, wherever people are putting up a fight, wherever they are showing character."

Fighting the good fight, leading to the light as many as he can. That's Vinayak Lohani for you; changing the world, one child at a time.

ADVICE TO YOUNG ENTREPRENEURS

Look, it's not that one needs to start an organisation like this to do something humanitarian or something good. Truly speaking, it is just about being positive and seeking out what is great, what is good in every person you interact with.

To have a positive outlook is to see extraordinariness everywhere, in ordinary situations and ordinary people.

This may sound very general, but I don't have any other thing to suggest. When I started I didn't know how to do this work. I just knew that I wanted to do this work. So many extraordinary people supported me and worked with me to make it possible.

I am overwhelmed with a sense of gratitude.

I think, at the end of day, sincerity and dedication are irreplaceable. Power of purity, power of sincere ideals…these are what matter. By pure I mean there should be no selfish intent, or desire to manipulate other people.

Many times gifted people have Emotional Intelligence, they understand the emotional dynamics of people. This power also brings tremendous responsibility. And I think sustained good work can only be done by a combination of gifts and responsibility, isn't it?

LEAD,
KINDLY LIGHT

Shreesh Jadhav,
Belur Math

Shreesh Jadhav graduated from IIT, knowing he did not want a conventional career. He toyed with social work but ultimately found his calling – as a monk. Through the path of renunciation, Shreesh holds up a candle. A light of hope in the darkness of a selfish, me-first world.

Connecting with Shreesh is a difficult task.

He is one of the rare breed which refuses to carry a cellphone.

But even rarer is an IIT graduate, choosing the monastic way of life.

Shreesh Jadhav is the registrar of Vivekananda University at Belur Math. When he is not handling academic affairs, he can be seen in class – or in the lab – teaching computer science.

"I don't know why you want to interview me," says Shreesh, with genuine reluctance.

But we persevere, and meet him in the serenity of his campus.

In a room overlooking a garden, the chirping of birds in the air, we await Shreesh. A simple breakfast is served with great love by the cook – making it truly special.

At exactly the appointed time, Shreesh arrives.

He is neither confident nor diffident.

With shaven head and saffron robes, he looks like a mendicant.

But even if you close your eyes, you can feel a *presence*.

Shreesh radiates calmness, consciousness. There is a sense of inclusion, which seems to come naturally.

It is only when you see yourself as separate from others, that you need to *practice* awareness...

To be one with Life, and to live in Oneness,

Because there is only Us, no Them.

LEAD,
KINDLY LIGHT

Shreesh Jadhav,
Belur Math

Shreesh Jadhav was born and brought up in Raipur.

"My father and mother were both engineers. My mother was teaching in Raipur Engineering College, father was working in Bhilai steel plant."

From early childhood, Shreesh and his three sisters visited the Ramakrishna Mission ashram in Raipur along with their parents. And they were influenced by Swami Atmananda Maharaj in a big way.

"My father used to stay in Raipur Ashram when he was studying in Raipur Engineering college. So he was very connected to the Ramakrishna movement."

However Shreesh attended St Paul's HS School – an all-boys, Hindi medium school run by Christian missionaries. The principal – John Samuel – was a man of extraordinary character and dedication. He was to be another major influence on Shreesh and the path he chose in life.

"I used to be a backbencher in school. You understand what it means to be a backbencher. Basically I was quite naughty – I would pick up fights and I also used to run away from the school to see cricket matches."

In those days everyone came to school on cycle. Now how did one sneak out in the middle of the day with one's cycle? Simple – throw your cycle over the fence.

"I was taller and heavy built, so I was the one who threw the cycles," recalls Shreesh with a faint grin.

One fine day, the Indian hockey team was visiting Raipur. Zafar Iqbal, Mohammad Shahid – these were big names at that time. Shreesh and some of his friends decided to bunk classes and watch them in action.

This time however, the *chowkidaar* saw them running and shouted, "*Kaun hai... kaun bhaag raha hai?*"

One of the boys panicked and ran back to the school. The gatekeeper locked his cycle and gave the key to the principal. All four boys were hauled up but John Samuel gave a dressing down only to Shreesh.

"That is when I realised he has special love for me," said Shreesh. "You see, my mother had also studied in the same school."

Actually, in her time, Raipur did not have any school for girls – so a special exception was made for her.

Principal Samuel said, "Shreesh, I cannot accept this from you – even your mother was my student."

"That affected me a lot. If he had merely scolded me then in fact I would have bragged about it. But because he chided me, with reference to my mother, it touched my heart."

From this point onwards, Shreesh decided to put more effort into studies. He excelled at the board exams and secured a high rank in IIT JEE and the state engineering entrance test. A rare thing in Raipur, those days.

Ultimately, Shreesh joined IIT Kanpur, in the computer science department.

"Which IIT you will study, which career you will take. In India, those things are actually decided by parents," he admits matter-of-factly.So essentially, 'life' started in IIT Kanpur. For the first time, Shreesh was on his own, taking his own decisions.

"What usually happens when you go to hostel is that there are bad influences and good influences. I was fortunate to go to IIT Kanpur because it had an academic atmosphere, so good influences were more."

Shreesh excelled at studies, but he was not focused on building a *career*.

"The atmosphere in IITs is deteriorating. It has become very westernised – very career oriented, very selfish. I don't think it is good for the health of the nation, for the health of society or the health of people also."

"I did not worry about money, or future prospects. I was pretty clear that these were not the only important things in life."

The words of Swami Vivekananda, resonated within, and gave him direction.

"From my second year, I was involved in the anti-ragging campaign. Then in third year I came into contact with Vivekananda Samithi. Actually, the organisation was defunct so some of us got together and revived it."

One of the activities the Samithi started was teaching the children in the nearby village. This village – known as Bharusarai – was located just outside the boundary of IIT Kanpur. However, it was extremely backward.

"There was a dividing line between the dalits and non-dalits. There were four schools in the village but dalits were not allowed to attend them."

Shreesh and his friends started informal classes for dalit children. Alongside, they made efforts to restart the non-functioning government school in the village.

"There were three teachers who collected salary every month but they never took a single class. We sent complaints to the education department and forced them to come to the school. Of course, they didn't like that!"

The school did open but no real 'teaching' took place there. The children attended for the sake of it, but continued flocking to the informal class. In the first year, sessions were held twice a week but quickly it became a daily affair.

"We started with ten student volunteers but as time went on, some dropped out," recalls Shreesh.

But with five dedicated volunteers and one passionate campus resident – Mrs Vijaya Ramachandran* – work continued. Apart from teaching kids, the volunteer group took up issues like sanitation and healthcare.

"In fact, in three years' time we were able to immunise 100% of the children in that village, which took a lot of effort. Because the first time you give injection it's easy, second time they see you and run away. We had to bribe them with sweets!"

The effort reached a stage where the volunteers were running more than a dozen informal 'schools' in *bastis* in and around Kanpur city. And although run on energy and enthusiasm, the activities did require some funding. These funds were raised on the IIT campus – from students and professors.

"We would put a register in the hostel mess, people would pledge some amount and then we would take it from the hostel."

So what was the outcome of all this effort? Difficult to say. Most of the students dropped out after class five and started working on construction sites – like their parents.

"Some of the children, mostly girls, went to college also. In fact one of them – Doojabai – studied upto BA and became a teacher in her village. But the rest at least learnt to read and write!"

And that was reason enough to carry on...

Meanwhile, Shreesh completed his BTech but found he had no interest in the usual career options. He enrolled for an integrated PhD program at IIT Kanpur. But while he was in between courses, he decided to explore the idea of doing social service.

"I finished BTech in the month of February and the post graduate program was to start in July. So in those three months my batchmate Alok Agrawal and I went to participate in the Narmada Bachao Andolan.

But while Alok decided to stay on**, Shreesh returned to IIT to pursue the PhD program. Alongside, he continued voluntary work in the villages.

Being of a different mindset, he got into a scrap with the authorities, on more than one occasion. Yet, after completing the

* *Wife of Professor R Ramachandran, Dept of Physics at IIT Kanpur and daughter of ex-President R Venkatraman*
** *Alok Agrawal is currently secretary of the Narmada Bachao Andolan and a close associate of Medha Patkar*

course, Shreesh was offered a faculty position at IIT Kanpur.

Shreesh asked his Head of Department, "Why do you want another eccentric person in your department?."

The HOD replied, "You are very idealistic – that's how people are in their youth. Later on you will be a big asset to the department."

But Shreesh declined. Why? Because his destiny lay elsewhere. And that destiny was to renounce the world, and live like a *sadhu*.

But *how* did that happen? There was no 'aha' moment, or event leading up to the decision. It was a very gradual process.

"I started thinking about this very deeply when I was doing my PhD. In my BTech days I had lots of friends – they all passed out and most went on to study in America."

In solitary days, and still nights, Shreesh contemplated what it might be like, to become a monk.

"But I was always in two minds. Sometimes I thought maybe I should become a social worker. At times I thought of staying in academics. So all these thoughts were churning inside me for 3-4 years."

So what swung the ball in favour of monkhood? Why is it that one person can say – at an intellectual level, "Money is not important" while only the rare individual can actually *believe* it and renounce the world?

"I am of the firm belief that influence of past lives – or past *sanskars* – play a major role. Because my decision cannot be rationally justified," says Shreesh.

It was these *sanskars* which probably guided Shreesh to visit Belur Math in 1994.

"Actually I did not come here to become a monk – I just wanted to see the place. But our President – Swami Atmasthanandaji Maharaj – quickly judged my real intentions."

He asked, "Where are you from and how long will you stay here?"

Shreesh replied, "One month."

Swamiji called one of the *bhramacharis* and told him to take Shreesh to 'PPTC'.

Shreesh had no idea what PPTC* was – he simply went along.

---

* PPTC is the Pre-Probationers Training Centre, a separate accomodation area where new brahmacharis live.

"Many a times we forget, money cannot be the aim. It is only the means to achieve something."

There, the bhramachari said, "Here is your *dhoti* and here is your plate. You have to wash your own plate and wash your own clothes."

Shreesh thought it was an odd request to make from a 'guest' but went along with it. In the evening, Swamiji holds a class for newly joined *bhramacharis*.

There he told Shreesh, "No one comes here to stay for a month... The moment you expressed that desire, I understood you are going to become a *sadhu*."

And that is how, without conscious effort, Shreesh entered the monkhood.

How did his family take the news?

"Definitely every parent will want their neighbour's son to become a monk, but not their own son!" he says matter-of-factly.

So what happened then?

"Nothing, what could they do! I was already convinced, I was on the path..."

That path is simple. Once you renounce the world, you are on the journey. After ten years as a *bhramachari*, you can take the vows and don saffron robes. And ultimately, by dissolving the self, by serving all of humanity – you strive for *mukti*, or liberation. From the cycle of birth and death.

"The concept of reincarnation – I keep coming back to it – because it is is pivotal in our philosophy. If you are not going to be reborn, then there is no need for ethics!"

Yavat jivet sukham jivet, rinam kritva ghritam pibet, bhasmibhutasya dehasya punaragamanam kutah...

"Means as long as you live, live happily. You take, you borrow money and you eat *ghee* because when you die, your body becomes *bhasma*, it's not going to come back. Basically this is the materialistic point of view."

> **"I don't have any bank account and I am totally dependent on the organisation to provide me food, to provide me clothes, to provide me medical help but I am not in the least bit worried about it."**

The Western view.

But ultimately, even those who are selfless and serve others – in doing so – serve themselves. By breaking the bonds of attachment, they move closer to their goal – of releasing the *atma* from the shackles of the body. Of liberating, the soul.

Sanyasis are torch-bearers – they illuminate the path for the rest of us, groping in the dark. Caught in *maya* – the illusion of this world.

"*Sanyasis* have to show people that indeed there is a path through renunciation. I am not saying *everyone* has to become a *sanyasi* but there should always be a segment of people who choose to renounce. Otherwise all of society will become very materialistic..."

In fact, nothing can be achieved unless you renounce something. And this applies to all of us, in our day to day lives.

"For example, to become a good student, you have to renounce. You have to give up pleasures like watching TV, watching movies, playing cricket in the gully. You have to focus on your studies."

If you are a sportsman also, you have to renounce. Spend long hours in training and practice.

"To achieve any higher goal, you have to renounce. And if you don't aim to achieve higher things, society will remain at stand still."

The goal of renunciation – in the words of Swami Vivekananda – is thus *atmamokshartham* (self-fulfillment) and *jagadhitayacha* (benefit of the world). Paraodoxical as it might sound, only if you do work for the others, can you get something for yourself.

"This is because at a deeper level, the *atman* is everywhere. The same *atman* that is inside me is also inside you – so I cannot ignore you and think about myself. Because of this unity, it is impossible to have 'liberation' by thinking only about oneself."

The liberation he is talking about is not 'nirvana'.

"Our liberation means existence. Basically we will exist, but exist in our true nature."

Hmmm.

"But you don't have to take those things very seriously," he adds.

You may believe, or not believe – you can simply experience the 'joy of giving'. And see the magic, for yourself.

"Actually in Ramakrishna Mission* we have four aims: *Annadaan, Jnanadaan, Prandaan* and *Mokshdaan. Annadaan* is basically food relief, *Jnandaan* is education, *Prandaan* is medical service and *Mokshdaan* is religious service."

Every person who joins the Mission is put into one of these four activities. With his PhD, Shreesh was a natural choice for *jnanadaan*. But the purpose of this activity is beyond marksheets, beyond degrees. The purpose is empowerment.

There is a famous incident where Swami Vivekananda was asked, "What do you think about the problems of women?"

He answered, "Am I a woman that you ask me about the problems of women? Give them education and they will be able to solve their own problems".

That is the spirit in which *Jnanadaan* is undertaken.

"We don't need to actually solve the problems of the poor, the dalits, the downtrodden. Give them education and they will become self-confident. They will solve their own problems. So 'education' is actually the solution to *all* problems!"

Of course, the definition of education is, in itself, debatable.

"Swamiji was talking about character-building education. Now, in most places, it is basically money-making education."

So all is lost?

"No, the important thing is people have started *thinking* about education. So after they have made money, they will realise money is not enough and will seek out something more."

That's a very different – optimistic! – way to look at it. For the monk is patient. He is planting his seeds, tending his grass, creating a small patch of beauty. The flowers are common but the fragrance is different.

It is the fragrance of peace, of dedication to a goal.

"Ramakrishna Mission schools are not 'different' as such. But they are different in the sense that they function properly, like all schools should!"

And that is a rare thing in Bengal. Most teachers do 'party work' and don't actually teach in school. The children must take private tuitions – to actually learn anything.

"In Ramakrishna Mission schools, we have regular classes. And we don't allow teachers to take tuitions for their own students. So basically we are showing other schools, other people, how education should be imparted."

This is the reason that Ramakrishna Mission schools are highly sought after.

"When students are here, they sometimes grumble because we have morning and evening prayers, lot of discipline, and focus on studies. But when they grow up – and become parents – they want to send their children to our schools."

Is it enough? Perhaps not. But 'scaling up' is not a goal for Shreesh, or for the Ramakrishna Mission. It is neither practical, nor desirable.

"We have limited manpower – and that is always going to be the case. Because not everyone becomes a monk!* So mainly we have to show the way, and society has to do it. The problem of the society, society has to solve. This is what Vedanta says."

A part of me finds all this difficult to digest. But a part of me feels – it is true. God only helps those who help themselves. And sometimes, the only 'help' we need is a lamp which lights the wick inside each of us.

But every lamp needs its oil.

The more you give, the more you get...

---

* Over the last 20 years, the number of monks in Ramakrishna Mission has increased marginally, from 1200 to 1400

<u>ADVICE TO YOUNG ENTREPRENEURS</u>

I think that unselfishness is the thing that you should strive for. If you strive for unselfishness then everything will come to you. Whether you are spiritual or non spiritual – it doesn't matter. Material things will also come to you and spiritual things will also come to you. For any kind of excellence, don't think about 'self' too much.

Swami Vivekananda always exhorted young people, because young people can do anything. Old people only sit and discuss the matters endlessly. Because eradicating poverty, illiteracy – these things actually need work. They can not be done by theory or philosophical discussion.

I am very hopeful that the young people of today are upto the challenge. My generation and the ones before me were actually very timid. In fact, we thought that the White Man is better than us. But nowadays children don't have that kind of an inferiority feeling. They are mentally strong. Positive.

They can solve any problem!

START UP RESOURCE

To contact any of the amazing entrepreneurs featured in this book, or contribute to their organisations, here are their email ids and websites. To improve your chances of response, be specific with your query or comment. But feel free even to just appreciate, and know that any small service you can offer can and will make a difference.

1. Bindeshwar Pathak - sulabhinfo@gmail.com
www.sulabhinternational.org

2. Anita Ahuja - info@conserveindia.org
www.conserveindia.org

3. Vineet Rai - vineet_rai@aavishkaar.org
www.aavishkaar.org

4. Sumita Ghose - sumita@rangsutra.com
www.rangsutra.com

5. Saloni Malhotra - saloni@desicrew.in
www.desicrew.in

6. Ishita Khanna - Spiti Ecosphere - ishita@spitiecosphere.com
www.spitiecosphere.com

7. Harish Hande - Selco - harish@selco-india.com
www.selco-india.com

8. Santosh Parulekar - Pipal Tree - sparulekar@pipaltreeventures.com
www.pipaltreeventures.com

9. Dinabandhu Sahoo - Project Chilika - dbsahoo@hotmail.com
website: not available

10. Anand Kumar - Super 30 - mail@super30.org
www.super30.org

11. Dhruv Lakra - Mirakle Courier - dhruv.lakra@miraklecouriers.com
www.miraklecouriers.com

12. Madhav Chavan - Pratham - madhavchavan@gmail.com
www.pratham.org

13. Anshu Gupta - Goonj - anshu@goonj.org
www.goonj.org

14. Trilochan Sastry - ADR - tsastry@gmail.com
www.adrindia.org

15. Shaheen Mistry - Akanksha & Teach for India - shaheen@teachforindia.org
www.akanksha.org & www.teachforindia.org

16. Arvind Kejriwal - Parivartan - parivartan_india@rediffmail.com
www.pcrf.in

17. Bhushan Punani - Blind Person's Association (BPA) - blinabad1@bsnl.in
www.bpaindia.org

18. Madhu Pandit Dasa - Akshaya Patra - mpd@iskconbangalore.org
www.akshayapatra.org

19. Vinayak Lohani - Parivaar Ashram - vinayak@parivaar.org
www.parivaar.org

20. Shreesh Jadhav - Belur Math - sarvottamananda@gmail.com
www.belurmath.org